1990
TOP 150
MINOR LEAGUE PROSPECTS

1990
TOP 150
MINOR LEAGUE PROSPECTS

Author/Top 150 Minor League Prospects
ROB RAINS

Statistical Compilation/Sabermetric Calculations
BROCK J. HANKE

Editor/Top 150 Minor League Prospects
STEVE ZESCH

Research/Top 150 Minor League Prospects
CRAIG CARTER
BARRY SIEGEL

Design/Top 150 Minor League Prospects
BILL PERRY

President-Chief Operating Officer
THOMAS G. OSENTON

Book Publisher
GREGORY WILEY

Editorial Director of Books and Periodicals
RON SMITH

Copyright © 1990 by THE SPORTING NEWS Publishing Co. All rights reserved.

Published in the United States by THE SPORTING NEWS Publishing Co., 1212 North Lindbergh Boulevard, St. Louis, Missouri 63132.

The 1990 Top 150 Minor League Prospects is protected by copyright. All information, in the form presented here, except playing statistics, was compiled by the publishers and proof is available.

Information from the 1990 Top 150 Minor League Prospects must not be used elsewhere without special written permission, and then only with full credit to the 1990 Top 150 Minor League Prospects, published by THE SPORTING NEWS, St. Louis, Missouri.

Library of Congress Catalog Card Number: 89-63679

ISSN: 1046-7025

ISBN: 0-89204-335-0

Table of Contents

Introduction .... Page 7

Position Player Rankings .... Pages 9-12

Position Player Reports .... Pages 13-100

Pitcher Rankings .... Pages 101-104

Pitcher Reports .... Pages 105-166

Statistical Explanation .... Page 168

(Complete team and player directory appears on Page 8)

Introduction

From Oneonta to Osceola and Visalia to Vancouver, approximately 4,000 professional baseball players shared the same dream last season.

It is a dream that is as real as the drone of a diesel engine as the team bus eats up six hours' worth of two-lane blacktop, the $10 daily allowance that buys a player two meals at the local fast-food barn, the cold showers and the not-quite-cold six pack.

For most of the players, it is the only lifestyle they will know during their baseball careers. It's called minor league baseball. The farm. The bushes.

And it is the dream that keeps them going, that makes all the petty annoyances and the dues-paying such a gas. Because one day, the dream says, it's going to be Show time. The bigs. Major league baseball.

Of the estimated 4,000 minor leaguers who had a rip at a fastball or at least a line in a box score in 1989, a minuscule number will live the dream. On these pages, The Sporting News has narrowed that list to a select 150 prospects it believes will use the minors to launch great major league careers.

Some of these players have been preceded by their reputations. Others were still adjusting to life without mom and dad in the rookie leagues in 1989.

The intent here is not to identify the first 150 minor leaguers likely to reach the majors. Instead, this scouting report profiles the prospects most likely to be impact players at the major league level, whether they arrive in 1990 or 1995.

The select group took shape after extensive interviews with scouts, farm directors, minor league managers, instructors and other baseball officials. All were granted anonymity, specifically to solicit honest and frank player assessments. Evaluations from at least two sources were sought in grading each prospect.

To be eligible for consideration, a player must have rookie status entering the 1990 season. Several criteria were weighed when drawing up the final list of prospects, including the player's age, his level of performance thus far and, perhaps most important, his potential for improvement.

The position players are evaluated in the key areas a scout uses to grade each prospect: hitting, hitting for power, speed, baserunning, fielding, range and throwing. In a chart separate from the text, players are given a current grade and a projected future mark. Each prospect's overall ranking is in part determined by his future grade but not fixed by it. Other intangible factors also were considered in the final rankings.

The chart grades pitchers on the three basic deliveries—fastball, curveball and changeup—along with their control, stamina, poise and fielding ability. Again, a present and future grade are assigned.

In addition to the subjective analyses of baseball officials, this scouting report offers an alternative projection of a prospect's potential through a Sabermetric evaluation of his minor league statistics.

By plugging those numbers into a complex calculation that adjusts for competition, ball park dimensions and environment, players are assigned a "Major League Equivalency" rating for each season they competed as high as the Class AA or AAA level. The result: a stat line that reflects performance as if it had occurred with the major league club.

And that's not all. For the position players, Brock Hanke's "Peak Projection" calculation examines what a prospect's statistics will look like in his best season as a major leaguer.

Essentially, these calculations make for a more interesting presentation of a player's minor league statistics. They are by no means a hard-and-fast evaluation of a player's ability. That's territory best left to the scouts and other baseball officials.

A detailed explanation of the formula is included in the back of the book.

A few notes on the text: References to All-Star honors indicate that a player was voted to a so-called "all-league" team, not necessarily that he participated in his league's All-Star game. In the player's personal information lines, the school listed is that at which the player last competed. Additionally, each prospect's draft line refers to the last time he was claimed in baseball's amateur draft.

The Sporting News' Top 150 Minor League Prospects is meant to be enjoyed by all fans, but especially by those who prefer to be on the cutting edge as they watch for the game's future stars. Many of these prospects will break into the major leagues in 1990. Others will continue to hone their skills in the minor leagues, bound with thousands of others by one thing:

The dream of making it to the Show.

—Rob Rains

Directory of Teams and Players

AMERICAN LEAGUE

BALTIMORE ORIOLES
Juan Bell, ss 86
Leo Gomez, 3b 80
Mike Linskey, p 128
Ben McDonald, p 106
Curt Schilling, p 117
David Segui, 1b 55

BOSTON RED SOX
Scott Cooper, 3b 65
Josias Manzanillo, p 153
Kevin Morton, p 111
Tim Naehring, ss 82
Mickey Pina, of 51
Phil Plantier, of 60

CALIFORNIA ANGELS
Glenn Carter, p 147
Gary Disarcina, ss 81
Mike Fetters, p 145
Lee Stevens, of/1b 47

CHICAGO WHITE SOX
Wilson Alvarez, p 113
Wayne Edwards, p 155
Scott Radinsky, p 163
Frank Thomas, 1b 46
Robin Ventura, 3b 17

CLEVELAND INDIANS
Beau Allred, of 79
Sandy Alomar Jr., c 14
Carlos Baerga, 3b 59
Mark Lewis, ss 21
Charles Nagy, p 110
Rudy Seanez, p 140

DETROIT TIGERS
Scott Aldred, p 130
Rico Brogna, 1b 44
Travis Fryman, ss 20
Rob Richie, of 42

KANSAS CITY ROYALS
Kevin Appier, p 127
Jose DeJesus, p 120
Bob Hamelin, 1b 63
Harvey Pulliam, of 48

MILWAUKEE BREWERS
Narciso Elvira, p 161
Bert Heffernan, c 93
John Jaha, 1b 99
Tim McIntosh, c 92
Greg Vaughn, of 15

MINNESOTA TWINS
Paul Abbott, p 143
Johnny Ard, p 146
Willie Banks, p 121
Terry Jorgensen, 3b 78
Scott Leius, ss 61
Pat Mahomes, p 154
Derek Parks, c 70
Paul Sorrento, 1b 40
Kevin Tapani, p 137

NEW YORK YANKEES
Steve Adkins, p 132
Kevin Maas, of 32
Hensley Meulens, 3b 74
Deion Sanders, of 38
Willie Smith, p 165
Bernie Williams, of 23

OAKLAND ATHLETICS
Scott Hemond, 3b 64
Dann Howitt, of/1b 69
Felix Jose, of 43
Darren Lewis, of 67
Stan Royer, 3b 71

SEATTLE MARINERS
Ruben Gonzalez, 1b 97
Tino Martinez, 1b 49
Roger Salkeld, p 116

TEXAS RANGERS
Kevin Belcher, of 26
Scott Coolbaugh, 3b 56
Juan Gonzalez, of 30
Eric McCray, p 144
Robb Nen, p 126
Dean Palmer, 3b 24
Ivan Rodriguez, c 98

TORONTO BLUE JAYS
Derek Bell, of 41
Nate Cromwell, p 142
Glenallen Hill, of 29
John Olerud, 1b/p 36
Alex Sanchez, p 114
Luis Sojo, ss 84

NATIONAL LEAGUE

ATLANTA BRAVES
Steve Avery, p 105
Pat Gomez, p 162
Tommy Greene, p 123
Tyler Houston, c 100
Brian Hunter, 1b/of 88
Mark Lemke, 2b 68
Kelly Mann, c 90
Kent Mercker, p 112
Tom Redington, 3b 83
Mike Stanton, p 150

CHICAGO CUBS
Shawn Boskie, p 159
Frank Castillo, p 152
Earl Cunningham, of 33
Ty Griffin, 3b 28
Mike Harkey, p 107
Derrick May, of 91
Greg Smith, 2b 96
Rick Wilkins, c 76

CINCINNATI REDS
Chris Hammond, p 138
Rodney Imes, p 141
Reggie Jefferson, 1b 77
Brian Lane, 3b 89
Hal Morris, of/1b 50
Reggie Sanders, ss 45
Luis Vasquez, p 136

HOUSTON ASTROS
Willie Ansley, of 34
Eric Anthony, of 16
Darryl Kile, p 109

LOS ANGELES DODGERS
Kiki Jones, p 118
Eric Karros, 1b 53
Jamie McAndrew, p 139
Jose Offerman, ss 18
Henry Rodriguez, 1b 58

MONTREAL EXPOS
Greg Colbrunn, c 95
Wilfredo Cordero, ss 57
Delino DeShields, ss 25
Howard Farmer, p 115
Mark Gardner, p 129
Marquis Grissom, of 22
Jeff Huson, ss 94
Richie Lewis, p 160
Mel Rojas, p 125
Larry Walker, of 19

NEW YORK METS
Blaine Beatty, p 148
Terry Bross, p 166
Chris Donnels, 3b 52
Todd Hundley, c 87
David Proctor, p 134
Jaime Roseboro, of 37
Julio Valera, p 131

PHILADELPHIA PHILLIES
Pat Combs, p 108
Jason Grimsley, p 122
Jeff Jackson, of 62
Mickey Morandini, 2b 39

PITTSBURGH PIRATES
Joe Ausanio, p 157
Stan Belinda, p 135
Wes Chamberlain, of 35
Willie Greene, ss 75
Keith Richardson, p 151

ST. LOUIS CARDINALS
Mark Clark, p 156
Paul Coleman, of 66
Rheal Cormier, p 149
John Ericks, p 124
Brian Jordan, of 54
Ray Lankford, of 27
Mike Milchin, p 133
Geronimo Pena, 2b 31
Todd Zeile, c 13

SAN DIEGO PADRES
Jerald Clark, of 85
Thomas Howard, of 72
Roger Smithberg, p 158
Rafael Valdez, p 119

SAN FRANCISCO GIANTS
Mike Benjamin, ss 73
Eric Gunderson, p 164

The Position Players

Catcher Sandy Alomar Jr.

The mention of one name brings to mind the other.

Todd Zeile ... Sandy Alomar Jr.

They have been compared for two years as the two best catching prospects in the minor leagues. And they are still together in 1990, arriving in The Show as not only the top young catchers, but as the two hottest prospects among all position players, according to a consensus of baseball officials.

The comparisons inevitably will continue as each vies for his place in the big time, Zeile with the St. Louis Cardinals, Alomar with the Cleveland Indians. But as they get set to launch their respective major league careers, Zeile emerged as the top-rated overall prospect by general agreement of scouts, minor league managers, farm directors, coaches and instructors.

"If somebody said you could have either one, it would take a coin flip," said Philadelphia Phillies General Manager Lee Thomas.

Zeile, however, edged Alomar for the top spot primarily because most officials believe he'll become a better hitter. Alomar, nevertheless, was more highly regarded defensively.

"There's no doubt (Zeile) is going to hit, hit home runs and drive in runs in the big leagues," said Fred McAlister, the Cardinals' director of scouting. "He's got a good swing and the ball jumps off his bat. The mark of a good player is that he does well every year. And you look to see if a player is better than the league. Everywhere Zeile has played, he has done that."

Drafted out of UCLA in 1986, Zeile is ticketed to become the Cardinals' starting catcher in 1990 and for years to come. Playing at Class AAA Louisville in 1989, he proved he was ready for the call, hitting .289 with 19 homers and 85 runs batted in before joining the Cardinals in mid-August.

"He's a real sensible kid, he's smart and he's aggressive," McAlister said. "He has everything you look for in a player, and he should be a good major league player. You would like for every player you sign to turn out like him."

Thomas echoed those sentiments. "Zeile will be a fine hitter, for average and home runs," he said. "And he's also a very good defensive catcher with a good arm."

Scouts also rave about Alomar, who had made steady progression through the San Diego Padres' farm system after being signed in 1983. The son of former major leaguer Sandy Alomar and the brother of Padres second baseman Roberto Alomar, he won the Most Valuable Player award in the Pacific Coast League in each of the last two seasons.

The prospect of serving a backup apprenticeship to entrenched San Diego catcher Benito Santiago excited neither Alomar nor the Padres. San Diego capitalized on his potential and made him the key in a three-player package to acquire slugger Joe Carter from Cleveland last December.

Catcher Todd Zeile

HOW THEY RANK

Position Players

1. Todd Zeile, St. Louis Cardinals, catcher
2. Sandy Alomar Jr., Cleveland Indians, catcher
3. Greg Vaughn, Milwaukee Brewers, outfielder
4. Eric Anthony, Houston Astros, outfielder
5. Robin Ventura, Chi. White Sox, third baseman
6. Jose Offerman, Los Angeles Dodgers, shortstop
7. Larry Walker, Montreal Expos, outfielder
8. Travis Fryman, Detroit Tigers, shortstop
9. Mark Lewis, Cleveland Indians, shortstop
10. Marquis Grissom, Montreal Expos, outfielder
11. Bernie Williams, N.Y. Yankees, outfielder
12. Dean Palmer, Texas Rangers, third baseman
13. Delino DeShields, Montreal Expos, shortstop
14. Kevin Belcher, Texas Rangers, outfielder
15. Ray Lankford, St. Louis Cardinals, outfielder
16. Ty Griffin, Chicago Cubs, third baseman
17. Glenallen Hill, Toronto Blue Jays, outfielder
18. Juan Gonzalez, Texas Rangers, outfielder
19. Geronimo Pena, St. Louis, second baseman
20. Kevin Maas, New York Yankees, outfielder
21. Earl Cunningham, Chicago Cubs, outfielder
22. Willie Ansley, Houston Astros, outfielder
23. Wes Chamberlain, Pittsburgh, outfielder
24. John Olerud, Toronto Blue Jays, 1b/p
25. Jaime Roseboro, New York Mets, outfielder
26. Deion Sanders, New York Yankees, outfielder
27. Mickey Morandini, Philadelphia, 2b
28. Paul Sorrento, Minnesota Twins, first baseman
29. Derek Bell, Toronto Blue Jays, outfielder
30. Rob Richie, Detroit Tigers, outfielder
31. Felix Jose, Oakland Athletics, outfielder
32. Rico Brogna, Detroit Tigers, first baseman
33. Reggie Sanders, Cincinnati Reds, shortstop
34. Frank Thomas, Chi. White Sox, first baseman
35. Lee Stevens, California Angels, of/1b
36. Harvey Pulliam, Kansas City Royals, outfielder
37. Tino Martinez, Seattle Mariners, first baseman
38. Hal Morris, Cincinnati Reds, of/1b
39. Mickey Pina, Boston Red Sox, outfielder
40. Chris Donnels, New York Mets, third baseman
41. Eric Karros, L.A. Dodgers, first baseman
42. Brian Jordan, St. Louis Cardinals, outfielder
43. David Segui, Baltimore Orioles, first baseman
44. Scott Coolbaugh, Texas, third baseman
45. Wilfredo Cordero, Montreal Expos, shortstop
46. Henry Rodriguez, L.A. Dodgers, first baseman
47. Carlos Baerga, Cleveland, third baseman
48. Phil Plantier, Boston Red Sox, outfielder
49. Scott Leius, Minnesota Twins, shortstop
50. Jeff Jackson, Philadelphia Phillies, outfielder
51. Bob Hamelin, K.C. Royals, first baseman
52. Scott Hemond, Oakland, third baseman
53. Scott Cooper, Boston Red Sox, third baseman

Outfielder Eric Anthony

54. Paul Coleman, St. Louis Cardinals, outfielder
55. Darren Lewis, Oakland Athletics, outfielder
56. Mark Lemke, Atlanta Braves, second baseman
57. Dann Howitt, Oakland Athletics, of/1b
58. Derek Parks, Minnesota Twins, catcher
59. Stan Royer, Oakland Athletics, third baseman
60. Thomas Howard, San Diego Padres, outfielder
61. Mike Benjamin, S.F. Giants, shortstop
62. Hensley Meulens, N.Y. Yankees, third baseman
63. Willie Greene, Pittsburgh Pirates, shortstop
64. Rick Wilkins, Chicago Cubs, catcher
65. Reggie Jefferson, Cincinnati, first baseman
66. Terry Jorgensen, Minnesota, third baseman
67. Beau Allred, Cleveland Indians, outfielder
68. Leo Gomez, Baltimore Orioles, third baseman
69. Gary Disarcina, California Angels, shortstop
70. Tim Naehring, Boston Red Sox, shortstop
71. Tom Redington, Atlanta, third baseman
72. Luis Sojo, Toronto Blue Jays, shortstop
73. Jerald Clark, San Diego Padres, outfielder
74. Juan Bell, Baltimore Orioles, shortstop
75. Todd Hundley, New York Mets, catcher
76. Brian Hunter, Atlanta Braves, 1b/of
77. Brian Lane, Cincinnati Reds, third baseman
78. Kelly Mann, Atlanta Braves, catcher
79. Derrick May, Chicago Cubs, outfielder
80. Tim McIntosh, Milwaukee Brewers, catcher
81. Bert Heffernan, Milwaukee Brewers, catcher
82. Jeff Huson, Montreal Expos, shortstop
83. Greg Colbrunn, Montreal Expos, catcher
84. Greg Smith, Chicago Cubs, second baseman
85. Ruben Gonzalez, Seattle, first baseman
86. Ivan Rodriguez, Texas Rangers, catcher
87. John Jaha, Milwaukee Brewers, first baseman
88. Tyler Houston, Atlanta Braves, catcher

Two power hitters, the Milwaukee Brewers' Greg Vaughn and the Houston Astros' Eric Anthony, follow Zeile and Alomar on the list of top prospects. Vaughn figures to break into the Milwaukee outfield after hitting 26 homers and driving in 92 runs in 110 games at Class AAA Denver in 1989. Moreover, he provided much-needed power in the Brewer lineup after joining the club down the stretch.

Anthony, who made the jump to Houston in 1989 after starting the season at the Class AA level, also will try to duplicate his minor league power numbers at the major league level. His 31 homers at Columbus and Tucson in 1989 led all minor leaguers.

A contact hitter in the Chicago White Sox's chain, third baseman Robin Ventura, is rated the No. 5 prospect. An All-America at Oklahoma State and a star with the 1988 U.S. Olympic team, Ventura made a very quick transition to the pro game at Class AA Birmingham last season.

Jose Offerman of the Los Angeles Dodgers is the first of three shortstop prospects ranked in the top 10. He checks in sixth, just ahead of No. 8 Travis Fryman of the Detroit Tigers and No. 9 Mark Lewis of Cleveland. All three have only outside chances to join the major leagues in 1990, but they figure to stick for years once they arrive.

Two prospects who might play side by side in the Montreal outfield in 1990 and beyond round out the Top 10: Larry Walker and Marquis Grissom. Both arrived in Montreal last August and showed the potential to become impact players, Walker as a power threat and Grissom as a leadoff-type hitter.

The Expos, in fact, placed more prospects among the position players than any other team in the majors. Of the 88 ranked position players, six are Expos. Following Walker and Grissom are three shortstops—Delino DeShields, Wilfredo Cordero and Jeff Huson—and catcher Greg Colbrunn.

Only the National League champion San Francisco Giants failed to place at least two position players on the list. Outfielders were the most popular pick, placing 32 on the list, followed by 14 shortstops, 14 third basemen, 13 first basemen, 11 catchers and only four second basemen.

Third Baseman Robin Ventura

Outfielder Greg Vaughn

TODD ZEILE

St. Louis Cardinals
Catcher
Cardinals' Supplemental Pick Following Second Round, June 1986 Draft

Personal
Height: 6-1 Weight: 190
Bats right, throws right
Born: September 9, 1965

School: UCLA

Ratings

	Present	Future
Hitting	5	6
Power	5	6
Baserunning	4	5
Speed	4	4
Fielding	5	6
Arm	4	5
Range	4	6

Rating Key
7 Outstanding
6 Major League Caliber, High
5 Major League Caliber
4 Minor League Caliber, High
3 Minor League Caliber
2 Below Average
1 Poor

General
Cardinal scouts and officials believe Zeile is the best catching prospect to come through the minor leagues in years. He has earned comparisons to Johnny Bench (perhaps those are premature) and has the physical build a catcher should have. Zeile showed considerable thump in each of his four minor league seasons and was a league All-Star selection each year. At Class AAA Louisville in 1989, he was voted the American Association's top rookie, ranking second in the league in home runs and runs batted in. In 1987, he was named the Midwest League's co-Most Valuable Player.

Hitting Tendencies
Zeile has the best mechanics of any hitter in the Cardinals' system. He has big-league power potential, having hit 19 home runs at both the Class AAA and AA levels. His best attribute as a hitter is his ability to drive in runs. He collected at least 75 RBIs in each of his last three seasons, including 106 to lead the Midwest League in 1987. A disciplined righthanded hitter who goes to all fields, Zeile seems to know what he wants in each at-bat. He's no wild swinger but instead works pitchers to get his pitch.

Fielding/Baserunning
Zeile blocks balls well and calls a good game. His only real weakness? He sometimes throws the ball before he has a good grip, resulting in a weak or wild throw. Otherwise, he has good arm speed and quickness. On the basepaths, Zeile has above-average speed for a catcher but isn't regarded as a stealing threat.

Projection
Zeile is the No. 1 candidate for the Cardinals' starting catcher job in 1990.

Career Statistics and Peak Projection

	G	AB	R	H	2B	3B	HR	RBI	BB	SO	AVG
1986 Erie (New York-Penn League-Class A)	70	248	40	64	14	1	14	63	37	52	.258
1987 Springfield (Midwest League-Class A)	130	487	24	142	24	4	25	106	70	85	.292
1988 Arkansas (Texas League-Class AA)	129	430	95	117	33	2	19	75	83	64	.272
1988 Major League Equivalency	129	412	72	99	31	2	12	57	62	65	.240
1989 Louisville (American Association-Class AAA)	118	453	71	131	26	3	19	85	45	78	.289
1989 St. Louis (National League)	28	82	7	21	3	1	1	8	9	14	.256
1989 Major League Equivalency	146	515	61	132	28	6	13	73	43	92	.256
Peak Projection	154	567	88	157	37	5	21	84	69		.277

Interpretation
Those Cardinal backers who think Zeile will hit 25 home runs per year should brace themselves for something less, according to the peak calculations. And since the Major League Equivalency doesn't take into account the beating his knees will take behind the plate, he likely won't hit the six triples projected in his 1989 MLE. Nitpicking aside, Zeile's projections are appealing across the board, particularly for a catcher. If his walk totals hadn't declined as he moved up the minor league ranks, he likely would have projected as a Jack Clark-type threat.

SANDY ALOMAR JR.

Cleveland Indians
Catcher
Signed by San Diego Padres as a Non-Drafted Free Agent, October 1983

Personal
Height: 6-5   Weight: 200
Bats right, throws right
Born: June 18, 1966

Ratings

	Present	Future
Hitting	4	5
Power	4	5
Baserunning	5	5
Speed	4	4
Fielding	6	6
Arm	6	6
Range	6	6

Rating Key
7 Outstanding
6 Major League Caliber, High
5 Major League Caliber
4 Minor League Caliber, High
3 Minor League Caliber
2 Below Average
1 Poor

General
Look at Sandy Alomar Jr. and you see a major league talent. Look at the circumstances in San Diego and you see why he was still in the minors in 1989: Benito Santiago. Alomar finally will be given his shot in Cleveland, where he's expected to take over the Indians' everyday catching chores after arriving in the off-season trade for Joe Carter. In 1989, Alomar had the mettle to overcome his fate and a monthlong slump and became only the second player (next to Steve Bilko) to win back-to-back Most Valuable Player awards in the Pacific Coast League. Alomar's name was constantly bandied about in trade rumors, yet he had the resolve and maturity to keep his focus on the game.

Hitting Tendencies
Alomar struggled offensively in his first three minor league seasons, never hitting above .240. The last three years, he has made tremendous progress. He makes good contact, hitting near .300 each season, and is tough to strike out. He emerged as a good hitter with runners on base, collecting 101 RBIs at Las Vegas last season and 71 RBIs in 93 games in 1988. He is developing a better understanding of hitting in specific situations, yet he needs to go more to the opposite field and resist trying for home runs. He has homer potential, but must let them come naturally.

Fielding/Baserunning
Alomar gets high marks for his defensive skills behind the plate. He blocks balls extremely well, and runners have been reluctant to test his arm. Last season, he displayed more confidence in his ability to call a game and handle a pitching staff. He is not a basestealing threat.

Projection
The Indians didn't part with Joe Carter to have Alomar sit on the bench.

Career Statistics and Peak Projection

	G	AB	R	H	2B	3B	HR	RBI	BB	SO	AVG
1984 Spokane (Northwest League-Class A)	59	219	13	47	5	0	0	21	13	20	.215
1985 Charleston (South Atlantic League-Class A)	100	352	38	73	7	0	3	43	31	30	.207
1986 Beaumont (Texas League-Class AA)	100	346	36	83	15	1	4	27	15	35	.240
1986 Major League Equivalency	100	328	24	65	12	1	3	18	10	37	.198
1987 Wichita (Texas League-Class AA)	103	375	50	115	19	1	8	65	21	37	.307
1987 Major League Equivalency	103	347	31	87	14	0	6	40	13	39	.251
1988 Las Vegas (Pacific Coast League-Class AAA)	93	337	59	100	9	5	16	71	28	35	.297
1988 San Diego (National League)	1	1	0	0	0	0	0	0	0	1	.000
1988 Major League Equivalency	94	311	35	73	7	2	11	42	17	38	.235
1989 Las Vegas (Pacific Coast League-Class AAA)	131	523	88	160	33	8	13	101	42	58	.306
1989 San Diego (National League)	7	19	1	4	0	0	1	6	3	3	.211
1989 Major League Equivalency	138	504	57	126	26	4	11	70	31	64	.250
Peak Projection	154	558	84	155	27	4	21	81	43		.278

Interpretation
Alomar's peak line shows him with Todd Zeile's power, an example of how stadium dimensions (Jack Murphy's vs. Busch) can affect various projections. Alomar's power numbers have lagged behind Zeile's through most of the minors. His Major League Equivalencies for doubles and walks also are weak for his reputation.

GREG VAUGHN

Milwaukee Brewers
Outfielder
Brewers' First-Round Pick, Secondary Phase of June 1986 Draft

Personal
Height: 6-0 Weight: 193
Bats right, throws right
Born: July 3, 1965

School: Miami

Ratings

	Present	Future
Hitting	5	6
Power	5	6
Baserunning	5	5
Speed	5	5
Fielding	4	5
Arm	4	5
Range	4	5

Rating Key
7 Outstanding
6 Major League Caliber, High
5 Major League Caliber
4 Minor League Caliber, High
3 Minor League Caliber
2 Below Average
1 Poor

General
"He gave us an electric jolt," was how one Milwaukee coach described it. Indeed, Vaughn added sock to the Brewers' lineup after being brought up from Class AAA Denver last August for the American League East title scramble. Slugging five homers with 23 runs batted in over 38 games, he was starting in the outfield in favor of Rob Deer and Glenn Braggs on most days down the stretch. At Denver, Vaughn was named the Most Valuable Player in the American Association. He led the league with both 26 home runs and 92 RBIs, and his average of one home run every 14.88 at-bats topped all Class AAA hitters.

Hitting Tendencies
Vaughn's bat and physique bring to mind Kirby Puckett. Like the Twins' outfielder, Vaughn has a compact, muscular build that can withstand the day-to-day grind. He has a quick, short swing that generates a lot of bat speed, which is primarily where he gets his power. Vaughn can hit the ball to all fields, but his muscle is mostly to left and left-center field. He led his league in home runs in each of the last three seasons and has averaged nearly 26 homers and 89 RBIs (in 410 at-bats) over four minor league campaigns. The Brewers believe he'll develop even more power once he learns major league pitchers. He'll strike out more often than some hitters, but he also knows the value of a walk.

Fielding/Baserunning
Vaughn is projected as a left fielder in the majors. He has room to improve his defense and master the fundamentals, but his speed helps him avoid some potential mistakes. He is a smart baserunner who averaged 25 steals per season in the minors.

Projection
Vaughn will bid to join the Brewers' everyday lineup in 1990.

Career Statistics and Peak Projection

	G	AB	R	H	2B	3B	HR	RBI	BB	SO	AVG
1986 Helena (Pioneer League-Rookie)	66	258	64	75	12	2	16	54	30	69	.291
1987 Beloit (Midwest League-Class A)	139	492	120	150	31	6	33	105	102	115	.305
1988 El Paso (Texas League-Class AA)	131	505	104	152	39	2	28	105	63	120	.301
1988 Major League Equivalency	131	466	59	113	28	1	16	60	37	135	.242
1989 Denver (American Association-Class AAA)	110	387	74	107	17	5	26	92	62	94	.276
1989 Milwaukee (American League)	38	113	18	30	3	0	5	23	13	23	.265
1989 Major League Equivalency	148	484	72	121	17	3	24	90	62	132	.250
Peak Projection	154	564	103	154	27	2	35	103	73		.273

Interpretation
Vaughn fits the mold of the prototype Milwaukee hitter—excellent home run potential, a decent batting average and never mind the strikeouts. Granted, Robin Yount and Paul Molitor have mastered other offensive skills, but the Brewers can turn to a budding talent like Vaughn to provide the traditional power wares. His 1989 Major League Equivalency shows only a .250 average, but the Brewers have been playing Rob Deer for three years.

ERIC ANTHONY

Houston Astros
Outfielder
Astros' 34th-Round Pick, June 1986 Draft

Personal
Height: 6-2 Weight: 195
Bats left, throws left
Born: November 8, 1967

School: Mount Carmel High in San Diego

Ratings

	Present	Future
Hitting	4	5
Power	6	6
Baserunning	5	5
Speed	5	5
Fielding	4	5
Arm	5	5
Range	5	5

Rating Key
7 Outstanding
6 Major League Caliber, High
5 Major League Caliber
4 Minor League Caliber, High
3 Minor League Caliber
2 Below Average
1 Poor

General
Few would have challenged the opinion back in 1988 that Eric Anthony was a one-man wrecking crew. Playing that season at Class A Asheville, the slugging outfielder pounded 29 home runs to lead all minor league hitters. Well, Anthony just got better in 1989. Not only did he top the minors again with 31 homers, but he climbed the ladder from Class AA ball to the major leagues and stamped himself as the Astros' best power prospect since Glenn Davis. And Anthony, who played high school ball only one season, is still learning. He is an outstanding pupil with good work habits, and he's gaining more confidence as he launches home run shots at each career stop. His first major league hit was a two-run homer off San Francisco Giants ace Rick Reuschel.

Hitting Tendencies
Scouts and instructors have no doubts that Anthony will be a home run hitter. He is very strong and generates additional power with his excellent bat speed. If his shots don't have home run distance, they often reach the wall for extra bases. He'll also rack up a lot of strikeouts. At this stage, Anthony needs to learn the strike zone and take a walk on occasion. At Class AA Columbus and Class AAA Tucson in 1989, he fanned 138 times and drew only 41 walks.

Fielding/Baserunning
Anthony's improvement in the outfield has been encouraging and he's probably best suited for right field in the majors. His arm has gotten stronger (17 assists at Columbus in 1989) and his mechanics have improved. He can steal a base but doesn't loom as a big threat.

Projection
Anthony will have a shot at Houston's opening-day roster in 1990 but likely will start the year at Class AAA Tucson.

Career Statistics and Peak Projection

	G	AB	R	H	2B	3B	HR	RBI	BB	SO	AVG
1986 Sarasota Astros (Gulf Coast League-Rookie)	13	12	2	3	0	0	0	0	5	5	.250
1987 Sarasota Astros (Gulf Coast League-Rookie)	60	216	38	57	11	6	10	46	26	58	.264
1988 Asheville (South Atlantic League-Class A)	115	439	73	120	36	1	29	89	40	101	.273
1989 Columbus (Southern League-Class AA)	107	403	67	121	16	2	28	79	35	127	.300
1989 Tucson (Pacific Coast League-Class AAA)	12	46	10	10	3	0	3	11	6	11	.214
1989 Houston (National League)	25	61	7	11	2	0	4	7	9	16	.180
1989 Major League Equivalency	144	495	68	127	21	2	26	79	41	169	.257
Peak Projection	154	567	122	170	28	2	49	131	65		.300

Interpretation
What the projection line says is that Clark Kent here uses the phone booth in the Judge's old offices to change into his uniform, knock out a couple of homers and then fly off to rescue Lois Lane. A 49-homer projection in the Astrodome borders on the unthinkable. Someone, however, might be that good someday. And it will be someone who tore apart the minor leagues the way Anthony did.

ROBIN VENTURA

Chicago White Sox
Third Baseman
White Sox's First-Round Pick, June 1988 Draft

Personal
Height: 6-1   Weight: 185
Bats left, throws right
Born: July 14, 1967

School: Oklahoma State

Ratings

	Present	Future
Hitting	5	6
Power	4	5
Baserunning	5	5
Speed	5	5
Fielding	5	5
Arm	5	5
Range	5	5

Rating Key
7 Outstanding
6 Major League Caliber, High
5 Major League Caliber
4 Minor League Caliber, High
3 Minor League Caliber
2 Below Average
1 Poor

General
With Ventura, the White Sox anticipate having their most productive regular third baseman since Bill Melton held down the position in the early 1970s. Ventura, the 10th player selected in the 1988 draft, is a smart, hard-nosed player committed to winning. Making his pro debut with Class AA Birmingham in 1989, he was named the All-Star third baseman in the Southern League and was promoted to the White Sox in September. As an amateur player, Ventura was a career .428 hitter at Oklahoma State and set an NCAA record with a 58-game hitting streak. He batted .409 for the gold medal-winning U.S. team at the Seoul Olympics and received the 1988 Golden Spikes award, given annually to baseball's top amateur player.

Hitting Tendencies
Ventura made a quick, smooth adjustment from aluminum to wood bats, hitting a respectable .278 at Birmingham. He is a good contact hitter who sprays line drives to all fields. Scouts see him as a good RBI man with gap power, although he isn't expected to display the home run stroke he had at Oklahoma State (68 home runs in three seasons). Ventura has an outstanding eye at the plate. He drew 93 walks at Birmingham last season and posted a .403 on-base percentage.

Fielding/Baserunning
Ventura is a steady third baseman who makes the plays he's expected to. He charges the ball well and can make the barehanded pickup and quick throw. He committed 27 errors at Birmingham but led the league's third basemen in fielding. On the bases, he has average speed.

Projection
Ventura is expected to be entrenched as the White Sox's regular third baseman by the end of the 1990 season.

Career Statistics and Peak Projection

	G	AB	R	H	2B	3B	HR	RBI	BB	SO	AVG
1989 Birmingham (Southern League-Class AA)	129	454	75	126	25	2	3	67	93	51	.278
1989 Chicago (American League)	16	45	5	8	3	0	0	7	8	6	.178
1989 Major League Equivalency	145	474	56	109	21	2	2	53	74	56	.230
Peak Projection	154	533	85	144	27	2	4	47	99		.270

Interpretation
The projected peak calculation says Ventura is a poor man's Wade Boggs—he'll get on base in the leadoff slot but won't carry Boggs' average. His 1989 Major League Equivalency doesn't show he's ready to advance to the White Sox. And for those who expected peak seasons in the neighborhood of .300, keep in mind that the projection is based only on one season at the Class AA level.

JOSE OFFERMAN

Los Angeles Dodgers
Shortstop
Signed by Dodgers as a Non-Drafted Free Agent, July 1986

Personal
Height: 6-0 Weight: 150
Bats left and right, throws right
Born: November 8, 1968

School: Dominican Republic

Ratings

	Present	Future
Hitting	4	6
Power	4	5
Baserunning	5	6
Speed	6	6
Fielding	4	5
Arm	5	5
Range	5	5

Rating Key
7 Outstanding
6 Major League Caliber, High
5 Major League Caliber
4 Minor League Caliber, High
3 Minor League Caliber
2 Below Average
1 Poor

General
Another highly touted prospect from San Pedro de Macoris in the Dominican Republic, Offerman already has been tabbed by scouts as the Dodgers' shortstop of the future. He moved another step closer in 1989, finishing the season in the Class AA Texas League after an outstanding start with Class A Bakersfield. In 62 games there, Offerman batted .306 and stole 37 bases, leaving behind enough of an impression to receive California League All-Star honors at shortstop. He received similar recognition in the Pioneer League in 1988, his first minor league campaign.

Hitting Tendencies
Offerman is a switch-hitter who makes contact from both sides of the plate. Although he's slight of build, he has some punch in his bat and continues to get stronger as he physically matures. He can look pitches over for a walk (75 in 1989) and steal a base to advance into scoring position. He always seems to be getting on, stealing and scoring a run. He scored 100 times last season, tying for the No. 2 spot among all minor leaguers.

Fielding/Baserunning
Offerman has been praised for his defense, or at least defensive potential. He has a rifle-like arm, outstanding range and good hands. He has, however, been prone to commit errors—some mental, others due to wild or risky throws. He has distinguished himself as one of the best baserunners in the minors. Last season, he led all players with 69 stolen bases; in 1988, he set a Pioneer League mark with 57 thefts.

Projection
Offerman is ticketed to begin the 1990 season at Class AAA Albuquerque and could make the jump to the majors by year's end.

Career Statistics and Peak Projection

	G	AB	R	H	2B	3B	HR	RBI	BB	SO	AVG
1988 Great Falls (Pioneer League-Rookie)	60	25	75	83	11	5	2	28	38	42	.331
1989 Bakersfield (California League-Class A)	62	245	53	75	9	4	2	22	35	48	.306
1989 San Antonio (Texas League-Class AA)	68	278	47	80	6	3	2	22	40	39	.288
1989 Major League Equivalency	68	283	31	65	5	3	1	15	27	41	.230
Peak Projection	154	559	93	157	15	6	3	49	74		.280

Interpretation
Dodger fans won't like the fact that the projection system doesn't look kindly on Offerman, but the calculations note that he's played in minor league home parks conducive to offense.

LARRY WALKER

Montreal Expos
Outfielder
Signed by Expos as a Non-Drafted Free Agent, November 1984

Personal
Height: 6-2 Weight: 195
Bats left, throws right
Born: December 1, 1966

School: Maple Ridge Senior Secondary in British Columbia

Ratings

	Present	Future
Hitting	4	5
Power	5	5
Baserunning	5	6
Speed	5	5
Fielding	5	6
Arm	5	5
Range	5	5

Rating Key
7 Outstanding
6 Major League Caliber, High
5 Major League Caliber
4 Minor League Caliber, High
3 Minor League Caliber
2 Below Average
1 Poor

General
Walker sat idle the 1988 season after injuring a knee in winter ball but bounced back strong at Class AAA Indianapolis in 1989. Still wearing a knee brace after undergoing reconstructive surgery, he stole bases with abandon and showed signs of hitting for the same kind of power that saw him propel 33 and 26 homers in the two years prior to his injury. He's capable of hitting for a high average and has decent speed that helps him in all phases of the game. Walker has shown he's a well-rounded player and has been an All-Star selection in each of his last two active seasons. He was called up by Montreal late last year.

Hitting Tendencies
Once the top power prospect in the Expos' system, Walker saw his home run production decline in 1989 due to his yearlong layoff. The more pitching he saw, however, the more he looked like his former self. Walker started driving the ball and was a dangerous hitter with men on base. Over his last three seasons, he has 236 runs batted in. He does have to learn to adjust to good fastballs inside and has some trouble against lefthanders. The Expos believe instruction and experience will take care of those weaknesses.

Fielding/Baserunning
Walker probably is best suited for either left or right field in the major leagues. He is a sound defensive player with an above-average arm. As a baserunner, he is improving all the time and has good speed for a man his size. Last season, he vied for the American Association stolen base lead until he was promoted to Montreal.

Projection
Walker is expected to challenge for a spot in the Expos' regular lineup in 1990.

Career Statistics and Peak Projection

	G	AB	R	H	2B	3B	HR	RBI	BB	SO	AVG
1985 Utica (New York-Penn League-Class A)	62	215	24	48	8	2	2	26	18	57	.223
1986 Burlington (Midwest League-Class A)	95	332	67	96	12	6	29	74	46	112	.289
1986 West Palm Beach (Florida State League-Class A)	38	113	20	32	7	5	4	16	26	32	.283
1987 Jacksonville (Southern League-Class AA)	128	474	91	136	25	7	26	83	67	120	.287
1987 Major League Equivalency	128	455	69	117	23	4	20	63	49	131	.257
1988				Injured—Did not play							
1989 Indianapolis (American Association-Class AAA)	114	385	68	104	18	2	12	59	50	87	.270
1989 Montreal (National League)	20	47	4	8	0	0	0	4	5	13	.170
1989 Major League Equivalency	134	424	63	104	18	1	11	55	46	109	.245
Peak Projection	154	550	128	158	28	3	28	93	71		.287

Interpretation
Walker projects quite well, although his 1989 Major League Equivalency indicates he might not be ready to move up to the big show. If the shape of the MLEs holds, Walker may have to sacrifice some power to bring up his batting average.

TRAVIS FRYMAN

Detroit Tigers
Shortstop
Tigers' Supplemental Pick Following First Round, June 1987 Draft

Personal
Height: 6-1 Weight: 180
Bats right, throws right
Born: April 25, 1969

School: Tate High
in Gonzalez, Fla.

Ratings

	Present	Future
Hitting	4	5
Power	4	6
Baserunning	4	5
Speed	4	4
Fielding	5	6
Arm	6	6
Range	5	6

Rating Key
7 Outstanding
6 Major League Caliber, High
5 Major League Caliber
4 Minor League Caliber, High
3 Minor League Caliber
2 Below Average
1 Poor

General
After batting .234 in each of his first two minor league seasons, Fryman recaptured the scouts' attention in 1989. Moving up to the Class AA level, he started to put his total game together and received Eastern League All-Star honors at shortstop. Fryman made major strides offensively and defensively, with observers attributing much of his improvement to his maturing mentally and physically. He is regarded as a hard worker who is driven to be successful. He was drafted 30th overall in 1987 as compensation for the Tigers' loss of free-agent Lance Parrish.

Hitting Tendencies
Fryman appears to be more than a singles-hitting shortstop. He made his presence felt by flashing extra-base power at Class AA London last season, stroking nine home runs and a league-leading 30 doubles. In his first two seasons, he had totaled just two home runs. He still has problems with breaking pitches but was able to raise his batting average 31 points in 1989 as he made adjustments. He also is working to hit the ball where it's pitched rather than trying to hammer everything to left field. He still strikes out frequently and rarely has the patience to stick around for a walk (78 strikeouts, 19 walks last season).

Fielding/Baserunning
Fryman has all the tools a scout looks for in a shortstop. He's smooth making plays and has an above-average arm, even for a major league shortstop. He did, however, commit a league-high 27 errors at London in 1989. He has average skills as a baserunner but swiped just five bases last season after stealing 18 in 1988.

Projection
Fryman, who turns just 21 this season, likely will begin 1990 at Class AAA Toledo but could be brought along quickly.

Career Statistics and Peak Projection

	G	AB	R	H	2B	3B	HR	RBI	BB	SO	AVG
1987 Bristol (Appalachian League-Rookie)	67	248	25	58	9	0	2	20	22	40	.234
1988 Fayetteville (South Atlantic League-Class A)	123	411	44	96	17	4	0	47	24	83	.234
1989 London (Eastern League-Class AA)	118	426	52	113	30	1	9	56	19	78	.265
1989 Major League Equivalency	118	411	43	98	27	1	9	47	16	84	.238
Peak Projection	154	527	85	150	38	1	19	78	33		.285

Interpretation
Fryman's Major League Equivalency and, to a lesser degree, his peak projection question his on-base ability. There are red flags over the walks column in both lines, yet there's nothing in the MLE to offset that weakness. Again, however, this prospect's figures are based on just one Class AA season.

MARK LEWIS

Cleveland Indians
Shortstop
Indians' First-Round Pick, June 1988 Draft

Personal
Height: 6-1   Weight: 170
Bats right, throws right
Born: November 30, 1969

School: Hamilton High
in Hamilton, Ohio

Ratings

	Present	Future
Hitting	3	5
Power	3	5
Baserunning	4	5
Speed	5	5
Fielding	5	6
Arm	6	6
Range	5	6

Rating Key
7 Outstanding
6 Major League Caliber, High
5 Major League Caliber
4 Minor League Caliber, High
3 Minor League Caliber
2 Below Average
1 Poor

General
Scouts say Lewis is gifted with skills and instincts that can't be taught to other players. Often likened to a young Robin Yount, he is a quiet, intense player who has a tremendous feel for the game. He is very demanding of himself and is driven to excel. Lewis has been a league All-Star pick at shortstop in each of his two minor league seasons. Playing at 19 years old last year, he moved up to the Class AA Eastern League from Class A Kinston late in the season. Before his junior year in high school, Lewis received the highest rating of any prospect, college or pro, by the Major League Scouting Bureau. The second player drafted in 1988, he is credited with setting national high school records for career hits and runs batted in.

Hitting Tendencies
Lewis has the quickest wrists of any hitter in the Indians' organization. When he matures and fills out physically, he'll handle the bat better and start hitting for average and more power. At this stage, he is struggling with curves and sliders, but the Indians have noted steady improvement as he acquires at-bats. He's a fixture of concentration when he digs in and tough to strike out. His biggest hindrance offensively is a body that hasn't caught up with a sharp mind.

Fielding/Baserunning
Lewis has above-average skills at shortstop with outstanding range, particularly into the hole. He did commit 32 errors in 89 games at short for Kinston, proof that he's still learning. He runs well and could be a 20-steals major leaguer.

Projection
Lewis is ticketed for Class AA Canton-Akron in 1990 and could climb a level by year's end. The step to Cleveland is probably two years away.

Career Statistics

	G	AB	R	H	2B	3B	HR	RBI	BB	SO	AVG
1988 Burlington (Appalachian League-Rookie)	61	227	39	60	13	1	7	43	25	44	.264
1989 Kinston (Carolina League-Class A)	93	349	50	94	16	3	1	32	34	50	.269
1989 Canton-Akron (Eastern League-Class AA)	7	25	4	5	1	0	0	1	1	3	.200

(Projections unavailable due to player's limited Class AA experience)

MARQUIS GRISSOM

Montreal Expos
Outfielder
Expos' Third-Round Pick, June 1988 Draft

Personal
Height: 5-11   Weight: 192
Bats right, throws right
Born: April 17, 1967

School: Florida A&M

Ratings

	Present	Future
Hitting	4	5
Power	3	4
Baserunning	5	6
Speed	6	6
Fielding	5	5
Arm	6	6
Range	5	5

Rating Key
7 Outstanding
6 Major League Caliber, High
5 Major League Caliber
4 Minor League Caliber, High
3 Minor League Caliber
2 Below Average
1 Poor

General
Grissom's rapid ascent through the Montreal system culminated with his reaching the majors in just his second season out of Florida A&M. In his first minor league campaign, he ranked among the leaders in the Class A New York-Penn League in virtually every offensive category. He climbed all the way to Montreal in 1989, stopping long enough at Class AA Jacksonville and Class AAA Indianapolis to showcase the bat, speed, arm and defensive range that indicate he'll be the complete big-league player. Scouts say all he needs is experience to become a great one. In 1988, his final year at Florida A&M (Andre Dawson's alma mater), the multitalented Grissom ranked sixth among Division I players in batting (.448) and posted a 9-3 record in 12 starts—all complete games—as a pitcher.

Hitting Tendencies
Grissom can make things happen at the plate and could become the leadoff hitter the Expos are looking for. He's a good contact hitter with a good knowledge of the strike zone, and he's capable of drawing his share of walks. He's had power in his swing on occasion, but speed is probably his best attribute as an offensive threat. Last season, he did appear overmatched at times by Class AAA pitching but hung in better once he made some adjustments.

Fielding/Baserunning
Grissom has a major league arm and is an outstanding defensive center fielder. In a one-month stint with Montreal, however, he had trouble going back on fly balls. As a basestealer, he's especially dangerous.

Projection
Grissom could stick with the Expos if he hits big-league pitching in spring training. If not, he'll return to Class AAA Indianapolis.

Career Statistics and Peak Projection

	G	AB	R	H	2B	3B	HR	RBI	BB	SO	AVG
1988 Jamestown (New York-Penn League-Class A)	74	291	69	94	14	7	8	39	35	39	.323
1989 Jacksonville (Southern League-Class AA)	78	278	43	83	15	4	3	31	24	31	.299
1989 Indianapolis (American Association-Class AAA)	49	187	28	52	10	4	2	21	14	23	.278
1989 Montreal (National League)	26	74	16	19	2	0	1	2	12	21	.257
1989 Major League Equivalency	153	529	78	144	27	6	6	47	43	82	.272
Peak Projection	154	571	110	174	32	6	10	68	62		.306

Interpretation
Grissom shot up the minor league ladder, and the system liked the way he hit. The Expos will find a place for Grissom, who could really flourish as a leadoff man if he exceeds his projected peak walk total. Even with a modest 62 projected walks, he figures to score 110 runs.

BERNIE WILLIAMS

New York Yankees
Outfielder
Signed by Yankees as a Non-Drafted Free Agent, September 1985

Personal
Height: 6-2   Weight: 180
Bats left and right, throws right
Born: September 13, 1968

School: Vega Alta, Puerto Rico

Ratings

	Present	Future
Hitting	4	5
Power	4	5
Baserunning	4	5
Speed	6	6
Fielding	5	6
Arm	6	6
Range	5	5

Rating Key
7 Outstanding
6 Major League Caliber, High
5 Major League Caliber
4 Minor League Caliber, High
3 Minor League Caliber
2 Below Average
1 Poor

General
Williams earns high marks from scouts in all five important major league skill areas: hitting, hitting for power, speed, fielding and throwing. The Yankees are not rushing his development, allowing him to gain some experience at the minor league level. Still, despite having played only Class A ball, he was one of the last three players the Yankees cut from camp in spring training in 1989. He struggled at Class AAA Columbus to start the year and was sent to Class AA Albany to get his game back in order. He had missed parts of the previous two seasons due to injuries but led the Carolina League in 1988 with a .335 batting mark.

Hitting Tendencies
Williams is a switch-hitter who packs power from both sides of the plate. He's a hitter who looks good swinging, and he has the speed to stretch hits to extra bases. He has learned to use the entire field and has good power going the opposite way. Williams has displayed a good eye through his career but last season wasn't nearly as selective, striking out 110 times. Over his first three seasons, he had averaged nearly a walk for every strikeout (133 walks, 142 strikeouts). Still just 21 years old, he's apt to become a stronger hitter as he matures mentally and physically.

Fielding/Baserunning
Williams contributes good center-field defense and speed on the bases. He is a gliding runner who gets a good jump on fly balls, and he has a strong arm. He could be a perennial 30-steals man.

Projection
Williams is expected to stick at Class AAA Columbus in 1990 and compete for a spot in the major leagues in 1991.

Career Statistics and Peak Projection

	G	AB	R	H	2B	3B	HR	RBI	BB	SO	AVG
1986 Sarasota Yankees (Gulf Coast League-Rookie)	61	230	95	62	5	3	2	25	39	40	.270
1987 Fort Lauderdale (Florida State League-Class A)	25	71	11	11	3	0	0	4	18	22	.155
1987 Oneonta (New York-Penn League-Class A)	25	93	13	32	4	0	0	15	10	14	.344
1988 Prince William (Carolina League-Class A)	92	337	72	113	16	7	7	45	66	66	.335
1989 Columbus (International League-Class AAA)	50	162	21	35	8	1	2	16	25	38	.216
1989 Albany (Eastern League-Class AA)	91	314	63	79	11	8	11	42	60	72	.252
1989 Major League Equivalency	141	472	78	110	18	6	12	54	74	117	.233
Peak Projection	154	512	127	143	23	7	22	80	95		.279

Interpretation
He has only one season of usable data, and Williams winds up with mixed results in his lone Major League Equivalency. The power totals increase significantly on the peak projection line, and his runs scored total reaches league-leading proportions.

DEAN PALMER

Texas Rangers
Third Baseman
Rangers' Third-Round Pick, June 1986 Draft

Personal
Height: 6-2   Weight: 187
Bats right, throws right
Born: December 27, 1968

School: Florida High
in Tallahassee, Fla.

Ratings

	Present	Future
Hitting	4	5
Power	4	6
Baserunning	4	5
Speed	4	4
Fielding	4	5
Arm	5	6
Range	4	5

Rating Key
7 Outstanding
6 Major League Caliber, High
5 Major League Caliber
4 Minor League Caliber, High
3 Minor League Caliber
2 Below Average
1 Poor

General
The numbers don't lie, but Palmer's are set in a slightly bolder typeface in many scouts' memories. Why? His age, enthusiasm and aggressiveness. He's a player who can bring a lift to a club, with both his bat and field presence. Just 20 years old last season, Palmer was named the Class AA Texas League's All-Star third baseman in his fourth year of pro ball. He led the league in home runs and ranked among the top five in total bases, runs scored, runs batted in and doubles. He was called up by Texas in September. In 1988, Palmer played just 74 games before undergoing wrist surgery.

Hitting Tendencies
Palmer has the best bat speed of any prospect in the Rangers' organization. He has above-average power potential, and he set a Tulsa club record last season by homering in five consecutive games. Palmer finished with a league-leading 25 home runs but also struck out too much: a league-high 152 times (plus 12 strikeouts in 19 at-bats with Texas). The Rangers believe he'll stop chasing bad pitches the more he bats against good pitching. If he does develop a hitter's strike zone, he should hit for a better average as well.

Fielding/Baserunning
Palmer has a very strong arm from third base. He has good hands and good range, but he committed a league-high 30 errors at his position last season. Many of those were due to carelessness on routine plays. Palmer has decent speed on the bases but is not projected to be a stealing threat.

Projection
Palmer figures to move on to Class AAA Oklahoma City to start the 1990 season but could be in the major leagues by year's end.

Career Statistics and Peak Projection

	G	AB	R	H	2B	3B	HR	RBI	BB	SO	AVG
1986 Sarasota Rangers (Gulf Coast League-Rookie)	50	163	19	34	7	1	0	12	22	34	.209
1987 Gastonia (South Atlantic League-Class A)	128	484	51	104	16	0	9	54	36	126	.215
1988 Charlotte (Florida State League-Class A)	74	305	38	81	12	1	4	35	15	69	.266
1989 Tulsa (Texas League-Class AA)	133	498	82	125	32	5	25	90	41	152	.251
1989 Texas (American League)	8	19	0	2	2	0	0	1	0	12	.105
1989 Major League Equivalency	141	502	68	112	27	4	23	76	34	176	.223
Peak Projection	154	536	120	145	33	4	42	115	49		.271

Interpretation
The enormous growth between Palmer's 1989 Major League Equivalency and his peak projection is due to his youth—he's still seven years away from his peak season. If the home run projection is on target, he'll probably get pitched around and at least double his walk total. If his power doesn't develop, the walks will be well below the major league average. His peak is based on just one season in the Texas League.

DELINO DeSHIELDS

Montreal Expos
Shortstop
Expos' First-Round Pick, June 1987 Draft

Personal
Height: 6-1 Weight: 170
Bats left, throws right
Born: January 15, 1969

School: Seaford High
in Seaford, Del.

Ratings

	Present	Future
Hitting	4	5
Power	3	5
Baserunning	5	6
Speed	6	6
Fielding	4	5
Arm	5	5
Range	4	5

Rating Key
7 Outstanding
6 Major League Caliber, High
5 Major League Caliber
4 Minor League Caliber, High
3 Minor League Caliber
2 Below Average
1 Poor

General
DeShields has a wealth of raw talent that needs some refining. He has the potential to be a dependable on-base man, with a good enough cut to flash some power on occasion. The Expos want him to become a better contact hitter, however, and take advantage of the speed that's suited for extra-base hits, turf singles and stolen bases. He has a flair for making acrobatic plays in the field, but his error totals have kept the faithful from getting overly excited. DeShields did show overall improvement in 1989, splitting time between Class AA Jacksonville and Class AAA Indianapolis.

Hitting Tendencies
As he moved up the minor league ladder in 1989, DeShields hit for his highest average to date. Nevertheless, he still needs some at-bats before he's ready for major league pitching. Only 21, he needs to reduce his strikeouts 133 in 1989, 110 in 1988) and make better contact. At times, he has the discipline to work pitchers for walks (92 in 1989, 95 in 1988), and he's often running when he's on base. When he hits the gaps, he has the speed to stretch hits for extra bases (10 triples overall last year).

Fielding/Baserunning
DeShields has good range, a strong arm and turns the double play well at short, but the only consistency he's shown is his tendency to commit errors: 47 last season, 42 in 1988 and 43 in 1987. The Expos are planning to work him some at second base in 1990. He has the potential to be a big basestealer in the major leagues, with 112 thefts over the last two seasons.

Projection
DeShields likely will play at Class AAA Indianapolis in 1990 and make a bid for the majors in 1991.

Career Statistics and Peak Projection

	G	AB	R	H	2B	3B	HR	RBI	BB	SO	AVG
1987 Bradenton Expos (Gulf Coast League-Rookie)	31	111	17	24	5	2	1	4	21	30	.216
1987 Jamestown (New York-Penn League-Class A)	34	96	16	21	1	2	1	5	24	28	.219
1988 Rockford (Midwest League-Class A)	129	460	97	116	26	6	12	46	95	110	.252
1989 Jacksonville (Southern League-Class AA)	93	307	55	83	10	6	3	35	76	80	.270
1989 Indianapolis (American Association-Class AAA)	47	181	29	47	8	4	2	14	16	53	.260
1989 Major League Equivalency	140	477	73	119	18	7	4	43	77	145	.249
Peak Projection	154	523	96	144	22	7	6	53	89		.276

Interpretation
DeShields has only one season to project with, but his offensive numbers from Class A through Triple-A have been pretty consistent. The only mystery is the collapse in walks at the Class AAA level. His projected line is made to order for a No. 2 man in the order, provided his strikeouts don't approach his 1989 Major League Equivalency.

KEVIN BELCHER

Texas Rangers
Outfielder
Rangers' Sixth-Round Pick, June 1987 Draft

General
Belcher is the hardest worker in the Texas organization and one of the reasons the club surrendered prized prospect Sammy Sosa to Chicago to get Harold Baines. Belcher has earned high grades in the five important skill areas: hitting, hitting for power, running, throwing and fielding. Before a broken collarbone ended his 1989 season a month early, he was one of the hitting terrors of the Class A South Atlantic League. In just 338 at-bats, Belcher ripped 14 homers and knocked in 59 runs to warrant a berth on the league's All-Star team. He healed in time to play in the Florida Instructional League, where he was named the Ranger team's co-captain (the first time captains had been appointed) due to his work ethic.

Hitting Tendencies
Belcher has a quick bat that generates a lot of offense. He has muscle to reach the fences and slash line drives into the alleys for extra-base hits and RBIs. His strength will help him get his hits, and he emerged as a more complete hitter in 1989, batting a career-high .296 with power. The Rangers would like him to start reading pitchers and reduce his strikeouts (one every 5.1 at-bats in two years at Gastonia).

Fielding/Baserunning
Belcher continues to improve defensively in center field. He's starting to find the mark with his strong throws and he has the speed to run down balls in the gaps. Although he totaled only 35 steals in two seasons at Gastonia, he could develop into a major stealing threat.

Projection
Belcher appears destined for Class AA Tulsa to start the 1990 season. If he shows as much improvement as in 1989, the Rangers could bring him up before season's end.

Personal
Height: 6-0 Weight: 170
Bats right, throws right
Born: August 8, 1967

School: Navarro College in Corsicana, Tex.

Ratings

	Present	Future
Hitting	4	5
Power	4	6
Baserunning	4	5
Speed	6	6
Fielding	4	5
Arm	5	5
Range	4	5

Rating Key
7 Outstanding
6 Major League Caliber, High
5 Major League Caliber
4 Minor League Caliber, High
3 Minor League Caliber
2 Below Average
1 Poor

Career Statistics

	G	AB	R	H	2B	3B	HR	RBI	BB	SO	AVG
1987 Sarasota Rangers (Gulf Coast League-Rookie)	58	215	32	45	8	2	2	10	32	38	.209
1988 Gastonia (South Atlantic League-Class A)	105	392	56	96	13	1	8	44	40	81	.245
1989 Gastonia (South Atlantic League-Class A)	93	338	61	100	21	1	14	59	31	62	.296

(Projections unavailable because player has not competed at Class AA or Class AAA levels)

RAY LANKFORD

St. Louis Cardinals
Outfielder
Cardinals' Third-Round Pick, June 1987 Draft

Personal
Height: 5-11 Weight: 180
Bats left, throws left
Born: June 5, 1967

School: Modesto Junior College in Modesto, Calif.

Ratings

	Present	Future
Hitting	5	6
Power	4	5
Baserunning	5	6
Speed	5	5
Fielding	5	5
Arm	5	5
Range	5	5

Rating Key
7 Outstanding
6 Major League Caliber, High
5 Major League Caliber
4 Minor League Caliber, High
3 Minor League Caliber
2 Below Average
1 Poor

General
Lankford looks like another prototype Cardinal outfielder who should thrive in spacious Busch Stadium. He's a strong lefthanded hitter with appealing power—not necessarily home run power, but punch to hammer doubles and triples into the gaps. Lankford has good speed (he once rushed for a school-record 1,026 yards as a running back at Modesto Junior College) and can steal bases. He swiped 37 in 1989 at Class AA Arkansas, where he put together numbers that placed him among the top five players in the Cardinal organization in virtually every offensive category. Among all minor leaguers, he ranked in the top 10 in runs batted in, triples and runs scored. He's a diligent worker who takes instruction well and plays the game hard.

Hitting Tendencies
The only concern about Lankford's hitting is his unconventional batting style. Scouts and instructors say he holds his hands too high and too tight, yet his stance hasn't affected his hitting at any stop in his career. Indeed, Lankford was voted the Texas League's Most Valuable Player last season. At times, he has tried to change his stance but reverted back to old—and successful—ways. He has good bat speed and a good knowledge of the strike zone, rarely swinging at bad pitches.

Fielding/Baserunning
Lankford is a good defensive outfielder with enough speed to cover the roomy outfield at Busch. He has a strong arm and plays aggressively. On the bases, he always looms as a stealing threat, yet he picks his spots intelligently.

Projection
Lankford figures to open the 1990 season in center field at Class AAA Louisville. He is a candidate to make the majors in late 1990 or in 1991.

Career Statistics and Peak Projection

	G	AB	R	H	2B	3B	HR	RBI	BB	SO	AVG
1987 Johnson City (Appalachian League-Rookie)	66	253	45	78	17	4	3	32	19	43	.308
1988 Springfield (Midwest League-Class A)	135	532	90	151	26	16	11	66	60	92	.284
1989 Arkansas (Texas League-Class AA)	134	498	98	158	28	12	11	98	65	57	.317
1989 Major League Equivalency	134	467	67	127	25	11	6	67	44	58	.272
Peak Projection	154	530	97	162	31	12	10	68	61		.305

Interpretation
Lankford's projected peak and Major League Equivalency are both solid across the board. He maintains his high triples total due to the expansive home park in St. Louis. The calculations are based on just one season at the Class AA level.

TY GRIFFIN

Chicago Cubs
Third Baseman
Cubs' First-Round Pick, June 1988 Draft

Personal
Height: 6-0   Weight: 187
Bats left and right, throws right
Born: September 5, 1967

School: Georgia Tech

Ratings

	Present	Future
Hitting	4	5
Power	3	4
Baserunning	5	6
Speed	5	5
Fielding	4	5
Arm	4	5
Range	4	5

Rating Key
7 Outstanding
6 Major League Caliber, High
5 Major League Caliber
4 Minor League Caliber, High
3 Minor League Caliber
2 Below Average
1 Poor

General
Griffin started his pro career in 1989 as a second baseman at Class A Peoria but soon was moved to third base and promoted to Class AA Charlotte. He plays with confidence and has outstanding physical abilities. Griffin has a knack for getting the big hit or making the key play with a game on the line, and he's the type of player who makes others on his team play better. As a member of the 1988 U.S. Olympic squad, he led the team in hitting (.416) and steals. At Georgia Tech, he received All-America recognition, hit .333 for his career and stole 127 bases in 140 attempts. The Cubs are confident he'll be an impact player.

Hitting Tendencies
Griffin has a good handle on the hitting fundamentals and is a smart situational hitter. He has line-drive power that probably won't produce many home runs in National League parks. Instead, the Cubs expect the switch-hitting speedster to hit for average, draw walks and have a high on-base percentage. Although he had his problems against Class AA pitching after his promotion in 1989, he's been a productive batter with men on base. On the U.S. Olympic team, Griffin ranked third in runs batted in (52) and second in home runs (16).

Fielding/Baserunning
Griffin responded well to the move from second to third base but still needs time to learn the position. The Cubs are willing to live with some of his early mistakes (23 errors in 73 games at third). He puts his speed to use on the basepaths, always looming as a stealing threat.

Projection
Some within the Chicago organization believe Griffin can jump directly from the Class AA level to the majors in 1990, like Jerome Walton did a year ago. More likely, Griffin will play at Class AAA Iowa.

Career Statistics and Peak Projection

	G	AB	R	H	2B	3B	HR	RBI	BB	SO	AVG
1989 Peoria (Midwest League-Class A)	82	296	45	85	15	6	10	64	49	74	.287
1989 Charlotte (Southern League-Class AA)	45	143	25	33	6	0	3	21	25	29	.231
1989 Major League Equivalency	45	137	18	27	5	0	2	15	17	31	.197
Peak Projection	154	493	111	128	22	0	13	57	73		.259

Interpretation
Griffin's limited experience doesn't lend itself to the system, what with only a third of one season to work with and the calculations trying to project for a full season five years down the road. The only real positive in the peak line is the high number of walks.

GLENALLEN HILL

Toronto Blue Jays
Outfielder
Blue Jays' Ninth-Round Pick, June 1983 Draft

Personal
Height: 6-2 Weight: 210
Bats right, throws right
Born: March 22, 1965

School: Santa Cruz High in Santa Cruz, Calif.

Ratings

	Present	Future
Hitting	5	6
Power	5	6
Baserunning	5	5
Speed	5	5
Fielding	3	4
Arm	4	4
Range	4	5

Rating Key
7 Outstanding
6 Major League Caliber, High
5 Major League Caliber
4 Minor League Caliber, High
3 Minor League Caliber
2 Below Average
1 Poor

General
Hill finally made the strides the Blue Jays have been awaiting, both on and off the field, in his seventh minor league campaign. Playing most of 1989 at Class AAA Syracuse, he showcased all of his offensive tools. He led the International League in home runs, hits, triples, total bases and runs; ranked second in batting, and fourth in runs batted in. But just as important, Hill grew up mentally. A bad attitude had cost him a demotion from Syracuse to Class AA Knoxville in 1988 and he was dropped from the Blue Jays' 40-man winter roster. He was a changed player when he returned in 1989, earning International League All-Star honors and a September promotion to Toronto.

Hitting Tendencies
Hill's power was never in question. He is very strong and can hit the ball out of the park to any field. But Hill became a more complete hitter in 1989. Laying off bad breaking balls and high fastballs, he was able to make better contact and reduce his strikeout total to 107 (with Syracuse) after averaging 160 strikeouts over the previous five seasons. He also showed the ability to hit to the opposite field when he trailed in the count. If he continues to be selective and make good contact, Hill is expected to post good numbers across the board.

Fielding/Baserunning
Hill is an above-average baserunner with good speed and has the potential to steal 20 bases a year. He probably is best suited to play left field, although he currently is regarded as only average in the field. He has an adequate arm but takes too long to get rid of the ball.

Projection
Hill likely will be competing for a spot on the Blue Jays' opening-day roster in 1990.

Career Statistics and Peak Projection

	G	AB	R	H	2B	3B	HR	RBI	BB	SO	AVG
1983 Medicine Hat (Pioneer League-Rookie)	46	133	26	34	3	4	6	27	17	49	.256
1984 Florence (South Atlantic League-Class A)	129	440	75	105	19	5	16	64	63	150	.239
1985 Kinston (Carolina League-Class A)	131	466	57	48	13	0	20	56	57	211	.210
1986 Knoxville (Southern League-Class AA)	141	570	87	159	23	6	31	96	39	153	.279
1986 Major League Equivalency	141	536	57	125	19	4	21	63	28	155	.233
1987 Syracuse (International League-Class AAA)	137	536	65	126	25	6	16	77	25	152	.235
1987 Major League Equivalency	137	512	46	102	21	4	11	54	19	154	.199
1988 Syracuse (International League-Class AAA)	51	172	21	40	7	0	4	19	15	59	.233
1988 Knoxville (Southern League-Class AA)	79	269	37	71	13	2	12	38	28	75	.264
1988 Major League Equivalency	130	430	50	100	19	2	14	49	41	135	.233
1989 Syracuse (International League-Class AAA)	125	483	86	155	31	15	21	72	34	107	.321
1989 Toronto (American League)	19	52	4	15	0	0	1	7	3	12	.288
1989 Major League Equivalency	125	465	72	137	29	12	18	60	31	108	.295
Peak Projection	154	541	85	154	31	9	27	93	50		.285

Interpretation
Hill's projected batting average winds up lower than his 1989 Major League Equivalency because the peak system factors in his earlier seasons as well. Generally, the more data the system has, the more accurate the projections. Whether Hill played beyond his potential or not in 1989, the calculations indicate he's ready for Toronto.

JUAN GONZALEZ

Texas Rangers
Outfielder
Signed by Rangers as a Non-Drafted Free Agent, May 1986

Personal
Height: 6-3   Weight: 175
Bats right, throws right
Born: October 16, 1969

School: Vega Baja, Puerto Rico

Ratings

	Present	Future
Hitting	5	6
Power	4	6
Baserunning	4	4
Speed	4	4
Fielding	5	5
Arm	5	6
Range	5	5

Rating Key
7 Outstanding
6 Major League Caliber, High
5 Major League Caliber
4 Minor League Caliber, High
3 Minor League Caliber
2 Below Average
1 Poor

General
Gonzalez has drawn some early comparisons to veteran Dale Murphy, essentially because of his big bat and ability to hold down center field despite a lack of speed. Gonzalez did a lot of growing up at Class AA Tulsa in 1989. Once lacking in concentration and inclined to emotional outbursts, he displayed a mature, professional attitude and, consequently, prospered at the plate. He led the Texas League in total bases and received All-Star honors in the outfield. In September, Gonzalez was called up by the Rangers at age 19. Despite his youth, he has logged four seasons in the minors.

Hitting Tendencies
Gonzalez made big strides at Tulsa in the second half of 1989, hitting for a higher average and with more power. He wound up third in the Texas League in home runs, fourth in hits and posted a career-best .293 batting average. The Rangers were particularly encouraged by his improved discipline at bat. He was able to lay off breaking balls in the dirt, but statistics show he drew only 31 walks and struck out 98 times for the Drillers. Gonzalez likely will add some muscle to his good athletic build. He hits the ball hard and has consistent 20-homer, .280 potential.

Fielding/Baserunning
Gonzalez doesn't have the speed of most center fielders, but he offsets that with a strong arm, good positional play and quick reaction to fly balls. As a baserunner, he rates slightly below average and is not a stealing threat.

Projection
Gonzalez likely will begin the 1990 season at Class AAA Oklahoma City but could reach the majors before the end of the season.

Career Statistics and Peak Projection

	G	AB	R	H	2B	3B	HR	RBI	BB	SO	AVG
1986 Sarasota Rangers (Gulf Coast League-Rookie)	60	233	24	56	4	1	0	36	21	57	.240
1987 Gastonia (South Atlantic League-Class A)	127	509	69	135	21	2	14	74	30	92	.265
1988 Charlotte (Florida State League-Class A)	77	277	25	71	14	3	8	43	25	64	.256
1989 Tulsa (Texas League-Class AA)	133	502	73	147	30	7	21	85	31	98	.293
1989 Texas (American League)	24	60	6	9	3	0	1	7	6	17	.150
1989 Major League Equivalency	157	545	67	139	26	5	21	78	32	123	.255
Peak Projection	154	581	109	173	31	5	37	113	49		.298

Interpretation
The Major League Equivalency is mostly favorable except for a horrible strikeouts-to-walks ratio. There seems to be a new breed of hitter these days, one who flails for home runs without any strike zone judgment. Remember the home run hitters of yesteryear, the ones who might approach 100 strikeouts but would walk more than 100 times? Even if he doesn't develop an eye, Gonzalez's other offensive projections are downright appealing.

GERONIMO PENA

St. Louis Cardinals
Second Baseman
Signed by Cardinals as a Non-Drafted Free Agent, August 1984

Personal
Height: 6-1 Weight: 170
Bats left and right, throws right
Born: March 29, 1967

School: District Nacional
(High) in Dominican Republic.

Ratings

	Present	Future
Hitting	5	6
Power	4	5
Baserunning	5	6
Speed	5	5
Fielding	5	5
Arm	5	5
Range	5	5

Rating Key
7 Outstanding
6 Major League Caliber, High
5 Major League Caliber
4 Minor League Caliber, High
3 Minor League Caliber
2 Below Average
1 Poor

General
Pena missed nearly the first two months of the 1989 season with a broken hand but came back stronger than ever at Class AA Arkansas. He has all the tools a prospect needs to play in the major leagues: he can hit, drive the ball for extra bases, play good defense and steal bases. He once stole 80 bases in a season (at Class A Savannah in 1987) but hasn't run as much the last two years.

Hitting Tendencies
Pena is very strong for his size, with power to pop the ball for doubles, triples and an occasional home run. He showed as much last season, along with a flair for driving in runs (44 in 77 games at Arkansas). He does, however, need to have better command of the strike zone, having fanned 275 times over the last three seasons. If he can make adjustments in his swing from both sides of the plate, the Cardinals believe he'll cut down on his strikeouts and start drawing walks. Still maturing physically, Pena added about 20 pounds in the last year, which accounted for much of his improvement at the plate.

Fielding/Baserunning
Pena makes all the plays he should—and then some—at second base. He has excellent range, soft hands, a good arm and turns the double play well. On the basepaths, he isn't attempting as many stolen bases as he did early in his minor league career. He'll need to revert back to old ways to have an impact in the majors. So far, he's been able to score a lot of runs, ranking among the league leaders whenever he's played a full season.

Projection
Pena figures to be the starting second baseman at Class AAA Louisville in 1990. He's a candidate to reach the majors in late 1990 or 1991.

Career Statistics and Peak Projections

	G	AB	R	H	2B	3B	HR	RBI	BB	SO	AVG
1986 Johnson City (Appalachian League-Rookie)	56	202	55	60	7	4	3	20	46	33	.297
1987 Savannah (South Atlantic League-Class A)	134	505	95	136	28	3	9	51	73	98	.269
1988 St. Petersburg (Florida State League-Class A)	130	484	82	125	25	10	4	35	88	103	.258
1989 St. Petersburg (Florida State League-Class A)	6	21	2	4	1	0	0	2	3	6	.190
1989 Arkansas (Texas League-Class AA)	77	267	61	79	16	8	9	44	38	68	.296
1989 Major League Equivalency	77	252	42	64	14	7	5	30	26	69	.254
Peak Projection	154	509	114	149	30	14	16	76	64		.292

Interpretation
Pena hasn't yet played a full season at the Class AA level, but the system likes what it sees. His peak season shows plenty of line-drive power and extra-base hit potential.

KEVIN MAAS

New York Yankees
Outfielder
Yankees' 22nd-Round Pick, June 1986 Draft

Personal
Height: 6-3 Weight: 195
Bats left, throws left
Born: January 20, 1965

School: California

Ratings

	Present	Future
Hitting	5	6
Power	5	6
Baserunning	4	5
Speed	4	4
Fielding	4	5
Arm	4	5
Range	4	5

Rating Key
7 Outstanding
6 Major League Caliber, High
5 Major League Caliber
4 Minor League Caliber, High
3 Minor League Caliber
2 Below Average
1 Poor

General
The Yankees have shifted Maas from first base to the outfield, a move designed to accelerate his rise to the major leagues. Although a knee injury cut short his 1989 season at Class AAA Columbus, he hit well enough to receive International League All-Star honors at designated hitter. The Yanks expect him to be fully healed for 1990. Healthy in 1988, Maas was named the Yankees' minor league Player of the Year. Playing at the Class A and AA levels, he led the farm system with 28 home runs (just one off the minor league lead) and drove in 90 runs. He has been a league All-Star selection in each of his last three seasons.

Hitting Tendencies
Maas is regarded as the best lefthanded hitter on the Yankee farm. He has a short, powerful stroke that allows him to use the whole field, with especially good power into the gaps. He is a strong, aggressive player with good RBI potential. Maas does tend to strike out too much (once every four at-bats in his career) but the Yanks believe experience will give him a better knowledge of the strike zone.

Fielding/Baserunning
The Yankees are confident Maas will make the switch from first base to the outfield without major difficulty. He has a good enough arm to play either left or right field. He has enough speed to the point where he isn't a liability in the field, but he won't steal many bases at the big-league level.

Projection
Because he missed valuable playing time last year, Maas likely will return to Class AAA Columbus to start the 1990 season. If he makes progress in the outfield and continues to hit, he could join the Yankees by season's end.

Career Statistics and Peak Projection

	G	AB	R	H	2B	3B	HR	RBI	BB	SO	AVG
1986 Oneonta (New York-Penn League-Class A)	28	101	14	36	10	0	0	18	7	9	.356
1987 Fort Lauderdale (Florida State League-Class A)	116	439	77	122	28	4	11	73	53	108	.278
1988 Prince William (Carolina League-Class A)	29	108	24	32	7	0	12	35	17	28	.296
1988 Albany (Eastern League-Class AA)	109	372	66	98	14	3	16	55	64	103	.263
1988 Major League Equivalency	109	367	60	93	13	2	15	50	54	110	.253
1989 Columbus (International League-Class AAA)	83	291	42	93	23	2	6	45	40	70	.320
1989 Major League Equivalency	83	285	37	87	22	1	5	39	33	75	.305
Peak Projection	154	521	78	159	32	2	21	81	74		.304

Interpretation
Maas' minor league numbers project well. His peak batting average is heavily influenced by his hot 1989 season at Columbus, but his 1988 and 1989 lines both have their strengths. The strikeouts are the only real concern, but they seem to be fashionable these days.

EARL CUNNINGHAM

Chicago Cubs
Outfielder
Cubs' First-Round Pick, June 1989 Draft

Personal
Height: 6-2 Weight: 225
Bats right, throws right
Born: July 3, 1970

School: Lancaster High
in Lancaster, S.C.

Ratings

	Present	Future
Hitting	3	6
Power	3	6
Baserunning	3	5
Speed	4	5
Fielding	3	5
Arm	4	5
Range	3	5

Rating Key
7 Outstanding
6 Major League Caliber, High
5 Major League Caliber
4 Minor League Caliber, High
3 Minor League Caliber
2 Below Average
1 Poor

General
Cunningham's legend won't soon be forgotten by the Lancaster, S.C., faithful who watched him set the state's high school record for career home runs. Packing thunder in his bat and flashing good speed afoot, he was selected No. 8 overall in the June 1989 draft. The Cubs called him clearly the best power prospect available. The slugging young outfielder measured up to early expectations by pounding seven home runs in 49 games in the rookie Appalachian League. Just 19 years old last season, he is very raw but long on star potential. He is quick to listen to suggestions and is a hard worker.

Hitting Tendencies
At 225 pounds, Cunningham is very strong and aggressive at the plate. No one doubts his home run potential, but he also ties into line drives that bode well for his batting average. With his good speed, he'll be an extra-base threat in the wide-open stadiums in the National League. Cunningham crushed some tape-measure home runs during his rookie year at Wytheville but also struck out 40 times in 182 at-bats. He had an easy, compact stroke in high school, but at times last season needed to cut back on his swing and make other adjustments. He has time to make those refinements.

Fielding/Baserunning
Cunningham's speed, on the bases and in the field, rates well above average, particularly for a player his size. He played center field in rookie ball but is far from being a finished product, as evidenced by his seven errors. His arm strength is above average.

Projection
Cunningham is tabbed to play for a Class A team in 1990 and is at least three years away from the majors.

Career Statistics

	G	AB	R	H	2B	3B	HR	RBI	BB	SO	AVG
1989 Wytheville (Appalachian League-Rookie)	49	182	20	47	6	2	7	38	12	40	.258

(Projections unavailable because player has not competed at Class AA or Class AAA levels)

WILLIE ANSLEY

Houston Astros
Outfielder
Astros' First-Round Pick, June 1988 Draft

General
Ansley, the seventh pick overall in the 1988 draft, did it all in his first season of pro ball. By year's end, the Class A South Atlantic League had voted him its outstanding major league prospect and Ansley had jumped to the Class AA level for a late-season stint with Columbus in the Southern League. Ansley lit up the field on both offense and defense. He batted .309 at Asheville to rank second in the South Atlantic and was voted to an All-Star berth in the outfield. The hard-working center fielder has a bounty of athletic ability and a willingness to learn. He is not the type who will be intimidated at any level and is a very coachable player.

Hitting Tendencies
To opposing teams, the sight of Ansley at the plate is unnerving. He can beat out ground balls he slaps toward holes in the infield. He has the patience to draw walks. He appears to be getting stronger, and while he'll probably never be a long-ball threat, he is developing a line-drive stroke to plug the gaps for doubles and triples. Like most young players, the 20-year-old Ansley is vulnerable to breaking pitches. Although he drew 99 walks last season, he struck out 127 times in 444 at-bats. He must learn which pitches he can handle.

Fielding/Baserunning
Ansley covers a lot of territory in center field and has an above-average arm. As a baserunner, he has outstanding acceleration and ranked among the minor leagues' top thiefs with 59 steals in 1989.

Projection
Ideally, Ansley would benefit from a stint with an upper-caliber Class A team in 1990, perhaps at Osceola in the Florida State League. At most, he is three years away from the majors.

Personal
Height: 6-2 Weight: 200
Bats right, throws right
Born: December 15, 1969

School: Plainview High in Plainview, Tex.

Ratings

	Present	Future
Hitting	4	5
Power	3	4
Baserunning	5	6
Speed	5	5
Fielding	4	6
Arm	5	5
Range	5	5

Rating Key
7 Outstanding
6 Major League Caliber, High
5 Major League Caliber
4 Minor League Caliber, High
3 Minor League Caliber
2 Below Average
1 Poor

Career Statistics and Peak Projection

	G	AB	R	H	2B	3B	HR	RBI	BB	SO	AVG
1989 Asheville (South Atlantic League-Class A)	103	340	81	105	14	2	6	55	73	90	.309
1989 Columbus (Southern League-Class AA)	30	104	16	26	3	0	0	7	26	37	.250
1989 Major League Equivalency	30	101	13	23	3	0	0	6	21	41	.228
Peak Projection	154	503	98	145	20	0	0	39	127		.288

Interpretation
Ansley's miniscule data sample is incapable of supporting any real analysis. His Class A season is very encouraging, particularly his ability to reach base. The projected peak line would be a good one for a leadoff hitter.

WES CHAMBERLAIN

Pittsburgh Pirates
Outfielder
Pirates' Fourth-Round Pick, June 1987 Draft

Personal
Height: 6-2 Weight: 210
Bats right, throws right
Born: April 13, 1966

School: Jackson State
in Jackson, Miss.

Ratings

	Present	Future
Hitting	4	5
Power	4	5
Baserunning	4	5
Speed	4	4
Fielding	5	6
Arm	5	5
Range	5	6

Rating Key
7 Outstanding
6 Major League Caliber, High
5 Major League Caliber
4 Minor League Caliber, High
3 Minor League Caliber
2 Below Average
1 Poor

General
A player who has the tools—that's the consensus opinion of Chamberlain, who blossomed in 1989 in his first season at the Class AA level. Indeed, Chamberlain has the potential to be an impact player both offensively and defensively. Playing at Harrisburg last season, he waged an onslaught against Eastern League pitching (ranking first in hits and RBIs and second in batting and home runs) and was voted the league's Most Valuable Player as well as the Pirates' top minor leaguer for 1989. Part of his success can be traced to a more focused approach to the game. He tried to do too much in Class A ball and usually wound up hitting in the .260 to .270 range.

Hitting Tendencies
Chamberlain developed his power potential in 1989 while maintaining a high batting average. He was the man pitchers least wanted to see with runners on base, particularly late in the season: In his final 60 games, Chamberlain knocked in 57 runs. He has been able to sit on fastballs in his three minor league seasons, but he needs to adjust to hit the breaking ball. The Pirates believe he'll do that if he continues to improve his mental approach. He's maturing physically, too, adding muscle to an already powerful build.

Fielding/Baserunning
Chamberlain is a good defensive outfielder with a strong enough arm to play right field in the majors. He is an average runner who can steal a base on occasion, although he was thrown out 11 times in 22 attempts in 1989.

Projection
The Pirates figure to assign Chamberlain to Class AAA Buffalo to begin the 1990 season. They could send for him before year's end.

Career Statistics and Peak Projection

	G	AB	R	H	2B	3B	HR	RBI	BB	SO	AVG
1987 Watertown (New York-Penn League-Class A)	66	258	50	103	13	4	5	35	25	48	.260
1988 Augusta (South Atlantic League-Class A)	27	107	22	36	7	2	1	17	11	11	.336
1988 Salem (Carolina League-Class A)	92	365	66	100	15	1	11	50	38	59	.274
1989 Harrisburg (Eastern League-Class AA)	129	471	65	144	26	3	21	87	32	82	.306
1989 Major League Equivalency	129	452	51	125	23	2	17	68	28	85	.277
Peak Projection	154	534	80	163	29	2	29	96	43		.306

Interpretation
The calculations look favorably on Chamberlain's Eastern League debut. His Major League Equivalency might have been even better if he'd taken more walks, yet the peak line likes the fact that he swings away—and makes good contact.

JOHN OLERUD

Toronto Blue Jays
First Baseman/Pitcher
Blue Jays' Third-Round Pick, June 1989 Draft

Personal
Height: 6-5   Weight: 210
Bats left, throws left
Born: August 5, 1968

School: Washington State

Ratings

	Present	Future
Hitting	4	6
Power	4	5
Baserunning	5	5
Speed	4	4
Fielding	5	5
Arm	5	5
Range	5	5

Rating Key
7 Outstanding
6 Major League Caliber, High
5 Major League Caliber
4 Minor League Caliber, High
3 Minor League Caliber
2 Below Average
1 Poor

General
Two-sport stars fascinate their public these days, but Olerud rekindles a memory from a bygone era: baseball's two-way pitcher/position player. Pardon the pun, Bo, but if the Jays say, "Just do it," Olerud knows pitching and hitting. In three seasons at Washington State, he fashioned a 26-4 record on the mound and batted .434. In 1988, he posted a perfect 15-0 record and shattered scores of hitting records in the Washington State books. But most remarkable is the fact that Olerud started at first base for Toronto in the final game of the 1989 season. Never mind that he hadn't played an inning in the minors. Only seven months before, Olerud lay on an operating table to have an aneurysm removed from the base of his brain.

Hitting/Pitching Tendencies
As a hitter, Olerud sends line drives to all fields with a smooth, compact lefthanded stroke. He's not overly strong, but he always seems to drive the ball because he's coordinated and disciplined. He rarely offers at bad pitches and makes solid contact with the good ones. Control is Olerud's forte on the mound. He changes speeds effectively and makes good use of his changeup. When he regains the strength he had before surgery, he should add some velocity to his mid-80s fastball.

Fielding/Baserunning
Olerud is a good fielder, whether on the mound or at first base. He has a long reach and makes quick, accurate throws. His move to first base is good for his experience and he's an intelligent baserunner.

Projection
Olerud's future, either as a first baseman or pitcher, will be clearer once the 1990 season unfolds. Either way, he's a candidate to reach Toronto sometime during the year.

Career Statistics

	G	AB	R	H	2B	3B	HR	RBI	BB	SO	AVG
1989 Toronto (American League)	6	8	2	3	0	0	0	0	0	1	.375

(Projections unavailable because player has not competed enough on professional level).

JAIME ROSEBORO

New York Mets
Outfielder
Mets' 11th-Round Pick, June 1986 Draft

Personal
Height: 6-2 Weight: 190
Bats right, throws right
Born: May 27, 1966

School: Los Angeles City College

Ratings

	Present	Future
Hitting	4	5
Power	3	4
Baserunning	5	6
Speed	5	6
Fielding	4	5
Arm	4	5
Range	4	5

Rating Key
7 Outstanding
6 Major League Caliber, High
5 Major League Caliber
4 Minor League Caliber, High
3 Minor League Caliber
2 Below Average
1 Poor

General
Roseboro, the son of former major league catcher John Roseboro, reaffirmed in 1989 that he is a player on the rise. Playing at Class A St. Lucie, he was in top form at the plate for the second straight year, which, for Roseboro, means stroking the ball for a good average and knocking in runs. Had he totaled enough plate appearances, he would have ranked third in the Florida State League with a .309 batting average. Nevertheless, he was an all-star pick among the league's outfielders. Playing center field, the fleet Roseboro saw his stock rise with his best season defensively to date.

Hitting Tendencies
Although home runs seldom fly off his bat, Roseboro has gap power that should translate into doubles and triples. He is getting stronger as he matures physically, and scouts aren't discounting his potential to hit the occasional long ball. For now, he shows promise as a leadoff-type batter who will hit for average and steal bases. He's a good contact hitter (he averaged only one strikeout every 9.6 at-bats in 1989) who has thrived in the clutch: Over the last two seasons, he drove home 120 runs in 220 games.

Fielding/Baserunning
Roseboro is a very good defensive outfielder who can get the ball with anybody. He's fast and graceful, too, although his arm rates as only average. As a basestealer, he's tremendous. He reads pitchers to get big leads and excellent jumps. He was a blur at St. Lucie in 1989, stealing 54 bases in 62 attempts.

Projection
Roseboro likely will open the 1990 season at Class AA Jackson but could move up to Class AAA Tidewater by year's end.

Career Statistics

	G	AB	R	H	2B	3B	HR	RBI	BB	SO	AVG
1986—Little Falls (New York-Penn League-Class A)	68	234	26	63	5	2	2	17	12	24	.269
1987—Columbia (South Atlantic League-Class A)	113	340	41	84	8	1	5	40	39	54	.247
1988—Columbia (South Atlantic League-Class A)	125	486	53	132	24	4	2	72	23	74	.272
1989—St. Lucie (Florida State League-Class A)	95	337	60	104	17	4	1	48	31	35	.309

(Projections unavailable because player has not competed at Class AA or Class AAA levels)

DEION SANDERS

New York Yankees
Outfielder
Yankees' 30th-Round Pick, June 1987 Draft

Personal
Height: 6-1 Weight: 195
Bats left, throws left
Born: August 9, 1967

School: Florida State

Ratings

	Present	Future
Hitting	4	5
Power	4	5
Baserunning	5	5
Speed	6	6
Fielding	5	6
Arm	4	4
Range	5	5

Rating Key
7 Outstanding
6 Major League Caliber, High
5 Major League Caliber
4 Minor League Caliber, High
3 Minor League Caliber
2 Below Average
1 Poor

General
Sanders did not have the same immediate impact on a baseball diamond as he did on a professional football field in 1989. Minutes into his first game with the Atlanta Falcons, Sanders returned a punt 68 yards for a touchdown. Not even Bo Jackson had scored a touchdown in the National Football League and hit a major league home run in the same week. Sanders has. Brought up twice by the Yankees last season, he finished with two homers and a .234 batting average in New York before checking out in early September to join the Falcons. The Yankees believe Sanders has definite star potential and want him to focus on baseball. "Prime Time" likely will tackle both sports.

Hitting Tendencies
Sanders is a line-drive hitter who displayed more power than the Yankees expected in 1989, hitting eight homers in a combined 425 at-bats. Any punch he has will be a bonus, since his objective is to put the ball in play and turn on the afterburners. With 4.2 speed in the 40, Sanders will regularly wind up on third base when he drives the ball into the gaps. He can hit a fastball, but he struggles against good breaking-ball pitchers due to his inexperience. To be a successful leadoff hitter, he'll need to reduce his strikeouts and draw more walks.

Fielding/Baserunning
Sanders is an above-average defensive outfielder who can run down almost any ball. He has a below-average arm, but he covers it up with a very quick release. He could become one of the game's top thiefs if he masters the fundamentals of basestealing. Last season, he had 34 thefts.

Projection
Sanders himself says his baseball skills aren't "Prime Time." He appears ticketed for Class AAA Columbus in 1990—at least to start the year.

Career Statistics and Peak Projection

	G	AB	R	H	2B	3B	HR	RBI	BB	SO	AVG
1988 Sarasota Yankees (Gulf Coast League-Rookie)	17	75	7	21	4	2	0	6	2	10	.280
1988 Fort Lauderdale (Florida State League-Class A)	6	21	5	9	2	0	0	2	1	3	.429
1988 Columbus (International League-Class AAA)	5	20	3	3	1	0	0	0	1	4	.150
1988 Major League Equivalency	5	20	3	3	1	0	0	0	1	4	.150
1989 Albany (Eastern League-Class AA)	33	119	28	34	2	2	1	6	11	20	.286
1989 Columbus (International League-Class AAA)	70	259	38	72	12	7	5	30	22	48	.278
1989 New York (American League)	14	47	7	11	2	0	2	7	3	8	.234
1989 Major League Equivalency	117	420	68	112	16	5	8	40	31	81	.267
Peak Projection	154	577	122	170	25	6	16	77	56		.296

Interpretation
Without taking the flash into account, Sanders still projects as a balanced, solid player. Sanders ran amok in Class AA ball, and the results inflate his runs scored total in the peak line.

MICKEY MORANDINI

Philadelphia Phillies
Second Baseman
Phillies' Fifth-Round Pick, June 1988 Draft

Personal
Height: 5-11 Weight: 170
Bats left, throws right
Born: April 22, 1966

School: Indiana

Ratings

	Present	Future
Hitting	4	5
Power	3	4
Baserunning	4	5
Speed	4	4
Fielding	4	5
Arm	4	4
Range	4	5

Rating Key
7 Outstanding
6 Major League Caliber, High
5 Major League Caliber
4 Minor League Caliber, High
3 Minor League Caliber
2 Below Average
1 Poor

General
Morandini is not the type of player who dazzles you on first impression but, instead, steadily grows on you. The Phillies voted him their minor league Player of the Year in 1989, when he led the farm system in batting, hits and runs scored. He earned two promotions in his first pro season, from Class A Spartanburg to Clearwater to Class AA Reading, and batted .302 or better at each level. At Indiana, he was an All-Big Ten Conference shortstop, his position last season. But with Dickie Thon returning to form at short in Philadelphia, Morandini was sent to the Instructional League to work at second base. He is a gung-ho player with intelligence and played on the 1988 U.S. Olympic team.

Hitting Tendencies
Morandini is a contact hitter who improved as he rose through the Phillies' system in 1989. He is a patient, disciplined hitter who sees the ball extremely well because he waits extra long on the pitch. He can get that look because of his quick bat, and he's able to hang in against lefthanders because he commits only at the last second. He isn't overly strong, but his bat speed gives him the drive to get the ball into the gap. A good situational hitter who understands the game, Morandini is a good bunter and can hit to all fields.

Fielding/Baserunning
Due to Thon's revival, the Phillies see Morandini's immediate future at second base. He has good range and turns the double play well, but he needs to adjust to the ball coming at him from a different angle. He is a smart baserunner with slightly above-average speed.

Projection
Because of his move to second, Morandini likely will begin the 1990 season at Class AA Reading. The majors aren't far away.

Career Statistics and Peak Projection

	G	AB	R	H	2B	3B	HR	RBI	BB	SO	AVG
1989 Spartanburg (South Atlantic League-Class A)	63	231	43	78	19	1	1	30	35	45	.338
1989 Clearwater (Florida State League-Class A)	17	63	14	19	4	1	0	4	7	8	.302
1989 Reading (Eastern League-Class AA)	48	188	39	66	12	1	5	29	23	32	.351
1989 Major League Equivalency	48	179	31	57	11	1	4	23	18	34	.318
Peak Projection	154	564	112	187	34	3	17	83	67		.332

Interpretation
Based on a very small sample at the Class AA level, the system grades out Morandini as the second coming of Von Hayes. His projected peak batting average of .332 rates tops among the 88 prospects.

PAUL SORRENTO

Minnesota Twins
First Baseman
California Angels' Fourth-Round Pick, June 1986 Draft

Personal
Height: 6-2 Weight: 210
Bats left, throws right
Born: November 17, 1965

School: Florida State

Ratings

	Present	Future
Hitting	4	5
Power	4	6
Baserunning	3	4
Speed	4	4
Fielding	4	5
Arm	4	4
Range	4	5

Rating Key
7 Outstanding
6 Major League Caliber, High
5 Major League Caliber
4 Minor League Caliber, High
3 Minor League Caliber
2 Below Average
1 Poor

General
Sorrento was one of three players the Twins obtained from California in the Bert Blyleven trade after the 1988 season. He is a big, strong hitter who has worked hard to become a better defensive player at first base. His biggest asset, however, is his offensive power. Playing most of the 1989 season at Class AA Orlando, Sorrento led the Southern League with 112 runs batted in and 35 doubles. Among all minor leaguers, he was tied for second with 27 home runs. He was named the Southern League's All-Star first baseman and called up by the Twins in September.

Hitting Tendencies
Sorrento has the stroke to reach any fence in any park. He has excellent gap power that makes him a good doubles hitter and RBI threat (211 RBIs in his last two minor league seasons). He hangs in against both lefties and righties, always getting his cuts. He does, however, strike out frequently (a total of 224 in two years), yet the Twins don't want to shorten his swing for fear it will reduce his power. Sorrento doesn't chase many bad balls and, accordingly, draws a lot of walks. He'd be an ideal designated hitter, but the Twins don't want to hang that label on him this early in his career.

Fielding/Baserunning
A former outfielder, Sorrento has worked hard to become a better first baseman. Granted, his 24 errors were a league high for his position in 1989, but he showed substantial improvement in all areas. He is a slow runner who doesn't risk steals.

Projection
Sorrento likely will begin the 1990 season at Class AAA Portland and could advance to the major leagues by season's end.

Career Statistics and Peak Projection

	G	AB	R	H	2B	3B	HR	RBI	BB	SO	AVG
1986 Quad City (Midwest League-Class A)	53	177	33	63	11	2	6	34	24	40	.356
1986 Palm Springs (California League-Class A)	16	62	5	15	3	0	1	7	4	15	.242
1987 Palm Springs (California League-Class A)	114	370	66	83	14	2	8	45	78	95	.224
1988 Palm Springs (California League-Class A)	133	465	91	133	30	6	14	99	110	101	.286
1989 Orlando (Southern League-Class AA)	140	509	81	130	35	2	27	112	84	119	.255
1989 Minnesota (American League)	14	21	2	5	0	0	0	1	5	4	.238
1989 Major League Equivalency	154	512	66	117	31	1	20	89	69	130	.229
Peak Projection	154	550	101	146	36	1	33	100	83		.266

Interpretation
Sorrento appears to be a player who will blend into the background if his batting average doesn't increase. Nonetheless, he has attractive power projections and should wind up with a good enough on-base percentage, given the 83 projected walks. The runs scored column is significant in the peak line.

DEREK BELL

Toronto Blue Jays
Outfielder
Blue Jays' Second-Round Pick, June 1987 Draft

Personal
Height: 6-2 Weight: 195
Bats right, throws right
Born: December 11, 1968

School: King High
in Tampa, Fla.

Ratings

	Present	Future
Hitting	4	5
Power	4	5
Baserunning	4	5
Speed	4	4
Fielding	4	5
Arm	4	4
Range	4	5

Rating Key
7 Outstanding
6 Major League Caliber, High
5 Major League Caliber
4 Minor League Caliber, High
3 Minor League Caliber
2 Below Average
1 Poor

General
Bell grades out with above-average marks in most phases of the game. He has a genuine enthusiasm and is eager to improve his skills with hard work. Just 20 years old last season, Bell held his own in the Class AA Southern League. Voted the team's Most Valuable Player at Knoxville, he ranked second in the Blue Jays' chain with 75 runs batted in. It was a big lift for the young outfielder, who had suffered a broken hand 14 games after he was promoted to Knoxville in 1988. Even with the promotion, he qualified as the batting champion in the Class A South Atlantic League, hitting .344. Overall, he is an alert player who just needs to work on some fundamental skills.

Hitting Tendencies
Bell is a high fastball hitter who is beginning to adapt to the breaking ball. Relying mostly on raw talent, he posted a .242 mark batting full time against Class AA pitching in 1989. Scouts say he has the potential to hit .300 when he masters the mechanics. He still tends to jump at the ball but otherwise has no major flaws. Bell has been a good run producer and is expected to become more of a power threat as he matures physically. His career strikeouts-to-walks (233-60) indicate he can be more selective.

Fielding/Baserunning
Bell probably is best suited for left field in the majors. He has an adequate arm, although he occasionally hesitates, and is generally solid defensively. He is an average runner who's had success stealing bases.

Projection
Because of his youth, Bell could return to the Class AA level in 1990, depending on his progress in spring training. He likely will join the major leagues in 1992.

Career Statistics and Peak Projection

	G	AB	R	H	2B	3B	HR	RBI	BB	SO	AVG
1987 St. Catharines (New York-Penn League-Class A)	74	273	46	72	11	3	10	42	18	60	.264
1988 Myrtle Beach (South Atlantic League-Class A)	91	352	55	121	29	5	12	60	15	67	.344
1988 Knoxville (Southern League-Class AA)	14	52	5	13	3	1	0	4	1	14	.250
1988 Major League Equivalency	14	51	4	12	3	1	0	3	1	14	.235
1989 Knoxville (Southern League-Class AA)	136	513	72	124	22	6	16	75	26	92	.242
1989 Major League Equivalency	136	497	58	108	20	5	13	60	23	93	.217
Peak Projection	154	548	103	146	27	6	23	83	37		.267

Interpretation
Bell's sub-.250 season in 1989 doesn't translate well to the Major League Equivalency or peak projection calculations. The formula takes particular note of his low number of hits and walks. He makes a lot of outs for the number of runs he creates, yet he's still young and has displayed consistent home run power.

ROB RICHIE

Detroit Tigers
Outfielder
Tigers' Second-Round Pick, June 1987 Draft

Personal
Height: 6-2 Weight: 190
Bats left, throws right
Born: September 5, 1965

School: Nevada-Reno

Ratings

	Present	Future
Hitting	4	5
Power	4	5
Baserunning	4	5
Speed	5	5
Fielding	5	5
Arm	6	6
Range	5	5

Rating Key
7 Outstanding
6 Major League Caliber, High
5 Major League Caliber
4 Minor League Caliber, High
3 Minor League Caliber
2 Below Average
1 Poor

General
Richie missed the first half of the 1989 season as he recovered from shoulder surgery but put a hurt on opposing pitchers once he returned. Richie is a triple threat offensively—he can run, hit for average and has power—and his skills in the outfield are consistent with a major leaguer's. He played mostly at Class AAA Toledo last season but had an impressive late-season stint with Detroit. In 19 games, he collected 13 hits, seven for extra bases. Richie was voted the Most Valuable Player of the Class AA Eastern League in 1988. He led the league in hits, total bases and runs batted in, and ranked among the top four in runs, doubles, triples and home runs.

Hitting Tendencies
Richie's lefthanded bat is ideal for Tiger Stadium. At this point, he's a straightaway hitter who can drive the ball to all fields, but the Tigers see him flourishing as a power threat once he starts to pull the ball. If he can learn to turn on the pitch without getting his swing out of sync, his confidence and home run totals could shoot up. He has an excellent eye, makes good contact and runs hard enough to rate as an above-average extra-base threat.

Fielding/Baserunning
Provided his shoulder holds up, Richie is targeted as a right fielder due to his strong arm. He doesn't have a burner's raw speed, but he gets to balls in the gaps quickly. He's steadily learning the fundamentals on defense although his progress as a basestealer has been delayed by his limited playing time. In his only full season, he showed his potential by stealing 24 bases. The Tigers also would like him to be more aggressive.

Projection
Richie will compete for a spot on Detroit's major league roster in 1990.

Career Statistics and Peak Projection

	G	AB	R	H	2B	3B	HR	RBI	BB	SO	AVG
1987 Bristol (Appalachian League-Rookie)	3	12	2	3	0	0	0	5	1	2	.250
1987 Lakeland (Florida State League-Class A)	60	204	31	60	8	3	1	32	22	27	.294
1988 Glens Falls (Eastern League-Class AA)	137	501	75	155	24	7	14	82	60	69	.309
1988 Major League Equivalency	137	479	61	133	21	8	13	67	51	74	.278
1989 Toledo (International League-Class AAA)	69	215	42	63	9	3	6	26	30	40	.293
1989 Detroit (American League)	19	49	6	13	4	2	1	10	5	10	.265
1989 Major League Equivalency	88	256	42	68	12	8	7	32	32	53	.266
Peak Projection	154	546	107	162	27	12	21	86	69		.297

Interpretation
The projection system ignores Richie's lost half-season in 1989, but there's enough impressive data to warrant a glowing peak season: Richie hits for power, average, gets on base and has the speed to collect 12 triples.

FELIX JOSE

Oakland Athletics
Outfielder
Signed by Athletics as a Non-Drafted Free Agent, January 1984

Personal
Height: 6-1   Weight: 185
Bats left and right, throws right
Born: May 8, 1965

School: Santo Domingo, Dominican Republic

Ratings

	Present	Future
Hitting	5	5
Power	4	5
Baserunning	5	5
Speed	6	6
Fielding	5	5
Arm	5	5
Range	5	5

Rating Key
7 Outstanding
6 Major League Caliber, High
5 Major League Caliber
4 Minor League Caliber, High
3 Minor League Caliber
2 Below Average
1 Poor

General
Some scouts said Jose had a reputation for worrying about mistakes in the minor leagues. After last winter, his baseball fears should seem trivial. Jose, the intended victim in a shooting incident in the Dominican, escaped with only a superficial head wound and was playing winter league baseball days later. Heading into 1990, he appears to be a talent who needs to play each day to take full advantage of his ability. An emotional player, Jose often feared making mistakes when he came off the bench. He batted .193 for the Athletics in 20 games last season but led Class AAA Tacoma in hitting for the second straight year.

Hitting Tendencies
After some lean early years, Jose has developed into one of the top hitting prospects in the Oakland chain. The switch-hitting outfielder can occasionally hit with the power associated with the current crop of A's bashers and still keep his batting average near .300. He makes good contact from both sides of the plate, delivers hits to all fields and has excellent RBI potential. At this stage, he's still bothered some by off-speed deliveries and doesn't always wait on the pitch. If he stays back on the ball, he'll make the solid contact that will produce even more extra-base blows.

Fielding/Baserunning
Jose has worked hard to stay mentally focused in the field. He has the physical talent to play any outfield position and his arm is easily right-field caliber. His speed allows him to cut off most balls hit into the gaps. Jose is similarly fast on the bases but attempts only about 20 steals per season.

Projection
Jose is ready to play in the major leagues in 1990.

Career Statistics and Peak Projection

	G	AB	R	H	2B	3B	HR	RBI	BB	SO	AVG
1984 Idaho Falls (Pioneer League-Rookie)	45	152	16	33	6	0	1	18	18	37	.217
1985 Madison (Midwest League-Class A)	117	409	46	89	13	3	3	33	33	82	.218
1986 Modesto (California League-Class A)	127	516	77	147	22	8	14	77	36	89	.285
1987 Huntsville (Southern League-Class AA)	91	296	29	67	11	1	5	42	28	61	.226
1987 Major League Equivalency	91	288	24	59	9	1	4	35	22	65	.205
1988 Tacoma (Pacific Coast League-Class AAA)	134	508	72	161	29	5	12	83	53	77	.317
1988 Oakland (American League)	8	6	2	2	1	0	0	1	0	1	.333
1988 Major League Equivalency	142	487	56	136	23	3	9	63	38	84	.279
1989 Tacoma (Pacific Coast League-Class AAA)	104	387	59	111	26	0	14	63	41	82	.287
1989 Oakland (American League)	20	57	3	11	2	0	0	5	4	13	.193
1989 Major League Equivalency	104	372	47	96	21	0	11	51	31	88	.258
Peak Projection	154	535	82	152	29	1	18	74	51		.283

Interpretation
Jose's Major League Equivalencies hint that he might have a problem reaching base and not quite enough power to compensate for that. The calculations put him over that hump by his peak season.

RICO BROGNA

Detroit Tigers
First Baseman
Tigers' First-Round Pick, June 1988 Draft

Personal
Height: 6-2 Weight: 190
Bats left, throws left
Born: April 18, 1970

School: Watertown High
in Watertown, Conn.

Ratings

	Present	Future
Hitting	4	5
Power	4	6
Baserunning	3	4
Speed	4	4
Fielding	5	6
Arm	5	5
Range	5	5

Rating Key
7 Outstanding
6 Major League Caliber, High
5 Major League Caliber
4 Minor League Caliber, High
3 Minor League Caliber
2 Below Average
1 Poor

General
Brogna is one of the best hopes for improving the aging Tigers from within. Only 19 years old last season, he was a starting first baseman playing a fast brand of ball in the Class A Florida State League. One manager said he already has the playing mannerisms of the San Francisco Giants' Will Clark. Drafted 26th overall in 1988, Brogna does have the raw tools to contribute both offensively and defensively. He was a highly recruited football player in high school and turned down a scholarship offer from Clemson to sign with Detroit.

Hitting Tendencies
The Tigers are developing Brogna as a pull hitter who should thrive in a park noted for its inviting right-field stands. His bat does indeed seem tailored for Tiger Stadium, but Brogna managed just five home runs last season playing in minor league parks with major league dimensions. Scouts say he may have tried to do too much too quickly. He made up for a rough start with a solid second half, a sign that he learned to make adjustments. Brogna did showcase his extra-base clout with 20 doubles and seven triples. He also struck out a lot and batted only .235. If he learns to make better contact and adjusts to breaking pitches, he'll carry a valuable RBI bat.

Fielding/Baserunning
Brogna's glove compares favorably to almost any major leaguer's. He moves well around the bag and has the range to snare grounders in the hole. He won't shake up the defense when he runs the bases, but he does go hard from first to third.

Projection
Brogna likely will move up to Class AA London in 1990 and probably is two seasons away from Detroit.

Career Statistics

	G	AB	R	H	2B	3B	HR	RBI	BB	SO	AVG
1988 Bristol (Appalachian League-Rookie)	60	209	37	53	11	2	7	33	25	42	.254
1989 Lakeland (Florida State League-Class A)	128	459	47	108	20	7	5	51	38	82	.235

(Projections unavailable because player has not competed at Class AA or Class AAA levels)

REGGIE SANDERS

Cincinnati Reds
Shortstop
Reds' Seventh-Round Pick, June 1987 Draft

Personal
Height: 6-1 Weight: 180
Bats right, throws right
Born: December 1, 1967

School: Spartanburg Methodist in Spartanburg, S.C.

Ratings

	Present	Future
Hitting	3	5
Power	3	5
Baserunning	4	5
Speed	6	6
Fielding	3	5
Arm	5	5
Range	4	5

Rating Key
7 Outstanding
6 Major League Caliber, High
5 Major League Caliber
4 Minor League Caliber, High
3 Minor League Caliber
2 Below Average
1 Poor

General
Opinion is divided on whether Sanders should remain a shortstop or switch to center field, but scouts agree unanimously that he creates excitement in the lineup. He was an All-Star pick at shortstop last season in the Class A South Atlantic League, but he clearly has the speed and arm to take care of center field. Both of Sanders' minor league campaigns have been cut short by injuries—a shoulder separation in 1988 and a broken ankle at Greensboro last season. The latter injury occurred shortly after he was voted player of the game in the South Atlantic League all-star contest. Sanders has been compared with Eric Davis at a similar stage.

Hitting Tendencies
The Reds believe Sanders has the tools to hit for power, average and drive in runs. His progress has been delayed by injuries, but he provided a glimpse of his potential last season by belting nine homers and driving in 53 runs in 81 games. With his speed, he'll be a good man to have running the bases, but he needs to reduce his strikeouts (one every five at-bats in 1989). Just turned 22, he has time to make adjustments.

Fielding/Baserunning
He has played exclusively at shortstop in the minor leagues, but Sanders has the talent to develop either at short or in the outfield. His speed would be better used in center field, but his range and arm in the infield leave a lasting impression. His 42 errors (in 77 games) last season were indicative of youth rather than any major weakness. He has the potential to be a big basestealer, with 21 steals in 28 attempts in 1989.

Projection
Sanders could open the 1990 season at the Class AA level. He likely is at least two years away from the major leagues.

Career Statistics

	G	AB	R	H	2B	3B	HR	RBI	BB	SO	AVG
1988 Billings (Pioneer League-Rookie)	17	64	11	15	1	1	0	3	6	4	.234
1989 Greensboro (South Atlantic League-Class A)	81	315	53	91	18	5	9	53	29	63	.289

(Projections unavailable because player has not competed at Class AA or Class AAA levels)

FRANK THOMAS

Chicago White Sox
First Baseman
White Sox's First-Round Pick, June 1989 Draft

Personal
Height: 6-5 Weight: 240
Bats right, throws right
Born: May 27, 1968

School: Auburn

Ratings

	Present	Future
Hitting	4	5
Power	4	6
Baserunning	4	5
Speed	5	5
Fielding	3	5
Arm	4	5
Range	3	5

Rating Key
7 Outstanding
6 Major League Caliber, High
5 Major League Caliber
4 Minor League Caliber, High
3 Minor League Caliber
2 Below Average
1 Poor

General
Thomas is brimming with that quality scouts look for in young prospects: confidence. When he was drafted seventh overall by the White Sox in 1989, Thomas predicted he'd be playing in the major leagues in 1990. That might be a tad optimistic, but Thomas did prove last season that he wasn't intimidated by the pro ranks. After a brief stop in the rookie Gulf Coast circuit, he joined Sarasota in the Class A Florida State League and hit four homers with 30 RBIs in just 55 games. He was drafted following his junior year at Auburn, where he also played football as a freshman. In three seasons on the baseball team, Thomas batted .382 with 49 home runs and 205 runs batted in.

Hitting Tendencies
At 6-foot-5, 240 pounds, Thomas is a strapping power specimen who blasts the ball a long way. What separates him from similar prospects is the lack of holes in other areas of his game. Thomas usually finds a way to get on base. He goes to the plate swinging yet has an outstanding eye and discipline. He walked 42 times in 240 at-bats last season and struck out only 36 times. With his power, eye and ability to make contact, he is regarded as an excellent clutch hitter. He's aggressive in all situations and isn't overmatched by breaking pitches.

Fielding/Baserunning
Thomas needs to improve his footwork around the base and work on fielding ground balls. He understands that, and he's committed to becoming a solid defensive player. The former tight end has decent speed that could catch some fielders off-guard.

Projection
Thomas likely will begin the 1990 season at Class AA Birmingham and is a candidate to be playing regularly in the major leagues in 1991.

Career Statistics

	G	AB	R	H	2B	3B	HR	RBI	BB	SO	AVG
1989 Sarasota White Sox (Gulf Coast League-Rookie)	17	52	8	19	5	0	1	11	11	3	.365
1989 Sarasota (Florida State League-Class A)	55	188	27	52	9	1	4	30	31	33	.277

(Projections unavailable because player has not competed at Class AA or Class AAA levels)

LEE STEVENS

California Angels
Outfielder/First Baseman
Angels' First-Round Pick, June 1986 Draft

Personal
Height: 6-4 Weight: 205
Bats left, throws left
Born: July 10, 1967

School: Lawrence High
in Lawrence, Kan.

Ratings

	Present	Future
Hitting	4	5
Power	4	6
Baserunning	4	5
Speed	4	4
Fielding	4	5
Arm	4	5
Range	4	5

Rating Key
7 Outstanding
6 Major League Caliber, High
5 Major League Caliber
4 Minor League Caliber, High
3 Minor League Caliber
2 Below Average
1 Poor

General
The Angels have allowed time for Stevens, a 1986 high school draftee, to enjoy some success at each minor league level. So far, so good. Stevens held his own as he made the transition in 1989 to Class AAA Edmonton, where he pulled double-duty in the outfield (64 games) and first base (73). The Angels like his versatility afield, and Stevens has lost none of his hitting touch (14 home runs and 74 runs batted in for the Trappers). At the Class AA level in 1988, he posted career highs in batting and home runs, and in 1987 collected 97 RBIs in the Class A California League. Just 22 years old, he needs only to play to refine his tools and sharpen his diamond I.Q.

Hitting Tendencies
Stevens' biggest attribute at this stage is his power potential. He's already displayed good long-ball punch, yet scouts predict he'll generate even more thunder if he develops his upper-body strength as he physically matures. He has a good swing and can hit the ball out in any direction. At times, he does develop bad habits, particularly when he tries to pull every pitch. Slumps usually follow. If he becomes more disciplined with experience, he should hit for a higher average. In each of the last three seasons, he has fanned more than 100 times.

Fielding/Baserunning
Stevens is an outstanding defensive first baseman and improving considerably in the outfield, to the point where he is no longer a liability. He'll get even better if he grasps the fundamentals of the position. He is an average baserunner who will pick his spots to steal a base.

Projection
The Angels likely will groom Stevens another season at the Class AAA level in 1990.

Career Statistics and Peak Projection

	G	AB	R	H	2B	3B	HR	RBI	BB	SO	AVG
1986 Salem (Carolina League-Class A)	66	186	27	45	9	1	9	28	14	54	.242
1987 Palm Springs (California League-Class A)	140	532	82	130	29	2	19	97	61	117	.244
1988 Midland (Texas League-Class AA)	116	414	79	123	26	2	23	76	58	108	.297
1988 Major League Equivalency	116	386	49	95	19	1	17	47	35	112	.246
1989 Edmonton (Pacific Coast League-Class AAA)	127	446	72	110	29	9	14	74	61	115	.247
1989 Major League Equivalency	127	429	53	93	24	6	12	55	44	119	.217
Peak Projection	154	513	101	138	31	5	28	89	62		.268

Interpretation
Stevens has posted some impressive power numbers but used up a lot of outs in the process. His Major League Equivalencies and peak projection indicate he needs to make better contact.

HARVEY PULLIAM

Kansas City Royals
Outfielder
Royals' Third-Round Pick, June 1986 Draft

General
Pulliam has the all-around tools to be a sound player offensively and defensively. Playing his first season at the Class AA level in 1989, he batted a team-leading .290 at Memphis and earned Southern League All-Star honors in the outfield. It was a clutch performance by Pulliam, considering he had batted just .250 over his first three seasons in the minors. He is aggressive on the bases and has a solid physique that should hold up well. Pulliam received the "Star of Stars" award in the Southern League's all-star contest, belting a home run and triple to key a win over the Toronto Blue Jays.

Hitting Tendencies
Pulliam is a line-drive hitter who uses the whole field. He has good gap power to both alleys (he ranked third in the Southern League in doubles in 1989) and has some potential as an RBI-type hitter. If he gets stronger, he'll get more loft on the ball and hit more home runs. Pulliam pulls the inside fastball well, and he's able to slap down-and-away breaking balls to right field. He makes good contact and is a fairly tough strikeout. Instructors say he needs only a little polishing to be ready for big-league pitching.

Fielding/Baserunning
Pulliam is most suited for left field in the major leagues. He makes the plays he should, although he won't overwhelm you with spectacular defense, and his arm rates about average. He has good instincts on the bases and goes from first to third well. He's gutsy enough to steal a base to help the team.

Projection
Pulliam appears destined for Class AAA Omaha in 1990. If he continues to hit, he'll arrive in the majors in 1991.

Personal
Height: 6-1 Weight: 190
Bats right, throws right
Born: October 20, 1967

School: McAteer High in San Francisco

Ratings

	Present	Future
Hitting	4	5
Power	4	5
Baserunning	4	5
Speed	5	5
Fielding	4	5
Arm	5	5
Range	5	5

Rating Key
7 Outstanding
6 Major League Caliber, High
5 Major League Caliber
4 Minor League Caliber, High
3 Minor League Caliber
2 Below Average
1 Poor

Career Statistics and Peak Projection

	G	AB	R	H	2B	3B	HR	RBI	BB	SO	AVG
1986 Sarasota Royals (Gulf Coast League-Rookie)	48	168	14	35	3	0	4	23	8	33	.208
1987 Appleton (Midwest League-Class A)	110	395	54	109	20	1	9	55	26	79	.276
1988 Baseball City (Florida State League-Class A)	132	457	56	111	19	4	4	42	34	87	.243
1989 Memphis (Southern League-Class AA)	116	417	67	121	28	8	10	67	44	65	.290
1989 Omaha (American Association-Class AAA)	7	22	3	4	2	0	0	2	3	6	.182
1989 Major League Equivalency	123	421	54	107	27	6	6	53	36	72	.254
Peak Projection	154	523	89	152	35	7	12	67	56		.291

Interpretation
Aside from a respectable .291 batting mark, Pulliam's peak projection is rather ordinary. It is, however, based on a single-season data sample and should be viewed as inconclusive.

TINO MARTINEZ

Seattle Mariners
First Baseman
Mariners' First-Round Pick, June 1988 Draft

Personal
Height: 6-2 Weight: 205
Bats left, throws right
Born: December 7, 1967

School: Tampa

Ratings

	Present	Future
Hitting	4	5
Power	4	6
Baserunning	4	4
Speed	4	4
Fielding	4	5
Arm	5	5
Range	4	5

Rating Key
7 Outstanding
6 Major League Caliber, High
5 Major League Caliber
4 Minor League Caliber, High
3 Minor League Caliber
2 Below Average
1 Poor

General
Martinez put the start of his professional career on hold in 1988 to tour with Team USA. He served his country well, smacking two home runs in the gold medal-winning game against Japan in the Seoul Olympics. For the summer, he led the U.S. team with 20 home runs and batted .402. Martinez's first minor league tour wasn't as star-spangled, but he impressed the Mariners with his work habits and improvement. Playing at Williamsport in the Class AA Eastern League, he rapped 13 home runs with 64 runs batted in, leading the club in both departments. In three seasons at the University of Tampa, Martinez established school records in career batting (.399), home runs (54) and RBIs (222).

Hitting Tendencies
Martinez has the kind of swing that must have been picture-perfect when he was 10 years old. It's that good. He is a line-drive hitter who can hammer the ball to the opposite field and reach the fence in the alleys. He's a good two-strike hitter, tough to fan (once every 10.7 plate appearances in 1989) and hangs in well against lefthanders. Flaws? Instructors say he needs more patience when he's ahead in the count, but not for the sake of sacrificing his aggressiveness. He has a good build and will be a durable player.

Fielding/Baserunning
Martinez isn't flashy, just fundamentally sound on defense. He was the Eastern League's fielding leader at first base in 1989, committing only seven errors in a league-high 137 games. He isn't gifted with speed and won't be much of a basestealing threat.

Projection
Martinez is ready to advance to Class AAA Calgary. He could be in Seattle before the end of the season.

Career Statistics and Peak Projection

	G	AB	R	H	2B	3B	HR	RBI	BB	SO	AVG
1989 Williamsport (Eastern League-Class AA)	137	509	51	131	29	2	13	64	59	54	.257
1989 Major League Equivalency	137	505	48	127	30	2	13	60	52	57	.251
Peak Projection	154	552	77	163	36	2	24	88	71		.295

Interpretation
Martinez met the challenge at the Class AA level in just his first season in the minors. The projection system has to build the whole sand castle out of just one year, but what a palace. Power, average, walks—Martinez projects well in each area.

HAL MORRIS

Cincinnati Reds
Outfielder/First Baseman
New York Yankees' Eighth-Round Pick, June 1986 Draft

Personal
Height: 6-4   Weight: 200
Bats left, throws left
Born: April 9, 1965

School: Michigan

Ratings

	Present	Future
Hitting	5	6
Power	4	5
Baserunning	4	4
Speed	4	4
Fielding	4	5
Arm	4	5
Range	4	5

Rating Key
7 Outstanding
6 Major League Caliber, High
5 Major League Caliber
4 Minor League Caliber, High
3 Minor League Caliber
2 Below Average
1 Poor

General
With a pretty fair hitter named Mattingly holding down first base in New York, Morris had begun to make the transition from first to the outfield to enhance his big-league chances. He got a bigger break once the season ended, getting dealt to the Cincinnati Reds. With his potent bat, Morris could contend for a job at either position in the Reds' lineup. He has always hit for a good average, but Morris showed growing lefthanded power last season at Class AAA Columbus. He belted 17 home runs in 417 at-bats, a tad better success rate than 11 home runs in 1,188 previous minor league at-bats. Morris was voted to an All-Star berth at first base in the International League in 1989 (he also appeared in 45 games in the outfield) and was called up by the Yankees three times.

Hitting Tendencies
Morris won the 1989 International League batting title with a .326 average, the best in the Yankee organization. He made his mark as a contact hitter with line-drive power through his first three seasons, but he's now generating the strength to push some of those shots over the fence. His added power hasn't affected his strikeout total, which is consistent with the best contact hitters'. Morris gets his share of extra-base hits to the opposite field and can punch shots into the alleys.

Fielding/Baserunning
Morris appears capable of making the switch full time to the outfield, if necessary. Although he is only an average runner, he has a good enough arm. On the bases, he attempts only a handful of steals.

Projection
Morris is ready to compete for a regular job in the major leagues in 1990.

Career Statistics and Peak Projection

	G	AB	R	H	2B	3B	HR	RBI	BB	SO	AVG
1986 Oneonta (New York-Penn League-Class A)	36	127	26	48	9	2	3	30	18	15	.378
1986 Albany (Eastern League-Class AA)	25	79	7	17	5	0	0	4	4	10	.215
1986 Major League Equivalency	25	78	6	16	5	0	0	3	3	11	.205
1987 Albany (Eastern League-Class AA)	135	530	65	173	31	4	5	73	36	43	.326
1987 Major League Equivalency	135	508	50	151	28	2	4	56	26	46	.297
1988 Columbus (International League-Class AAA)	121	452	41	134	19	4	3	38	36	62	.296
1988 New York (American League)	1	1	0	0	0	0	0	0	0	0	.000
1988 Major League Equivalency	122	453	41	134	19	3	3	38	34	66	.296
1989 Columbus (International League-Class AAA)	111	417	70	136	24	1	17	66	28	47	.326
1989 New York (American League)	15	18	2	5	0	0	0	4	1	4	.278
1989 Major League Equivalency	126	426	63	132	23	1	15	62	24	54	.310
Peak Projection	154	572	93	186	30	2	19	84	45		.326

Interpretation
Morris has rated high in the Major League Equivalencies for three straight seasons. He didn't project as a home run threat until last season, a year that heavily influenced his home run potential in the peak projection.

MICKEY PINA

Boston Red Sox
Outfielder
Signed by Red Sox as a Non-Drafted Free Agent, June 1987

Personal
Height: 6-0 Weight: 195
Bats right, throws right
Born: March 8, 1966

School: Eckerd College
in St. Petersburg, Fla.

Ratings

	Present	Future
Hitting	4	5
Power	4	6
Baserunning	4	5
Speed	4	4
Fielding	4	5
Arm	5	5
Range	5	5

Rating Key
7 Outstanding
6 Major League Caliber, High
5 Major League Caliber
4 Minor League Caliber, High
3 Minor League Caliber
2 Below Average
1 Poor

General
Pina has hit for power wherever he's played. He moved up from Class AA New Britain to Class AAA Pawtucket midway through the 1989 season and actually hit much better at the higher level. He was an All-Star selection and Most Valuable Player of the Class A Carolina League in 1988, when he led the league in homers and runs batted in. He has a lot of enthusiasm and is dedicated to making improvement. Pina has primarily played right field in the minor leagues but probably is better suited for left at the major league level. He was passed over in the 1987 draft and signed by the Red Sox as a free agent.

Hitting Tendencies
Pina has legitimate major league power that would fit well in the middle of the order. Once he learns the strike zone and stops chasing high pitches, scouts say he'll be even a bigger threat. Despite his high strikeout totals, Pina has been a consistent .270s hitter and displayed power to all fields. Granted, he doesn't get much to hit since he's usually been his team's biggest RBI bat. But if he sharpens his big cut and displays a measure of patience, he could thrive as a run producer at the big-league level when he's surrounded by good hitters in the lineup.

Fielding/Baserunning
Pina's outfield skills would fit best in left field. He has average speed and an accurate arm that is strong enough for the position. After Pina posted a league-high 20 assists in the Carolina League in 1988, opponents were reluctant to run on him last season. He runs the bases fairly well but won't steal much.

Projection
Pina likely will play the full 1990 season at Class AAA Pawtucket and probably will reach the major leagues in 1991.

Career Statistics and Peak Projection

	G	AB	R	H	2B	3B	HR	RBI	BB	SO	AVG
1987 Elmira (New York-Penn League-Class A)	60	196	44	54	15	2	12	45	28	64	.276
1988 Lynchburg (Carolina League-Class A)	136	472	91	129	31	4	21	108	84	118	.273
1989 New Britain (Eastern League-Class AA)	46	154	22	40	10	0	2	26	26	47	.260
1989 Pawtucket (International League-Class AAA)	71	260	32	74	15	0	14	45	22	68	.285
1989 Major League Equivalency	117	410	51	110	27	0	14	67	45	120	.268
Peak Projection	154	534	88	160	37	0	27	92	68		.299

Interpretation
Pina's Major League Equivalency believes he can nearly double his total of doubles and walks by moving to Fenway Park from Class AAA Pawtucket. What's more, he doesn't lose a home run. Pina projects as a solid, balanced hitter who apparently doesn't need much preparation to be ready for major league pitching.

CHRIS DONNELS

New York Mets
Third Baseman
Mets' First-Round Pick, June 1987 Draft

Personal
Height: 6-0 Weight: 185
Bats left, throws right
Born: April 21, 1966

School: Loyola Marymount

Ratings

	Present	Future
Hitting	4	5
Power	5	6
Baserunning	4	5
Speed	4	4
Fielding	4	5
Arm	4	5
Range	4	5

Rating Key
7 Outstanding
6 Major League Caliber, High
5 Major League Caliber
4 Minor League Caliber, High
3 Minor League Caliber
2 Below Average
1 Poor

General
Donnels made major strides as a hitter last season, his third in the minor leagues. Playing at Class A St. Lucie, he was named the Florida State League's Most Valuable Player, leading the league in runs batted in and ranking second in home runs and batting. His swing wasn't the only thing that improved, however. Coming off a disappointing 1988 season, Donnels showed up in 1989 with a better attitude and became a team leader. In a stellar collegiate career at Loyola Marymount (Calif.), he batted .389, .350 and .365 in three seasons and totaled 45 homers and 225 RBIs, both school records.

Hitting Tendencies
Donnels flashed his big-league power potential in 1989, blasting 17 home runs in the Florida State League parks that are home to the major leagues in spring training. A lefthanded batter, he can hit to all fields but has especially good power to left. He has a good eye and knows the strike zone, having ranked among the leaders in the Florida State League with 83 walks in 1989. Scouts like the way he hangs in against lefthanded pitching.

Fielding/Baserunning
Donnels has a major league arm from third base and is adequate defensively. His 25 errors in 1989 were the second most among his league's third basemen, although he did field the most chances. He has average speed but is a good, smart baserunner. With the big leads he gets, he'll be able to steal on occasion.

Projection
Donnels likely will begin the 1990 season at Class AA Jackson but could move up to Class AAA Tidewater before the end of the year. He is believed to be two years, at most, away from the major leagues.

Career Statistics

	G	AB	R	H	2B	3B	HR	RBI	BB	SO	AVG
1987 Kingsport (Appalachian League-Rookie)	26	86	18	26	4	0	3	16	17	17	.302
1987 Columbia (South Atlantic League-Class A)	41	136	20	35	7	0	2	17	24	27	.257
1988 St. Lucie (Florida State League-Class A)	65	198	25	43	14	2	3	22	32	53	.217
1988 Columbia (South Atlantic League-Class A)	42	133	19	32	6	0	2	13	30	25	.241
1989 St. Lucie (Florida State League-Class A)	117	386	70	121	23	1	17	78	83	65	.313

(Projections unavailable because player has not competed at Class AA or Class AAA levels)

ERIC KARROS

Los Angeles Dodgers
First Baseman
Dodgers' Sixth-Round Pick, June 1988 Draft

Personal
Height: 6-4 Weight: 205
Bats right, throws right
Born: November 4, 1967

School: UCLA

Ratings

	Present	Future
Hitting	4	5
Power	4	6
Baserunning	4	5
Speed	4	4
Fielding	4	5
Arm	5	5
Range	4	5

Rating Key
7 Outstanding
6 Major League Caliber, High
5 Major League Caliber
4 Minor League Caliber, High
3 Minor League Caliber
2 Below Average
1 Poor

General
Karros is an outstanding hitter, both for power and average, who has excelled wherever he's picked up a bat. A former All-America at UCLA, he waged an impressive assault on Class A pitching in just his second pro season in 1989. Karros led the California League in hits and doubles, ranked second in batting and runs scored, third in total bases and fourth in runs batted in. The slugging first baseman received the league's Rookie of the Year award and was just one of six players to receive All-Star honors on the Dodgers' talent-rich Bakersfield entry. Karros was an unmistakable team leader, the kind of winning player who spurs those around him to play extra hard.

Hitting Tendencies
Karros has the potential to be a genuine home run threat in the major leagues. A big righthanded batter with raw power, he hit 12 home runs in the short-season Pioneer League in 1988 and 15 homers last season for Bakersfield. But what makes Karros such an attractive prospect is everything else he does with the bat. He hits for average, cranks out doubles and drives in loads of runs. Last season, he led all minor leaguers with 165 hits, was No. 3 with 40 doubles and ranked second within the Dodger organization with 86 RBIs. Put him in the cleanup spot and pitchers beware. Karros does strike out frequently but will take a walk if he's served strictly junk (99 strikeouts, 63 walks in 1989).

Fielding/Baserunning
Karros is a capable first baseman who can fill in at third base in a pinch. He has decent speed but isn't expected to be a stealing threat.

Projection
Karros likely will begin the 1990 season at Class AA San Antonio and probably is two years away from the majors.

Career Statistics

	G	AB	R	H	2B	3B	HR	RBI	BB	SO	AVG
1988—Great Falls (Pioneer League-Rookie)	66	268	68	98	12	1	12	55	32	35	.366
1989—Bakersfield (California League-Class A)	142	545	86	165	40	1	15	86	63	99	.303

(Projections unavailable because player has not competed at Class AA or Class AAA levels)

BRIAN JORDAN

St. Louis Cardinals
Outfielder
Cardinals' Supplemental Pick Following First Round, June 1988 Draft

Personal
Height: 6-1   Weight: 205
Bats left and right, throws right
Born: March 29, 1967

School: Richmond

Ratings

	Present	Future
Hitting	4	5
Power	4	6
Baserunning	4	5
Speed	4	4
Fielding	4	5
Arm	4	5
Range	4	5

Rating Key
7 Outstanding
6 Major League Caliber, High
5 Major League Caliber
4 Minor League Caliber, High
3 Minor League Caliber
2 Below Average
1 Poor

General
The Cardinals have no doubts Jordan is major league material, even though he has played just 30 games in their farm system over the last two seasons. The only thing holding him back: football. Jordan, a former star cornerback and punt returner at the University of Richmond, was claimed by the National Football League's Atlanta Falcons in 1989 after being drafted—and released in camp—by the Buffalo Bills. His slow recovery from a broken fibula suffered in the Senior Bowl game upset plans the Cardinals had for Jordan at Class A St. Petersburg in 1989.

Hitting Tendencies
Jordan has major league power potential, even in St. Louis' cavernous Busch Stadium. What's more, he's flashed his ability to hit for a high average and drive in runs, too. He has good hitting mechanics, with a short stride and short swing, and is balanced in the box. Because of his football pursuits, Jordan hasn't played enough baseball to prove he can hit the breaking ball—which he'll need to do to be a productive hitter. If he concentrates on baseball, acquiring the seasoning he sorely needs, the Cardinals believe he'll accelerate his trek to the majors.

Fielding/Baserunning
Jordan has played mostly center field but could play in either right or left field in the majors. He is outstanding defensively, with good speed (timed at 4.47 in the 40) and a strong arm. He could become a better runner as he gains experience, stealing a fair number of bases.

Projection
Because of Jordan's interest in football, it's difficult to see where he immediately fits in. If he gives baseball a chance, he'll probably begin the 1990 season at Class AA Arkansas.

Career Statistics

	G	AB	R	H	2B	3B	HR	RBI	BB	SO	AVG
1988—Hamilton (New York-Penn League-Class A)	19	71	12	22	3	1	4	12	6	15	.310
1989—St. Petersburg (Florida State League-Class A)	11	43	7	15	4	1	2	11	0	8	.349

(Projections unavailable because player has not competed at Class AA or Class AAA levels)

DAVID SEGUI

Baltimore Orioles
First Baseman
Orioles' 18th-Round Pick, June 1987 Draft

Personal
Height: 6-1 Weight: 170
Bats left and right, throws right
Born: July 19, 1966

School: Louisiana Tech

Ratings

	Present	Future
Hitting	4	5
Power	3	4
Baserunning	3	4
Speed	3	3
Fielding	5	6
Arm	5	5
Range	5	5

Rating Key
7 Outstanding
6 Major League Caliber, High
5 Major League Caliber
4 Minor League Caliber, High
3 Minor League Caliber
2 Below Average
1 Poor

General
Segui was voted the Orioles' minor league Player of the Year in 1989, putting together a solid season split between the Class A and AA levels. He finished with a .319 batting average, best in the Baltimore chain, and totaled 77 runs batted in, only two off the organization lead. Segui started fast at Class A Frederick and earned a berth on the Carolina League All-Star team despite moving up midway through the season to the Class AA Eastern League. He stayed hot after his promotion, batting .324 for Hagerstown and earning praise for his hard work. Segui is the son of Diego Segui, who pitched in the major leagues from 1962 through 1977.

Hitting Tendencies
Segui is a switch-hitter without a dominant side. He hits well from both sides, sending out line drives by consistently making solid contact. Segui has a good knowledge of hitting and a disciplined approach at the plate. He has walked more than he's struck out in his career and had a .407 on-base percentage at Frederick last season. He doesn't shoot for home runs but may develop more power as he fills out and gains experience. He currently has a good doubles-type stroke and uses the entire field. Instructors say he drives the ball well to the opposite field.

Fielding/Baserunning
Segui is an outstanding first baseman who could play defense in the major leagues now. He committed just five errors in 1989 and has added appeal because he's lefthanded. He has below-average speed as a runner and has stolen only two bases in two seasons.

Projection
Segui will get a chance to join the Class AAA Rochester club in 1990 and likely will fit into the Orioles' plans sometime in 1991.

Career Statistics and Peak Projection

	G	AB	R	H	2B	3B	HR	RBI	BB	SO	AVG
1988 Hagerstown (Carolina League-Class A)	60	190	35	51	12	4	3	31	22	23	.268
1989 Frederick (Carolina League-Class A)	83	284	43	90	19	0	10	50	41	32	.317
1989 Hagerstown (Eastern League-Class AA)	44	173	22	56	14	1	1	27	16	16	.324
1989 Major League Equivalency	44	170	20	53	13	1	1	24	15	17	.312
Peak Projection	154	573	75	187	42	3	5	63	61		.327

Interpretation
Segui has just a one-season sample to project, but his peak batting average of .327 rates second among the prospects. He doesn't show any home run potential but note the 42 doubles in the peak line.

SCOTT COOLBAUGH

Texas Rangers
Third Baseman
Rangers' Third-Round Pick, June 1987 Draft

Personal
Height: 5-11 Weight: 185
Bats right, throws right
Born: June 13, 1966

School: Texas

Ratings

	Present	Future
Hitting	5	5
Power	4	5
Baserunning	5	5
Speed	4	4
Fielding	5	5
Arm	5	5
Range	5	5

Rating Key
7 Outstanding
6 Major League Caliber, High
5 Major League Caliber
4 Minor League Caliber, High
3 Minor League Caliber
2 Below Average
1 Poor

General
Coolbaugh has played his way into the Rangers' major league picture with quick success at all three minor league levels. He provided a sneak preview in Texas last September, starting 18 games and batting .275. Before his promotion, he earned All-Star honors in the Class AAA American Association, where he ranked third in the league in total bases and fourth in both home runs and runs batted in. Coolbaugh has a good fundamental knowledge of the game and reacts quickly—and correctly—on the field. He was the Most Valuable Player on the University of Texas' 1986 College World Series team.

Hitting Tendencies
Not a hit-or-miss type, Coolbaugh makes good contact and is capable of going deep. His batting average dipped slightly as he advanced through the Rangers' organization, but his home run total steadily rose, to a team-leading 18 homers at Oklahoma City (plus two at Texas) in 1989. Coolbaugh is a good situational hitter who knows what his job is each time he comes to the plate. He has a good eye and has the potential to provide a dependable RBI bat.

Fielding/Baserunning
Coolbaugh isn't flashy on defense, but he always gets the job done. He is especially adept at charging the ball and making the barehanded pick-up on bunt plays. He can turn the double play (a league-high 32 at his position in 1989) and has a strong arm. As a runner, he has slightly below-average speed but won't clog the bases because of his good fundamental skills.

Projection
Coolbaugh will compete for a spot on the Texas roster in spring training in 1990.

Career Statistics and Peak Projection

	G	AB	R	H	2B	3B	HR	RBI	BB	SO	AVG
1987 Charlotte (Florida State League-Class A)	66	233	27	64	21	0	2	20	24	56	.275
1988 Tulsa (Texas League-Class AA)	136	470	52	127	15	4	13	75	76	79	.270
1988 Major League Equivalency	136	457	45	114	12	3	12	64	65	85	.249
1989 Oklahoma City (American Assoc.-Class AAA)	144	527	66	137	28	0	18	74	57	93	.260
1989 Texas (American League)	25	51	7	14	1	0	2	7	4	12	.275
1989 Major League Equivalency	169	565	65	138	23	0	20	72	54	113	.244
Peak Projection	154	511	82	143	21	1	25	82	64		.279

Interpretation
This is your basic power hitter's profile. The Rangers might like to see 30 home runs or a .290 batting average in the peak years, but Coolbaugh projects close on both counts.

WILFREDO CORDERO

Montreal Expos
Shortstop
Signed by Expos as a Non-Drafted Free Agent, May 1988

Personal
Height: 6-2 Weight: 185
Bats right, throws right
Born: October 3, 1971

School: Mayaguez, Puerto Rico

Ratings

	Present	Future
Hitting	3	5
Power	3	5
Baserunning	4	5
Speed	4	4
Fielding	3	5
Arm	3	5
Range	3	5

Rating Key
7 Outstanding
6 Major League Caliber, High
5 Major League Caliber
4 Minor League Caliber, High
3 Minor League Caliber
2 Below Average
1 Poor

General
Cordero was one of the youngest players in the minor leagues in 1989, playing in the Class AA Southern League at age 17. He struggled offensively at that level, batting just .215 at Jacksonville, but did show well with a .277 average at Class A West Palm Beach before his promotion. The Expos believe the latter mark is indicative of his potential. He has good instincts for the game despite his youth and picks up things easily. A native of Puerto Rico, he was pursued by a number of clubs before signing with Montreal.

Hitting Tendencies
Cordero has a great deal of raw ability that he has time to refine. He possesses good hitting mechanics and appears to have some pop in his bat, having belted nine home runs in 1989 while driving in 46 runs. The Expos believe he'll have above-average power for a shortstop when he develops. He'll likely get stronger as he gets older and have better bat control. At this point, he just needs to get some at-bats. He can work to reduce his strikeouts total 91 in 410 at-bats last season) and become a better on-base threat.

Fielding/Baserunning
The book on the shortstop reads: good hands, good arm, good range, good positioning for different hitters. Which is why the Expos are not fretting his 36 errors last season. Some scouts have speculated Cordero will eventually move to another infield position, but the Expos are confident he'll settle down with experience. As a baserunner, he has average speed but will rarely steal.

Projection
Cordero likely will begin the 1990 season at Class AA Jacksonville and probably is close to three years away from the major leagues.

Career Statistics and Peak Projection

	G	AB	R	H	2B	3B	HR	RBI	BB	SO	AVG
1988 Jamestown (New York-Penn League-Class A)	52	190	18	49	3	0	2	22	15	44	.258
1989 West Palm Beach (Florida State League-Class A)	78	289	37	80	12	2	6	29	33	58	.277
1989 Jacksonville (Southern League-Class AA)	39	121	9	26	6	1	3	17	12	33	.215
1989 Major League Equivalency	39	119	8	24	6	1	3	15	10	36	.202
Peak Projection	154	486	61	132	29	5	23	80	54		.271

Interpretation
Cordero couldn't solve Class AA pitching in just 39 games in 1989, a fact borne out by his Major League Equivalency. Given Cordero's limited experience, the peak calculations could be a shot in the dark for a season seven years away.

HENRY RODRIGUEZ

Los Angeles Dodgers
First Baseman
Signed by Dodgers as a Non-Drafted Free Agent, July 1985

Personal
Height: 6-1 Weight: 180
Bats left, throws left
Born: November 8, 1967

School: Dominican Republic

Ratings

	Present	Future
Hitting	4	5
Power	4	6
Baserunning	3	4
Speed	4	4
Fielding	4	5
Arm	5	5
Range	4	5

Rating Key
7 Outstanding
6 Major League Caliber, High
5 Major League Caliber
4 Minor League Caliber, High
3 Minor League Caliber
2 Below Average
1 Poor

General
Rodriguez's potential surfaced at Class A Vero Beach in 1989, his third year in the Dodger organization. Voted the All-Star first baseman in the Florida State League, Rodriguez has a good deal of raw talent he's just starting to refine. Formerly prone to spells of sluggishness, he displayed a dedicated attitude and became a more complete hitter. Rodriguez ranked third among Florida State League players in runs batted in, fourth in total bases and fifth in slugging percentage. He led Vero Beach with 10 home runs and was the team's No. 2 hitter with a .284 average. With some strong first-base talent ahead of Rodriguez in the system, the Dodgers will see how he responds to a trial in the outfield.

Hitting Tendencies
Rodriguez has very good power potential, which he showed last season in the big Florida State League parks. He's handled the bat well at each stop in the Dodgers' minor league system, hitting for a good average while displaying a discriminating eye. He doesn't flail away at pitches, which makes him particularly appealing as a high average/power prospect. Just turned 22, he's getting stronger as he matures and becoming a smarter hitter as he moves up the ladder.

Fielding/Baserunning
Rodriguez's primary position is first base, but he has the arm and enough speed to play the outfield if the Dodgers decide to develop him there. He has good hands at first and was solid enough to rank second among Florida State League first basemen in fielding last season. He isn't expected to be a stealing threat.

Projection
Rodriguez is on schedule to play at Class AA San Antonio in 1990 and is probably two years away from the major leagues.

Career Statistics

	G	AB	R	H	2B	3B	HR	RBI	BB	SO	AVG
1987 Sarasota Dodgers (Gulf Coast League-Rookie)	49	148	23	49	7	3	0	15	16	15	.331
1988 Salem (Northwest League-Class A)	72	291	47	84	14	4	2	38	21	42	.289
1989 Vero Beach (Florida State League-Class A)	126	433	53	123	33	1	10	73	48	58	.284
1989 Bakersfield (California League-Class A)	3	9	2	2	0	0	1	2	0	3	.222

(Projections unavailable because player has not competed at Class AA or Class AAA levels)

CARLOS BAERGA

Cleveland Indians
Third Baseman
Signed by San Diego Padres as a Non-Drafted Free Agent, November 1985

Personal
Height: 5-11 Weight: 165
Bats left and right, throws right
Born: November 4, 1968

Ratings
	Present	Future
Hitting	4	5
Power	3	4
Baserunning	4	5
Speed	5	5
Fielding	4	5
Arm	5	5
Range	4	5

Rating Key
7 Outstanding
6 Major League Caliber, High
5 Major League Caliber
4 Minor League Caliber, High
3 Minor League Caliber
2 Below Average
1 Poor

General
Baerga reminds some observers of the St. Louis Cardinals' Jose Oquendo because of his versatility. Formerly a second baseman and shortstop, Baerga made the switch to third base at Class AAA Las Vegas last season without suffering ill consequences at the plate. Like Oquendo, he's a switch-hitter, but scouts believe he'll hit for more power than Jose at the major league level. Despite his smallish stature, Baerga totaled 22 home runs over the last two seasons and ranked fifth in the San Diego organization in 1989 with 74 runs batted in. Still only 21, he logged four seasons on the Padres' farm.

Hitting Tendencies
Baerga has particular appeal because he's a proven switch-hitter. He has batted .270 or better in each of his four seasons and last year bid for his second .300 campaign until a wrist injury triggered a late-season slump. He has good gap power, with 28 doubles in each of his last two years. Baerga does need to refine his knowledge of the strike zone, what with his walk total annually in the 30s and his strikeouts near 100. He has made adjustments to the curveball, and instructors predict he'll continue to develop as he matures.

Fielding/Baserunning
Having played just one season at third base, Baerga is still learning the position. His 25 errors were a high for Pacific Coast League third basemen in 1989, but he also fielded the most chances. Scouts like his range, his good first-step quickness and his arm. Baerga once stole 26 bases (in 1987) but has never swiped more than six in any other year.

Projection
Baerga likely will compete for a spot on the Indians' 1990 roster, but he'd get valuable playing time at the Class AAA level.

Career Statistics and Peak Projection

	G	AB	R	H	2B	3B	HR	RBI	BB	SO	AVG
1986 Charleston (South Atlantic League-Class A)	111	378	57	102	14	4	7	41	26	60	.270
1987 Charleston (South Atlantic League-Class A)	134	515	83	157	23	9	7	50	38	107	.305
1988 Wichita (Texas League-Class AA)	122	444	67	121	28	1	12	65	31	83	.273
1988 Major League Equivalency	122	418	45	95	22	1	9	44	22	88	.227
1989 Las Vegas (Pacific Coast League-Class AAA)	132	520	63	143	28	2	10	74	30	98	.275
1989 Major League Equivalency	132	486	40	109	21	1	7	47	20	104	.224
Peak Projection	154	550	71	150	28	1	14	65	35		.272

Interpretation
The Major League Equivalencies are virtually identical for 1988 and 1989. Despite Baerga's youth, only his batting average climbs significantly in the seven years it takes to reach his peak. His strikeouts-to-walks ratios are distressing.

PHIL PLANTIER

Boston Red Sox
Outfielder
Red Sox's 11th-Round Pick, June 1987 Draft

Personal
Height: 6-0 Weight: 175
Bats left, throws right
Born: January 27, 1969

School: Poway High
in Poway, Calif.

Ratings

	Present	Future
Hitting	4	5
Power	4	6
Baserunning	4	5
Speed	4	4
Fielding	4	5
Arm	3	4
Range	4	5

Rating Key
7 Outstanding
6 Major League Caliber, High
5 Major League Caliber
4 Minor League Caliber, High
3 Minor League Caliber
2 Below Average
1 Poor

General
The league was positively Class A, but Plantier opened eyes at the major league level in 1989 by staging a veritable hitting exhibition at Lynchburg. Playing his second full season of Class A ball, Plantier led the Carolina League in home runs and runs batted in to carry off the league's Most Valuable Player award. Add four hits and he would have won the batting title and Triple Crown. Originally signed as a third baseman, Plantier moved to left field full time in 1989 after playing 52 games in the outfield in 1988. He underwent shoulder surgery before last season.

Hitting Tendencies
At this stage, Plantier's bat has earned him comparisons with Mike Greenwell, the current Red Sox left fielder. Scouts say Plantier probably has even better power potential. He gets his home runs with a short, compact stroke, although his strikeout total (122 in 443 at-bats last season) is on par with a free swinger's. He did show some discipline, however, ranking second in the Carolina League with 74 walks in 1989. Plantier's quick stroke allows him to wait longer on the pitch, something he didn't do when he struggled through his first two minor league seasons. He has good power from left-center to the right-field line and isn't overmatched by breaking pitches.

Fielding/Baserunning
Plantier doesn't appear ready to play left field in the major leagues. He is adequate, but he needs to master the fundamentals of the position. His speed on the bases is about average.

Projection
Plantier likely will play at Class AA New Britain in 1990 and probably is two or three years away from the major leagues.

Career Statistics

	G	AB	R	H	2B	3B	HR	RBI	BB	SO	AVG
1988—Elmira (New York-Penn League-Class A)	28	80	7	14	2	0	2	9	9	9	.175
1989—Lynchburg (Carolina League-Class A)	131	443	73	133	26	1	27	105	74	122	.300

(Projections unavailable because player has not competed at Class AA or Class AAA levels)

SCOTT LEIUS

Minnesota Twins
Shortstop
Twins' 13th-Round Pick, June 1986 Draft

Personal
Height: 6-3 Weight: 180
Bats right, throws right
Born: September 24, 1965

School: Concordia College
in Bronxville, N.Y.

Ratings

	Present	Future
Hitting	4	5
Power	3	4
Baserunning	4	5
Speed	4	4
Fielding	5	6
Arm	5	5
Range	5	5

Rating Key
7 Outstanding
6 Major League Caliber, High
5 Major League Caliber
4 Minor League Caliber, High
3 Minor League Caliber
2 Below Average
1 Poor

General
Not even a broken foot—for the second straight year, no less—could prevent Scott Leius from taking a major stride in 1989, so to speak. After hitting below .240 in each of his two previous seasons, Leius appeared to come of age offensively in 1989, claiming the Class AA Southern League batting title with a .303 average. It was an important career juncture, and the shortstop wound up on the Southern League All-Star team. He missed the season's final month when a foul tip fractured a bone in his left foot, the same injury that prematurely ended his 1988 season. Scouts like his makeup and intensity, and he's the type of player who can lead on the field.

Hitting Tendencies
Leius made some off-season adjustments and flashed his offensive potential in 1989. He is mostly a contact-type hitter who won't back up outfielders to the fence. He will, however, sting the ball on occasion, sending a line drive into the gap for extra bases. He generally puts the ball in play but could stand to get on base more often via charity. Leius understands the need to be more selective and is starting to hold out for his pitch when he's ahead in the count.

Fielding/Baserunning
Leius' calling card is his smooth defense at shortstop. He has good hands, good range, a strong, accurate arm, and he's one of the best at turning the double play. He has good instincts and ability on the bases, but he'll attempt only a handful of steals per season.

Projection
Leius likely will play for Class AAA Portland in 1990. If he continues his offensive surge (and stays injury-free), he could be in the major leagues by year's end.

Career Statistics and Peak Projection

	G	AB	R	H	2B	3B	HR	RBI	BB	SO	AVG
1986 Elizabethton (Appalachian League-Rookie)	61	237	37	66	14	1	4	23	26	45	.278
1987 Kenosha (Midwest League-Class A)	126	414	65	99	16	4	8	51	50	88	.239
1988 Visalia (California League-Class A)	93	308	44	73	14	4	3	46	42	50	.237
1989 Orlando (Southern League-Class AA)	99	346	49	105	22	2	4	45	38	74	.303
1989 Major League Equivalency	99	332	38	91	20	1	3	35	29	78	.274
Peak Projection	154	518	71	154	32	1	7	56	53		.298

Interpretation
Leius has very little power and seldom draws a walk, but the system looked kindly on his 1989 season. He's already 24 years old and can't afford to revert to his pre-1989 form.

JEFF JACKSON

Philadelphia Phillies
Outfielder
Phillies' First-Round Pick, June 1989 Draft

Personal
Height: 6-2 Weight: 185
Bats right, throws right
Born: January 2, 1972

School: Simeon High
in Chicago

Ratings

	Present	Future
Hitting	2	5
Power	2	5
Baserunning	3	5
Speed	4	5
Fielding	2	5
Arm	3	5
Range	4	5

Rating Key
7 Outstanding
6 Major League Caliber, High
5 Major League Caliber
4 Minor League Caliber, High
3 Minor League Caliber
2 Below Average
1 Poor

General
Frustration set in for the Phillies' first-round draft choice when he struggled through a .227 season in the rookie Appalachian League in 1989. But time is on Jeff Jackson's side. He was, after all, only 17 years old and playing at stop No. 1 in what the Phillies expect to be a long career. Jackson began his senior year in high school as a virtual unknown in scouting circles yet was the fourth player picked in the 1989 draft. He has tremendous physical ability and the raw tools necessary to become a great player. He knows he has much to learn and is an eager student.

Hitting Tendencies
The Phillies have revamped Jackson's swing, his stance and virtually everything else related to hitting. He had a bad habit of pulling off the ball last season and was tied up by breaking pitches, just like many other young hitters. In 163 at-bats for Martinsville, he struck out 66 times. Instructors also are trying to teach him to use his lower body to help his swing. The tools are there for Jackson to hit for both power and average, but it will take time. In his senior year at Chicago's Simeon High School, he batted over .512 with power and stole 46 bases in 46 attempts.

Fielding/Baserunning
Jackson has room to improve in both areas. He has good speed, but he needs to learn the finer points of baserunning and how to take leads. He can go after the ball in the outfield and has an average arm that could get better.

Projection
Jackson is at least four years away from the major leagues. The next logical step is to a Class A team in 1990.

Career Statistics

	G	AB	R	H	2B	3B	HR	RBI	BB	SO	AVG
1989—Martinsville (Appalachian League-Rookie)	48	163	16	37	5	1	2	21	14	66	.227

(Projections unavailable because player has not competed at Class AA or Class AAA levels)

BOB HAMELIN

Kansas City Royals
First Baseman
Royals' Second-Round Pick, June 1988 Draft

Personal
Height: 6-1 Weight: 230
Bats left, throws left
Born: November 29, 1967

School: Rancho Santiago College in Santa Ana, Calif.

Ratings

	Present	Future
Hitting	4	5
Power	4	6
Baserunning	3	4
Speed	4	4
Fielding	4	5
Arm	4	5
Range	4	5

Rating Key
7 Outstanding
6 Major League Caliber, High
5 Major League Caliber
4 Minor League Caliber, High
3 Minor League Caliber
2 Below Average
1 Poor

General
Hamelin is the Royals' prized slugging prospect but missed almost half of the 1989 season with a strained back at Class AA Memphis. If he doesn't keep his weight under control, scouts say, he could go down with similar injuries in the future. When he's playing, Hamelin injects a megadose of power into a lineup. In his first two seasons, he cracked 33 home runs in 446 at-bats (one homer every 13.1 at-bats), including a league-leading 17 homers in the Class A Northwest League in 1988. He's been a league All-Star pick in each of his two seasons and displayed good work habits. As a collegian, Hamelin set a single-season California junior college record with 31 home runs in 1988.

Hitting Tendencies
Hamelin has the swing to produce upwards of 25 home runs a year in the big leagues. He's strong enough to hit the ball out to any field, but he's primarily a pull hitter who attacks fastballs with a quick, compact swing. He has a good sense of the strike zone and has displayed patience in the box (108 walks over the equivalent of one full season). He does have some holes on the outside part of the plate, particularly when he's served off-speed pitches. When he's healthy, he can hit the ball as far as anybody. Some observers predict he'll eventually wind up as a designated hitter.

Fielding/Baserunning
Hamelin is average defensively at first. The fact that he's a lefthander helps his cause, but his footwork needs improvement. He has limited speed on the bases and will not be a stealing threat.

Projection
Hamelin likely will move up to Class AAA Omaha to start the 1990 season but could be in Kansas City by September.

Career Statistics and Peak Projection

	G	AB	R	H	2B	3B	HR	RBI	BB	SO	AVG
1988 Eugene (Northwest League-Class A)	90	235	42	70	19	1	17	61	56	67	.298
1989 Memphis (Southern League-Class AA)	68	211	45	65	12	5	16	47	52	52	.308
1989 Major League Equivalency	68	202	34	56	11	4	10	36	40	53	.277
Peak Projection	154	477	114	151	28	9	38	112	110		.317

Interpretation
Hamelin's 1989 numbers sent the projection totals soaring. He winds up with Bo Jackson-like power and a George Brett-type batting average in his peak season. He dresses up the line even more with 110 projected walks. The down side? The calculations are based on the equivalent of half a season.

SCOTT HEMOND

Oakland Athletics
Third Baseman
Athletics' First-Round Pick, June 1986 Draft

Personal
Height: 6-0   Weight: 205
Bats right, throws right
Born: November 18, 1965

School: South Florida

Ratings

	Present	Future
Hitting	4	5
Power	4	5
Baserunning	5	6
Speed	5	5
Fielding	5	5
Arm	5	5
Range	5	5

Rating Key
7 Outstanding
6 Major League Caliber, High
5 Major League Caliber
4 Minor League Caliber, High
3 Minor League Caliber
2 Below Average
1 Poor

General
It took him almost two seasons to get untracked offensively at the Class AA level, but Hemond finally began showing the promise the Athletics anticipated when they made him the 12th overall pick in the 1986 draft. Sparked by a hot second half, he posted career-best totals in every major offensive category except home runs in 1989. He finished second in the Southern League in runs scored and tied for fourth with 45 stolen bases. Drafted as a catcher out of South Florida, Hemond is an enthusiastic player who likes to get his uniform dirty.

Hitting Tendencies
Hemond has potential as a hitter who can give his team the high on-base percentage it needs from a player in the top part of the order. Formerly a swinger who tried to pull every delivery, Hemond has started to go with the pitch and make use of the entire field. He stopped wasting at-bats and showed more patience last season; consequently, he came through more often in the clutch. When he tried to pull every pitch, he didn't make enough contact to do anything. Hemond has the pure strength to drive the ball. As he becomes comfortable with his abilities and limitations, he should hit for more power.

Fielding/Baserunning
Hemond was stationed mostly at third base last season but has the experience to move behind the plate. He can make the routine plays at third and pull off the great ones because of his quick reaction and strong arm. He has a catcher's build but the speed to be a legitimate 30-steals threat in the majors.

Projection
Hemond likely will advance to Class AAA Tacoma in 1990 and could make the jump to Oakland sometime in 1991.

Career Statistics and Peak Projection

	G	AB	R	H	2B	3B	HR	RBI	BB	SO	AVG
1986 Madison (Midwest League-Class A)	22	85	9	26	2	0	2	13	5	19	.306
1987 Madison (Midwest League-Class A)	90	343	60	99	21	4	8	52	40	79	.289
1987 Huntsville (Southern League-Class AA)	33	110	10	20	3	1	1	8	4	30	.182
1987 Major League Equivalency	33	107	8	17	2	1	1	7	3	32	.159
1988 Huntsville (Southern League-Class AA)	133	482	51	106	22	4	9	53	48	114	.220
1988 Major League Equivalency	133	470	43	94	18	2	8	45	39	122	.200
1989 Huntsville (Southern League-Class AA)	132	490	89	130	26	6	5	62	62	70	.265
1989 Oakland (American League)	4	0	2	0	0	0	0	0	0	0	.000
1989 Major League Equivalency	132	465	63	105	19	3	4	44	42	75	.226
Peak Projection	154	535	90	131	23	3	9	53	56		.244

Interpretation
Hemond fared well in the Class A Midwest League but has had difficulty adjusting to Class AA pitching. The calculations alone don't offer much hope now or down the road.

SCOTT COOPER

Boston Red Sox
Third Baseman
Red Sox's Third-Round Pick, June 1986 Draft

Personal
Height: 6-3 Weight: 205
Bats left, throws right
Born: October 13, 1967

School: Pattonville High in St. Louis

Ratings

	Present	Future
Hitting	4	5
Power	4	5
Baserunning	4	5
Speed	4	4
Fielding	4	5
Arm	5	5
Range	4	5

Rating Key
7 Outstanding
6 Major League Caliber, High
5 Major League Caliber
4 Minor League Caliber, High
3 Minor League Caliber
2 Below Average
1 Poor

General
He has been touted as the heir apparent to Wade Boggs, but Cooper struggled through his most disappointing season to date in 1989. Stepping up to the Class AA Eastern League, he didn't adjust well to tougher pitching and posted career lows in batting, home runs and runs batted in. Some observers believe he might have been intimidated by the size of New Britain's Beehive Field, not a particularly good offensive park. His performance did pick up toward the end of the season, a sign that he was starting to read pitchers. Cooper had a banner year at the Class A level in 1988, ranking second among all minor leaguers with 45 doubles and leading the Carolina League with 148 hits.

Hitting Tendencies
Cooper is a line-drive hitter with a quick, straightaway swing. He has hit home runs in the past, but he doesn't fit the mold of the traditional basher. Granted, the Red Sox believe he'll drive the ball a little better as he gets at-bats and becomes a smarter hitter, but Cooper is primarily a doubles threat who holds RBI promise. His strikeouts-to-walks ratio in 1989 wasn't as good as in the past, an indication he has some adjusting to do against good pitching.

Fielding/Baserunning
While his offense slipped, Cooper's defense at third base continued to improve. He has a strong presence at the corner, with good instincts and a strong arm. His baserunning speed is just average and he rarely attempts to steal.

Projection
Despite a down year in 1989, Cooper is expected to move up another grade to Class AAA Pawtucket in 1990. He likely is one to two years away from Boston.

Career Statistics and Peak Projection

	G	AB	R	H	2B	3B	HR	RBI	BB	SO	AVG
1986 Elmira (New York-Penn League-Class A)	51	191	23	55	9	0	9	43	19	32	.288
1987 Greensboro (South Atlantic League-Class A)	119	370	52	93	21	2	15	63	58	69	.251
1988 Lynchburg (Carolina League-Class A)	130	497	90	148	45	7	9	73	58	74	.295
1989 New Britain (Eastern League-Class AA)	127	421	50	104	24	2	7	39	55	84	.247
1989 Major League Equivalency	124	422	51	105	27	2	7	40	55	87	.249
Peak Projection	154	520	85	149	35	2	14	68	79		.286

Interpretation
Cooper has just one Class AA season to evaluate. Unfortunately for him, it was a down year offensively, and his Major League Equivalency suffered. At his peak, he projects as a line-drive hitter with a good eye for walks.

PAUL COLEMAN

St. Louis Cardinals
Outfielder
Cardinals' First-Round Pick, June 1989 Draft

Personal
Height: 5-11 Weight: 200
Bats right, throws right
Born: December 9, 1970

School: Frankston High
in Frankston, Tex.

Ratings

	Present	Future
Hitting	3	5
Power	2	6
Baserunning	3	5
Speed	4	4
Fielding	3	5
Arm	3	5
Range	3	5

Rating Key
7 Outstanding
6 Major League Caliber, High
5 Major League Caliber
4 Minor League Caliber, High
3 Minor League Caliber
2 Below Average
1 Poor

General
Just out of high school, Coleman is very raw and spent most of his first professional season adjusting to the differences between prep and rookie league ball. He struggled initially but did show marked improvement in the last month of the season at Johnson City. Tabbed by the Cardinals as their power hitter of the future, he was drafted sixth overall in 1989 after batting .498 with 39 home runs in his high school career. Coleman is a hard worker and takes instruction well.

Hitting Tendencies
With a chiseled physique similar to Bo Jackson's, Coleman has tremendous strength and outstanding power. Many scouts say the home runs he hit in high school were of the legendary variety, often traveling more than 500 feet. He'll be expected to drive in runs and hit for a good average, too, although he was inconsistent in his first minor league season. He struck out 58 times in 178 at-bats while adjusting to better pitching. The Cardinals will prescribe plenty of playing time and instruction, particularly on hitting the breaking ball. Once they fine tune his swing, Coleman is expected to show signs of being the dominating player he is capable of being in a few years.

Fielding/Baserunning
Coleman has an outstanding arm and runs well for a player his size. He played center field at Johnson City, but his arm is good enough to make him a right-field candidate in the majors. He will not be a prolific basestealer, but his speed will help him run down balls hit into the gaps in the outfield.

Projection
Coleman is ticketed to play a full season at the Class A level in 1990. At best, he is probably four years away from the majors.

Career Statistics

	G	AB	R	H	2B	3B	HR	RBI	BB	SO	AVG
1989 Johnson City (Appalachian League-Rookie)	53	172	26	40	11	0	3	24	16	58	.233

(Projections unavailable because player has not competed at Class AA or Class AAA levels)

DARREN LEWIS

Oakland Athletics
Outfielder
Athletics' 18th-Round Pick, June 1988 Draft

Personal
Height: 6-0 Weight: 175
Bats right, throws right
Born: August 28, 1967

School: California

Ratings

	Present	Future
Hitting	4	5
Power	3	4
Baserunning	4	5
Speed	6	6
Fielding	5	5
Arm	4	4
Range	5	5

Rating Key
7 Outstanding
6 Major League Caliber, High
5 Major League Caliber
4 Minor League Caliber, High
3 Minor League Caliber
2 Below Average
1 Poor

General
To opponents, Lewis is like the fly that won't go away. A good-hit, great-glove outfielder, he plays to make things happen—and usually does. He is an intelligent player whose enthusiasm makes him a favorite with instructors. Batting mostly leadoff at Class A Modesto in 1989, his first full season in the minors, Lewis rapped out 150 hits to rank fifth in the California League. He made a number of eye-popping catches in center field and won praise leaguewide for his ability in all phases of the game.

Hitting Tendencies
Lewis has shown potential as a leadoff hitter who takes full advantage of his speed. At this stage, however, he has a tendency to give in to pitchers simply to make contact. The Athletics are teaching him to take a good swing and to pull the ball to left field on occasion. Lewis nevertheless is a smart situational hitter. He has a short, compact swing but needs to cut down on his strikeouts (nearly one every six at-bats in 1989) to become more of a threat in the leadoff slot.

Fielding/Baserunning
If Lewis can be likened to a pesky fly, call him a fly on the wall on defense. He'll scale the wall to catch balls other center fielders play on the carom. Of all his defensive skills, only his arm rates average. He's outstanding in every other regard and gets a tremendous jump on the ball. With speed to burn, Lewis will be a major stealing threat when he learns to read pitchers. He swiped 27 bases in 1989 but was caught 23 times.

Projection
Lewis likely will move up to Class AA Huntsville in 1990 and is expected to be in the major leagues in 1992.

Career Statistics

	G	AB	R	H	2B	3B	HR	RBI	BB	SO	AVG
1988 Scottsdale (Arizona League-Rookie)	5	15	8	5	3	0	0	4	6	5	.333
1988 Madison (Midwest League-Class A)	60	199	38	49	4	1	0	11	46	37	.246
1989 Modesto (California League-Class A)	129	503	74	150	23	5	4	39	59	84	.298
1989 Huntsville (Southern League-Class AA)	9	31	7	10	1	1	1	7	2	6	.323

(Projections unavailable due to player's limited experience at Class AA level)

MARK LEMKE

Atlanta Braves
Second Baseman
Braves' 27th-Round Pick, June 1983 Draft

Personal
Height: 5-9 Weight: 167
Bats left and right, throws right
Born: August 13, 1965

School: Notre Dame High
in Utica, N.Y.

Ratings

	Present	Future
Hitting	4	5
Power	3	4
Baserunning	5	5
Speed	5	5
Fielding	5	5
Arm	5	5
Range	5	5

Rating Key
7 Outstanding
6 Major League Caliber, High
5 Major League Caliber
4 Minor League Caliber, High
3 Minor League Caliber
2 Below Average
1 Poor

General
Lemke's attitude is one of his biggest assets. He still approaches the game like a Little Leaguer, showing up at the ball park early and straggling out among the last departees. He is a hustling, hard-nosed player who, oddly, occasionally needs a shot of confidence. Observers say Lemke has to feel like he belongs before he can play like it. He had been tabbed to open the 1989 season at second base in Atlanta, but the Braves' acquisition of Jeff Treadway forced Lemke to Class AAA Richmond. He has been brought up by Atlanta in each of his last two seasons and been a league All-Star selection his last three years. After being called up from Richmond in 1989, he drove in seven runs in his first week with the Braves.

Hitting Tendencies
Lemke isn't expected to carry a lineup, but he should hit for a respectable average and have some punch, particularly for a middle infielder. Before slipping to seven home runs in 1989, he belted 54 homers over his previous three seasons. He is a switch-hitter who has a knack for getting on base. He led the Class AA Southern League in hits in 1988 and ranked fourth in the International League last season. Lemke is a tough strikeout and will hang in to work for a walk. With his discipline and hitting knowledge, he's averaged 73 RBIs over the last four years.

Fielding/Baserunning
Lemke is a solid second baseman in every regard and turns the double play extremely well. In each of the last three seasons, he led his league's second basemen in double plays, assists and chances. He has average speed but stole only four bases in 1989.

Projection
Lemke will compete for the Braves' second-base job in 1990.

Career Statistics and Peak Projection

	G	AB	R	H	2B	3B	HR	RBI	BB	SO	AVG
1983 Bradenton Braves (Gulf Coast League-Rookie)	53	209	37	55	6	0	0	19	30	19	.263
1984 Anderson (South Atlantic League-Class A)	42	121	18	18	2	0	0	5	14	14	.149
1984 Bradenton Braves (Gulf Coast League-Rookie)	63	243	41	67	11	0	3	32	29	14	.276
1985 Sumter (South Atlantic League-Class A)	90	231	25	50	6	0	0	20	34	22	.216
1986 Sumter (South Atlantic League-Class A)	126	448	99	122	24	2	18	66	87	31	.272
1987 Durham (Carolina League-Class A)	127	489	75	143	28	3	20	68	54	45	.292
1987 Greenville (Southern League-Class AA)	6	26	0	6	0	0	0	4	0	4	.231
1987 Major League Equivalency	6	25	0	5	0	0	0	3	0	4	.200
1988 Greenville (Southern League-Class AA)	143	567	81	153	30	4	16	80	52	52	.270
1988 Atlanta (National League)	16	58	8	13	4	0	0	2	4	5	.224
1988 Major League Equivalency	159	606	72	147	33	3	12	66	44	98	.243
1989 Richmond (International League-Class AAA)	146	518	69	143	22	7	5	61	66	45	.276
1989 Atlanta (National League)	14	55	4	10	2	1	2	10	5	7	.182
1989 Major League Equivalency	160	565	68	145	25	7	6	66	64	52	.257
Peak Projection	154	567	84	159	29	5	11	66	67		.280

Interpretation
Lemke's Major League Equivalencies reflect steady progress, a trend the peak system likes best. His peak year isn't mind-boggling, but there is no glaring weakness in his record.

DANN HOWITT

Oakland Athletics
Outfielder/First Baseman
Athletics' 18th-Round Pick, June 1986 Draft

Personal
Height: 6-5   Weight: 205
Bats left, throws right
Born: February 13, 1964

School: Cal State Fullerton

Ratings

	Present	Future
Hitting	4	5
Power	5	6
Baserunning	4	4
Speed	4	4
Fielding	4	5
Arm	5	5
Range	4	5

Rating Key
7 Outstanding
6 Major League Caliber, High
5 Major League Caliber
4 Minor League Caliber, High
3 Minor League Caliber
2 Below Average
1 Poor

General
An outfielder for most of his first three minor league seasons, Howitt played first base nearly full time in 1989 as the Athletics stepped up plans to make him a two-position player. At the same time, his offensive production mushroomed, carrying him to All-Star honors (in the outfield, ironically) in the Class AA Southern League. Howitt ranked among the league leaders in most batting categories and led the Athletics' minor league chain with 26 homers and 111 runs batted in. It was probably the jolt his career needed. Howitt turns 26 this season but at least had a peek at major league action in 1989. He is an intense, dedicated worker who is gaining confidence.

Hitting Tendencies
Howitt's most obvious asset is his explosive bat. He belted some tremendous home runs in the Southern League last season and cuts an imposing figure at the plate, standing 6-foot-5. He has the strength to hit the ball out in any direction and started to make better contact as the 1989 season progressed. He has a roundhouse swing that strikeout pitchers took a liking to but is starting to make adjustments. He's learning to hit the breaking ball consistently and could develop as a hitter who can't be pitched to any one particular way.

Fielding/Baserunning
Howitt has impressed scouts with his all-around ability in right field, his natural position, but the Athletics liked the way he responded at first base in 1989. He is an average runner—but not a stealing threat—once he gets on base. He's slow getting out of the box, however.

Projection
Howitt is set to advance to Class AAA Tacoma in 1990 and likely will play in the major leagues in 1991.

Career Statistics and Peak Projection

	G	AB	R	H	2B	3B	HR	RBI	BB	SO	AVG
1986 Medford (Northwest League-Class A)	66	208	36	66	9	2	6	37	49	37	.317
1987 Modesto (California League-Class A)	109	336	44	70	11	2	8	42	59	110	.208
1988 Modesto (California League-Class A)	132	480	75	121	20	2	18	86	81	106	.252
1988 Tacoma (Pacific Coast League-Class AAA)	4	15	1	2	1	0	0	0	0	4	.133
1988 Major League Equivalency	4	15	1	2	1	0	0	0	0	4	.133
1989 Huntsville (Southern League-Class AA)	138	509	78	143	28	2	26	111	68	107	.281
1989 Oakland (American League)	3	3	0	0	0	0	0	0	0	2	.000
1989 Major League Equivalency	138	482	55	116	21	1	18	78	46	115	.241
Peak Projection	154	536	76	140	25	1	27	85	56		.261

Interpretation
Howitt's age and his modest batting average at the Class AA level don't help his 1989 Major League Equivalency.

In his peak season, the power easily makes up for a projected .261 average.

DEREK PARKS

Minnesota Twins
Catcher
Twins' First-Round Pick, June 1986 Draft

Personal
Height: 6-0 Weight: 205
Bats right, throws right
Born: September 29, 1968

School: Montclair High
in Montclair, Calif.

Ratings

	Present	Future
Hitting	4	5
Power	4	6
Baserunning	3	4
Speed	4	4
Fielding	4	5
Arm	5	5
Range	4	5

Rating Key
7 Outstanding
6 Major League Caliber, High
5 Major League Caliber
4 Minor League Caliber, High
3 Minor League Caliber
2 Below Average
1 Poor

General
Parks remained high on the Twins' list of hopefuls despite missing all but 31 games in 1989 due to a broken thumb. He batted just .189 in 95 at-bats for Class AA Orlando, falling far short of expectations for the second straight season. His stock hasn't fallen because he's still just 21 years old. If he stays healthy, the Twins believe he can realize some of his early potential. Parks was a pitcher for much of his high school career but moved permanently behind the plate after being drafted 10th overall by the Twins in 1986. The future looked bright in 1987, when he belted 24 homers and knocked in 94 runs in the Class A Midwest League. After a fast start at the Class AA level in 1988, however, nagging injuries took their toll.

Hitting Tendencies
Parks has run-producing ability, with good power to the alleys and muscle to hit the ball over any fence. He is very aggressive and tends to be a big swinger with a big strikeout total. He is gradually showing better discipline, however, and will take his share of walks. His biggest concern is to stay healthy and allow his potential to resurface.

Fielding/Baserunning
Parks has the tools to be a good defensive catcher but missed valuable playing time last season. His throws have plenty of zip, but he hasn't mastered the moves behind the plate. Being a converted pitcher, he does have the background to call a good game and relate with a staff. He has a solid build but needs to prove he can withstand the grind. He doesn't have speed on the bases and has stolen exactly one base each season.

Projection
Depending on Parks' health, the Twins will assign him either to Orlando or Class AAA Portland in 1990. He'll control his destiny from there.

Career Statistics and Peak Projection

	G	AB	R	H	2B	3B	HR	RBI	BB	SO	AVG
1986 Elizabethton (Appalachian League-Rookie)	62	224	39	53	10	1	10	40	23	58	.237
1987 Kenosha (Midwest League-Class A)	129	466	70	115	19	2	24	94	77	111	.247
1988 Orlando (Southern League-Class AA)	118	400	52	94	15	0	7	42	49	81	.235
1988 Major League Equivalency	118	393	47	87	14	0	6	38	43	86	.221
1989 Orlando (Southern League-Class AA)	31	95	16	18	3	0	2	10	19	27	.189
1989 Major League Equivalency	31	93	13	16	3	0	1	8	14	29	.172
Peak Projection	154	500	144	131	21	0	13	57	75		.262

Interpretation
Parks hasn't fared well against Class AA pitching, primarily because of his injury problems. The peak formula likes his age, but his lost 1989 season isn't particularly desirable. The peak projection system does not deal well with MLEs that have a low batting average, thus the unreasonable total of 144 runs scored.

STAN ROYER

Oakland Athletics
Third Baseman
Athletics' First-Round Pick, June 1988 Draft

Personal
Height: 6-3 Weight: 195
Bats right, throws right
Born: August 31, 1967

School: Eastern Illinois

Ratings

	Present	Future
Hitting	4	5
Power	4	5
Baserunning	3	4
Speed	4	4
Fielding	4	6
Arm	5	5
Range	4	5

Rating Key
7 Outstanding
6 Major League Caliber, High
5 Major League Caliber
4 Minor League Caliber, High
3 Minor League Caliber
2 Below Average
1 Poor

General
Royer has made a smooth transition to third base after catching for part of his collegiate career at Eastern Illinois. Playing his first full professional season in 1989, he led the Class A California League in fielding at third base, a feat that may soon become routine. In his first stop out of college, Royer led the Northwest League in fielding at third as well. The 16th pick overall in the 1988 draft, he is an alert player who knows the game, especially considering his lack of experience. He has the makeup scouts look for in a prospect, although some say he needs to play a little more aggressively.

Hitting Tendencies
A well-built youngster, Royer has a good-looking swing with power behind it. He's put a charge on the ball in each of his minor league stints, leading Modesto last season with 11 homers and 69 runs batted in after collecting 48 RBIs in the short-season Northwest League in 1988. Royer can hit to all fields but has the most power into the left-center field alley. His biggest weakness is the strikeout. He fanned once every 3.6 at-bats last season and was vulnerable to pitches on the outside part of the plate. He's still not comfortable with curveballs and must learn to protect the plate.

Fielding/Baserunning
Royer has definite promise as a third baseman. He has good hands, a very quick release and makes accurate throws. He reacts well, especially considering his lack of seasoning. On the bases, he has slightly below-average speed and has stolen just four bases in the minors.

Projection
Royer appears ready to play at Class AA Huntsville in 1990 and could advance to the majors in 1992.

Career Statistics and Peak Projection

	G	AB	R	H	2B	3B	HR	RBI	BB	SO	AVG
1988 Southern Oregon (Northwest League-Class A)	73	286	47	91	19	3	6	48	33	71	.318
1989 Modesto (California League-Class A)	127	476	54	120	28	1	11	69	58	132	.252
1989 Tacoma (Pacific Coast League-Class AAA)	6	19	2	5	1	0	0	2	2	6	.263
1989 Major League Equivalency	6	18	2	4	1	0	0	2	2	6	.222
Peak Projection	154	541	94	159	28	0	0	44	73		.293

Interpretation
With only six Class AAA games to use as a sample, the peak system rewards Royer with a leadoff hitter's line. The strikeouts at Class A Modesto would have altered the final picture.

THOMAS HOWARD

San Diego Padres
Outfielder
Padres' First-Round Pick, June 1986 Draft

Personal
Height: 6-0   Weight: 198
Bats left and right, throws right
Born: December 11, 1964

School: Ball State

Ratings

	Present	Future
Hitting	4	5
Power	3	4
Baserunning	5	5
Speed	5	5
Fielding	5	5
Arm	5	5
Range	5	5

Rating Key
7 Outstanding
6 Major League Caliber, High
5 Major League Caliber
4 Minor League Caliber, High
3 Minor League Caliber
2 Below Average
1 Poor

General
Although he has missed parts of the last two seasons, Howard continues to move closer to a major league job. Knee and hip injuries limited him to 303 at-bats at Class AAA Las Vegas in 1989, but the switch-hitting outfielder finished with a .300 batting mark and 22 stolen bases. Howard also opened the 1988 season with Las Vegas but was sidelined for several weeks with a severely pulled leg muscle. He played out the year with Class AA Wichita, where in 1987 he ranked fifth in the Texas League with a .332 average. Howard is a good all-around athlete who also lettered in football at Ball State. He was the 11th pick overall in the 1986 draft.

Hitting Tendencies
Howard is a switch-hitter who at this stage is a more complete hitter from the left side. He does have punch from either side, although his power potential likely translates to gap power rather than home run pop in the major leagues. He makes good contact and uses the whole field. Instructors say Howard could stand to be more selective, which would make him more of an on-base threat and enable him to make better use of his outstanding speed. He is expected to drive in a fair number of runs.

Fielding/Baserunning
Howard is an adequate defensive outfielder who has particularly good range because of his speed. He has played mostly center field in the minors but probably is best suited for left field due to an arm that rates slightly below average. He's a scoring threat on the bases and is projected as a 20-plus steals man in the major leagues.

Projection
Howard likely will compete for a spot in the major leagues in 1990.

Career Statistics and Peak Projection

	G	AB	R	H	2B	3B	HR	RBI	BB	SO	AVG
1986 Spokane (Northwest League-Class A)	13	55	16	23	3	3	2	17	3	9	.418
1986 Reno (California League-Class A)	58	178	31	50	4	2	0	18	31	28	.281
1987 Wichita (Texas League-Class AA)	113	401	72	133	27	4	14	60	36	72	.332
1987 Major League Equivalency	113	368	44	100	20	2	10	37	23	76	.272
1988 Las Vegas (Pacific Coast League-Class AAA)	44	167	29	42	9	1	0	15	12	31	.251
1988 Wichita (Texas League-Class AA)	29	103	15	31	9	2	0	16	13	14	.301
1988 Major League Equivalency	73	252	27	55	14	2	0	20	16	48	.218
1989 Las Vegas (Pacific Coast League-Class AAA)	80	303	45	91	18	3	3	31	30	56	.300
1989 Major League Equivalency	80	281	28	69	14	2	2	20	20	59	.246
Peak Projection	154	533	65	146	31	4	3	49	45		.273

Interpretation
The calculations don't want to believe that Howard has made up for the time he lost in 1988. The peak system winds up reading his 1987 season as his offensive pinnacle, which probably throws off his projected totals.

MIKE BENJAMIN

San Francisco Giants
Shortstop
Giants' Third-Round Pick, June 1987 Draft

Personal
Height: 6-3   Weight: 195
Bats right, throws right
Born: November 22, 1965

School: Arizona State

Ratings

	Present	Future
Hitting	4	5
Power	3	4
Baserunning	4	5
Speed	5	5
Fielding	5	5
Arm	5	5
Range	5	5

Rating Key
7 Outstanding
6 Major League Caliber, High
5 Major League Caliber
4 Minor League Caliber, High
3 Minor League Caliber
2 Below Average
1 Poor

General
Benjamin is the type of prospect who doesn't impress scouts until they watch him day in, day out. The fact that he was brought up by the Giants in 1989 as they battled for the National League West title says something about his value. Benjamin does not have any single outstanding ability, but he makes the grade with steady skills in most phases of the game. He is beginning to make the adjustments, both offensively and defensively, that will make him a better player at the major league level. His minor league numbers indicate he's still learning, but he received his share of honors at Arizona State. As a senior in 1987, he earned All-America recognition and was voted the Most Valuable Player on the Sun Devils' College World Series team. Benjamin batted .327, hit 18 homers, drove in 55 runs and stole 30 bases.

Hitting Tendencies
Benjamin's biggest weakness offensively is his tendency to strike out. In three minor league seasons, he has fanned once every four at-bats, a ratio usually associated with undisciplined long-ball hitters. Benjamin occasionally has a charge in his bat, but not enough to justify the strikeouts. He's beginning to make strides by hitting the ball to the opposite field. Not surprisingly, his average is starting to climb.

Fielding/Baserunning
Benjamin isn't a showman in the field, but he plays the steady, no-frills defense that major league pitchers like to have behind them. He has good speed and instincts on the basepaths, and he'll steal his team a base when the need arises.

Projection
The Giants expect Benjamin to compete for a spot on their opening-day roster in 1990.

Career Statistics and Peak Projection

	G	AB	R	H	2B	3B	HR	RBI	BB	SO	AVG
1987 Fresno (California League-Class A)	64	212	25	51	6	4	6	24	24	71	.241
1988 Shreveport (Texas League-Class AA)	89	309	48	73	19	5	6	37	22	63	.236
1988 Phoenix (Pacific Coast League-Class AAA)	37	106	13	18	4	1	0	6	13	32	.170
1988 Major League Equivalency	126	402	46	78	21	5	5	33	26	99	.194
1989 Phoenix (Pacific Coast League-Class AAA)	113	363	44	94	17	6	3	36	18	82	.259
1989 San Francisco (National League)	14	6	6	1	0	0	0	0	0	1	.167
1989 Major League Equivalency	127	354	38	80	15	4	2	26	13	86	.226
Peak Projection	154	487	69	119	24	5	6	47	33		.245

Interpretation
Neither Benjamin's 1989 Major League Equivalency nor his peak projection look promising. No power, no walks, no batting average. That's three big strikes against him.

HENSLEY MEULENS

New York Yankees
Third Baseman
Signed by Yankees as a Non-Drafted Free Agent, October 1985

Personal
Height: 6-3   Weight: 190
Bats right, throws right
Born: June 23, 1967

School: Curacao

Ratings

	Present	Future
Hitting	4	5
Power	4	6
Baserunning	4	5
Speed	4	4
Fielding	4	5
Arm	4	5
Range	4	5

Rating Key
7 Outstanding
6 Major League Caliber, High
5 Major League Caliber
4 Minor League Caliber, High
3 Minor League Caliber
2 Below Average
1 Poor

General
Meulens likely would be closer to the major leagues if the Yankees hadn't rushed his development. Back in 1987, he had staged a hitting clinic at Class A Prince William, batting .300 with 103 runs batted in and a Carolina League-leading 28 home runs. The next season, the Yankees hurried him to Class AAA Columbus. Result: a .230 average in 55 games for the Clippers and one deep funk. Meulens appeared to regain some confidence last season, progressing from Class AA Albany to Columbus to New York. A native of Curacao, Netherlands Antilles, he'll start the 1990 season at just 22 years old.

Hitting Tendencies
Meulens has a very quick bat with above-average power potential. What's puzzling is his low number of extra-base hits. After collecting 23 doubles during his banner year at Prince William in 1987, he has totaled only 30 doubles in two seasons. That's not on par with his power capabilities. Although he has struggled trying to duplicate his success of 1987, Meulens did display a measure of patience last season, cutting his strikeouts from 158 in 1988 to 121 at Albany and Columbus. He's been a streaky hitter who needs to develop some confidence.

Fielding/Baserunning
Meulens has the hands, arm and quickness to play third base. Results, however, haven't always measured up to expectations. Scouts have noticed his tendency to flip the ball instead of throwing it, and his error totals have been high: 44 in 1987, 37 in '88, 32 in the minors last season. On the bases, he has average speed.

Projection
Meulens would benefit from a full season at Class AAA Columbus, where he could steady his game and prepare for the majors in 1991.

Career Statistics and Peak Projection

	G	AB	R	H	2B	3B	HR	RBI	BB	SO	AVG
1986 Sarasota Yankees (Gulf Coast League-Rookie)	59	219	36	51	10	4	4	31	28	66	.233
1987 Prince William (Carolina League-Class A)	116	430	76	129	23	2	28	103	53	124	.300
1987 Fort Lauderdale (Florida State League-Class A)	17	58	2	10	3	0	0	2	7	25	.172
1988 Albany (Eastern League-Class AA)	79	278	50	68	9	1	13	40	37	97	.245
1988 Columbus (International League-Class AAA)	55	209	27	48	9	1	6	22	14	61	.230
1988 Major League Equivalency	134	484	72	113	18	1	18	58	45	169	.233
1989 Albany (Eastern League-Class AA)	104	335	55	86	8	2	11	45	61	108	.257
1989 Columbus (International League-Class AAA)	14	45	8	13	4	0	1	3	8	13	.289
1989 New York (American League)	8	28	2	5	0	0	0	1	2	8	.179
1989 Major League Equivalency	126	401	58	97	11	2	11	44	63	135	.242
Peak Projection	154	565	106	155	24	1	32	95	69		.274

Interpretation
Meulens' two Major League Equivalencies are pretty consistent. Along with his peak projection, they indicate he'll live up to his nickname, "Bam Bam." The Yankees will have to live with his low batting average to get the power, however.

WILLIE GREENE

Pittsburgh Pirates
Shortstop
Pirates' First-Round Pick, June 1989 Draft

Personal
Height: 5-11 Weight: 160
Bats left, throws right
Born: September 23, 1971

School: Jones County High
in Gray, Ga.

Ratings

	Present	Future
Hitting	3	5
Power	3	5
Baserunning	4	5
Speed	4	4
Fielding	3	5
Arm	2	5
Range	4	5

Rating Key
7 Outstanding
6 Major League Caliber, High
5 Major League Caliber
4 Minor League Caliber, High
3 Minor League Caliber
2 Below Average
1 Poor

General
Greene impressed Pirates scouts with his ability in all phases of the game. He's fast, has a good lefthanded stroke with power potential and a strong arm. The 18th player drafted in 1989, he came out of high school to bat .324 in the rookie-level Appalachian League after a brief stop in the Gulf Coast circuit. Greene is unpolished, but all the natural talent is there. He'll fill out physically and get stronger as he gets older, and he loves to play the game.

Hitting Tendencies
Greene's quick hands whip the bat through the strike zone, supplying the kind of bat speed that generates power and line drives. He already has the strength to hit the ball out of the park, yet he's projected to become a better power hitter (especially for a shortstop) when he adds more muscle to his lean frame. As he refines his hitting mechanics, he should become more comfortable driving balls into the gaps and pick up his share of RBIs. He does need more discipline and a better knowledge of the strike zone, however, after walking only nine times and striking out 29 in 136 at-bats at Princeton.

Fielding/Baserunning
Greene was never regarded as a bad fielder, but he committed 19 errors in 35 games in the Appalachian League. The Pirates taught him to change the angle of release on his throws, hoping that will minimize his throwing errors. He had some other bad habits that got attention as well. He has average range and a strong arm. As a runner, he has some speed and the potential to steal a fair number of bases.

Projection
Greene likely will begin the 1990 season with a Class A team and is believed to be three or four years away from Pittsburgh.

Career Statistics

	G	AB	R	H	2B	3B	HR	RBI	BB	SO	AVG
1989—Bradenton Pirates (Gulf Coast League-Rookie)	23	86	17	24	3	3	5	11	9	6	.279
1989—Princeton (Appalachian League-Rookie)	39	136	22	44	6	4	2	24	9	29	.324

(Projections unavailable because player has not competed at Class AA or Class AAA levels)

RICK WILKINS

Chicago Cubs
Catcher
Cubs' 23rd-Round Pick, June 1986 Draft

Personal
Height: 6-2   Weight: 210
Bats left, throws right
Born: July 4, 1967

School: Florida Community College in Jacksonville

Ratings

	Present	Future
Hitting	3	5
Power	3	5
Baserunning	4	4
Speed	3	3
Fielding	5	5
Arm	6	6
Range	5	5

Rating Key
7 Outstanding
6 Major League Caliber, High
5 Major League Caliber
4 Minor League Caliber, High
3 Minor League Caliber
2 Below Average
1 Poor

General
At this stage, Wilkins reminds Cubs officials of another former catching prospect who's now a budding young big-league star: the Cubs' own Damon Berryhill. Wilkins, always regarded as an outstanding defensive catcher, is beginning to find the hitting stroke that scouts had anticipated all along. He hit a career-high 12 home runs at Class A Winston-Salem last season, his third in the minor leagues, while catching in a league-high 117 games. He has the size and natural ability to be a quality catcher.

Hitting Tendencies
Wilkins has adjusted his batting stance and is now better able to drive the ball. He's making other little changes, as well, which should start showing up in his home run totals and batting average. Thus far, his average has been restricted to .250 territory. Scouts say he needs to stop trying to hit home runs (with his size, they'll come anyway) and work on making contact. He already has a good knowledge of the strike zone, and he'll cut his strikeout total (197 in two full seasons) if he can cut down his swing.

Fielding/Baserunning
Opposing teams have had very limited success running against Wilkins' strong arm. In 1988, he threw out 42.7 percent of the runners attempting to steal. He blocks the ball extremely well and has a good presence behind the plate. Scouts predict he'll get even better defensively with experience. He will not be a basestealing threat, although he is a decent runner for a man his size.

Projection
The Cubs figure to send Wilkins to Class AA Charlotte in 1990. He is probably two years away from the majors.

Career Statistics

	G	AB	R	H	2B	3B	HR	RBI	BB	SO	AVG
1987 Geneva (New York-Penn League-Class A)	75	243	35	61	8	2	8	43	58	40	.251
1988 Peoria (Midwest League-Class A)	137	490	54	119	30	1	8	63	67	110	.243
1989 Winston-Salem (Carolina League-Class A)	132	445	61	111	24	1	12	54	50	87	.249

(Projections unavailable because player has not competed at Class AA or Class AAA levels)

REGGIE JEFFERSON

Cincinnati Reds
First Baseman
Reds' Third-Round Pick, June 1986 Draft

Personal
Height: 6-4 Weight: 210
Bats left and right, throws left
Born: September 25, 1968

School: Lincoln High
in Tallahassee, Fla.

Ratings

	Present	Future
Hitting	4	5
Power	4	6
Baserunning	4	4
Speed	3	3
Fielding	3	5
Arm	3	4
Range	3	5

Rating Key
7 Outstanding
6 Major League Caliber, High
5 Major League Caliber
4 Minor League Caliber, High
3 Minor League Caliber
2 Below Average
1 Poor

General
Jefferson's star continued to rise two years after a shin fracture forced him to miss almost the entire 1987 season. He shared team Most Valuable Player honors at Class AA Chattanooga in 1989, leading the club with 17 homers and finishing with 80 runs batted in. Only 21 years old, he is noted for his excellent work habits and enthusiasm for the game. Jefferson led the Reds' farm with 90 RBIs in 1988, when he received All-Star honors at first base in the Midwest League.

Hitting Tendencies
Jefferson has big-league power potential from both sides of the plate. He is probably a stronger, more dangerous hitter from the left side, but he's crushed some long home runs righthanded as well. He can drive the ball to any field, and he's become a tougher out after making adjustments in his stance that enable him to handle the hard stuff inside. Instructors say Jefferson is a good listener who wants to learn. Consequently, he keeps improving. He still has a weakness for high fastballs out of the strike zone but otherwise has a pretty good eye. He will strike out occasionally, but not as much as most other hitters with similar power.

Fielding/Baserunning
Jefferson made major strides defensively in 1989. Formerly at the mercy of infield throws he had to field on the short hop, he learned to move up to catch the ball instead of retreating. He has average range and below-average arm strength that isn't as much of a concern since he's lefthanded. He seldom attempts to steal a base.

Projection
Jefferson is on pace to play at Class AAA Nashville in 1990 and probably is two seasons away from the majors.

Career Statistics and Peak Projection

	G	AB	R	H	2B	3B	HR	RBI	BB	SO	AVG
1986 Sarasota Reds (Gulf Coast League-Rookie)	59	208	28	54	4	5	3	33	24	40	.260
1987 Billings (Pioneer League-Rookie)	8	22	10	8	1	0	1	9	4	2	.364
1987 Cedar Rapids (Midwest League-Class A)	15	54	9	12	5	0	3	11	1	12	.222
1988 Cedar Rapids (Midwest League-Class A)	135	517	76	149	26	2	18	90	40	89	.288
1989 Chattanooga (Southern League-Class AA)	135	487	66	140	19	3	17	80	43	73	.287
1989 Major League Equivalency	135	467	49	120	18	2	13	60	31	75	.257
Peak Projection	154	525	82	157	24	2	24	85	48		.300

Interpretation
His Major League Equivalency isn't particularly eye-catching, but it's darn good for a 21-year-old. He gets his home run power going by his peak season, although his doubles total could project low.

TERRY JORGENSEN

Minnesota Twins
Third Baseman
Twins' Second-Round Pick, June 1987 Draft

Personal
Height: 6-4 Weight: 208
Bats right, throws right
Born: September 2, 1966

School: Wisconsin-Oshkosh

Ratings

	Present	Future
Hitting	4	5
Power	4	5
Baserunning	3	4
Speed	4	4
Fielding	4	5
Arm	5	5
Range	4	5

Rating Key
7 Outstanding
6 Major League Caliber, High
5 Major League Caliber
4 Minor League Caliber, High
3 Minor League Caliber
2 Below Average
1 Poor

General
No one expects Jorgensen to put Gary Gaetti out of a job at third base, but the Twins' hard-hitting prospect handled his first full season at third in promising fashion in 1989. Formerly an outfielder, Jorgensen came through with his most productive offensive season to date while leading Southern League third basemen in putouts, assists, double plays and total chances. He has played just 2½ seasons in the minors (the last two at Class AA Orlando) and steadily improved in all areas. The Twins considered him their most improved player at the Class AA level in 1989. Jorgensen raised his batting average from .246 in 1988 to .263 last season, his home run total from three to 13, and runs batted in from 43 to 101. He played in 10 games for Minnesota down the stretch.

Hitting Tendencies
Most of Jorgensen's power is to left and left-center field. He has a strong, sturdy build and proved last season that he can reach the fences. With his extra-base swing (he ranked fifth in the Southern League in doubles), Jorgensen is a good man to have at the plate with runners on base. He was a more selective hitter last season, garnering a career-high 76 walks with only 78 strikeouts (one strikeout every eight plate appearances).

Fielding/Baserunning
Jorgensen held up well last season in everyday duty at third. His arm and range are acceptable and he's getting better with the glove. He still needs to master some of the fundamentals and mechanics. He doesn't have much speed on the bases and stole only one base last year.

Projection
Jorgensen likely will begin 1990 at Class AAA Portland but could be in the major leagues before the end of the season.

Career Statistics and Peak Projection

	G	AB	R	H	2B	3B	HR	RBI	BB	SO	AVG
1987 Kenosha (Midwest League-Class A)	67	254	37	80	17	0	7	33	18	43	.315
1988 Orlando (Southern League-Class AA)	135	472	53	116	27	4	3	43	40	62	.246
1988 Major League Equivalency	135	464	48	108	26	3	3	39	35	66	.233
1989 Orlando (Southern League-Class AA)	135	514	84	135	27	5	13	101	76	78	.263
1989 Minnesota (American League)	10	23	1	4	1	0	0	2	4	5	.174
1989 Major League Equivalency	145	519	67	121	25	3	10	81	62	88	.233
Peak Projection	154	559	91	149	31	3	13	66	69		.267

Interpretation
Jorgensen's Major League Equivalencies are consistent, if nothing else. They also agree with his Minnesota trial last season. In spite of the 101 runs batted in at Class AA Orlando in 1989, the other categories hold his peak production down.

BEAU ALLRED

Cleveland Indians
Outfielder
Indians' 25th-Round Pick, June 1987 Draft

Personal
Height: 6-0 Weight: 193
Bats left, throws left
Born: June 4, 1965

School: Lamar

Ratings

	Present	Future
Hitting	4	5
Power	4	5
Baserunning	4	5
Speed	4	4
Fielding	5	5
Arm	5	5
Range	5	5

Rating Key
7 Outstanding
6 Major League Caliber, High
5 Major League Caliber
4 Minor League Caliber, High
3 Minor League Caliber
2 Below Average
1 Poor

General
Some scouts predict Allred will become a valuable role player in the major leagues, comparing him with former Cleveland-Baltimore outfielder John Lowenstein. Allred has the tools to be a key contributor for a big-league club, with a good line-drive stroke and a steady glove. He finished the 1989 season in Cleveland after playing most of the year at Class AA Canton-Akron. Allred ranked third in the Eastern League in batting, fifth in runs batted in and was voted to a league All-Star berth in the outfield. In 1987, he topped the rookie Appalachian League with a .341 batting mark.

Hitting Tendencies
Some observers question whether Allred will become an everyday big-league star because of his inability thus far to consistently hit lefthanded pitching. He has average to above-average power and hits righthanders well, the kinds of things clubs look for when searching for a good platoon player. He can hit to all fields and has made some noise as a dangerous clutch hitter. Allred always seems to be in the middle of a big inning and has driven home 74 and 75 runs, respectively, in his last two seasons. If he presses, he is more apt to strike out, although he reduced his strikeout total to 98 in 459 minor league at-bats last season, down from 113 strikeouts in 397 at-bats in 1988.

Fielding/Baserunning
Allred is fundamentally sound in the outfield and has an above-average arm. On the bases, he has decent speed but is not regarded as a major stealing threat.

Projection
Allred likely will get some experience at Class AAA Colorado Springs in 1990 and could be in the major leagues by the end of the season.

Career Statistics and Peak Projection

	G	AB	R	H	2B	3B	HR	RBI	BB	SO	AVG
1987 Burlington (Appalachian League-Rookie)	54	167	39	57	14	1	10	38	35	33	.341
1988 Kinston (Carolina League-Class A)	126	397	66	100	23	3	15	74	59	112	.252
1989 Canton-Akron (Eastern League-Class AA)	118	412	67	127	23	5	14	75	56	88	.303
1989 Colorado Springs (P. Coast League-Class AAA)	11	47	8	13	3	0	1	4	2	10	.277
1989 Cleveland (American League)	13	23	0	6	3	0	0	1	2	10	.261
1989 Major League Equivalency	142	470	65	134	28	5	12	70	53	113	.285
Peak Projection	154	554	92	170	34	5	20	84	69		.307

Interpretation
The peak system likes Allred. He has no outstanding strengths or weaknesses—he's just solid in all phases of the game. The Indians have players on their roster who aren't.

LEO GOMEZ

Baltimore Orioles
Third Baseman
Signed by Orioles as a Non-Drafted Free Agent, December 1985

Personal
Height: 6-0 Weight: 180
Bats right, throws right
Born: March 2, 1967

School: Luis Hernaes Nevones High in Puerto Rico

Ratings

	Present	Future
Hitting	4	5
Power	4	6
Baserunning	3	3
Speed	3	3
Fielding	4	5
Arm	5	5
Range	3	4

Rating Key
7 Outstanding
6 Major League Caliber, High
5 Major League Caliber
4 Minor League Caliber, High
3 Minor League Caliber
2 Below Average
1 Poor

General
Gomez is regarded as the best hitting prospect in the Baltimore organization. He bounced back strong in 1989 after missing all but one month of the 1988 season with a broken right leg. Playing last year at Class AA Hagerstown, Gomez was named the Eastern League's All-Star third baseman on the merit of a strong all-around campaign. He led the Orioles' chain in home runs and runs batted in and ranked among the Eastern League leaders in most hitting departments. His batting prowess was hardly news around Hagerstown. In 1987, when the club was a Class A affiliate, Gomez led the Carolina League with a .326 batting mark and knocked in 110 runs. He was honored that season as the Orioles' minor league Player of the Year.

Hitting Tendencies
Coming off an injury-shortened season, Gomez started slow in 1989 but found his hitting groove in the second half. He is a very strong right-handed batter who drives the ball well to the opposite field. He has long-ball power, enough to hit 15 to 20 home runs in the major leagues, and can muscle balls into the gaps for doubles, despite his slowness afoot. Gomez has a very good eye and has approached 100 walks in each of his two full seasons. And since he's swinging at good pitches, he looks as if he'll hit for a good average in the big leagues. He'd be an ideal No. 3 hitter with a good RBI bat.

Fielding/Baserunning
Gomez is an average fielder with a strong arm. His range is somewhat limited, but he catches what he gets to. His speed is well below average.

Projection
Gomez figures to play one season at Class AAA Rochester and reach the majors in 1991.

Career Statistics and Peak Projection

	G	AB	R	H	2B	3B	HR	RBI	BB	SO	AVG
1986 Bluefield (Appalachian League-Rookie)	27	88	23	31	7	1	7	28	25	27	.352
1987 Hagerstown (Carolina League-Class A)	131	466	94	152	38	2	19	110	95	85	.326
1988 Charlotte (Southern League-Class AA)	24	89	6	26	5	0	1	10	10	17	.292
1988 Major League Equivalency	24	86	5	23	4	0	1	8	8	18	.267
1989 Hagerstown (Eastern League-Class AA)	134	448	71	126	23	3	18	78	89	102	.281
1989 Major League Equivalency	134	441	64	119	21	2	16	70	83	111	.270
Peak Projection	154	510	95	154	27	2	26	88	102		.303

Interpretation
Gomez shows good power in both the Major League Equivalency and projected peak totals. The calculations reflect a good on-base percentage, one that might enable him to surpass his peak total of 95 runs scored if he's in the right spot in the order.

GARY DISARCINA

California Angels
Shortstop
Angels' Sixth-Round Pick, June 1988 Draft

Personal
Height: 6-1   Weight: 170
Bats right, throws right
Born: November 19, 1967

School: Massachusetts

Ratings

	Present	Future
Hitting	4	5
Power	3	3
Baserunning	4	5
Speed	5	5
Fielding	5	5
Arm	5	5
Range	5	5

Rating Key
7 Outstanding
6 Major League Caliber, High
5 Major League Caliber
4 Minor League Caliber, High
3 Minor League Caliber
2 Below Average
1 Poor

General
Disarcina took the fast track to the major leagues, arriving in California just one year after being drafted. He played the bulk of the 1989 season at Class AA Midland, where he earned All-Star honors at shortstop in the Texas League. Disarcina already had returned home and enrolled for classes at the University of Massachusetts when he received the call to join the Angels for the final 2½ weeks of last season. He jumped to Class AA ball after playing just 71 games as a minor league rookie in 1988. He is a coachable player who doesn't have to be told things twice.

Hitting Tendencies
Some scouts questioned whether Disarcina could handle the jump to the Class AA level. He put doubts to rest within the Angels' organization, batting .286 with 54 runs batted in, generally hitting in the No. 9 spot in the order. Despite his inexperience, he didn't give Texas League pitchers many breaks, striking out just 54 times in 441 at-bats. Disarcina is a line-drive hitter who usually makes contact. His hard-hit balls seldom will carry for home runs, but he does have a good stroke into the gaps and goes to right field well. If he can place shots in the outfield holes, he'll have run-producing ability.

Fielding/Baserunning
Disarcina is a steady player who makes the routine plays and the occasional sensational one. He has the range to go into the hole and the arm to put a strong throw on target. He has good speed and good baserunning skills. If opponents aren't watching, he'll take the stolen base.

Projection
Disarcina is on schedule to play at Class AAA Edmonton in 1990 and could join the major leagues as a regular in 1991.

Career Statistics and Peak Projection

	G	AB	R	H	2B	3B	HR	RBI	BB	SO	AVG
1988 Bend (Northwest League-Class A)	71	295	40	90	11	5	2	39	27	35	.305
1989 Midland (Texas League-Class AA)	126	441	65	126	18	7	4	54	24	54	.286
1989 California (American League)	2	0	0	0	0	0	0	0	0	0	.000
1989 Major League Equivalency	128	414	41	99	14	4	3	34	15	56	.239
Peak Projection	154	503	74	143	21	5	6	51	30		.285

Interpretation
Taken out of the Texas League, Disarcina isn't nearly the hitter, according to his Major League Equivalency. His lack of power and low walk total both affect his batting average in the bigger major league parks. Since he's still young, his average comes around in the peak projection line.

TIM NAEHRING

Boston Red Sox
Shortstop
Red Sox's Eighth-Round Pick, June 1988 Draft

General
All five minor league managers in Boston's spring training camp in 1989 wanted Naehring on their team. Another minor league instructor called him the best prospect he saw all season. Indeed, Naehring brings a winning spirit to a club with his hard-nosed play. In 1988, he received the Red Sox's annual award given to their most enthusiastic player in the Florida Instructional League. Last season, his second as a pro, Naehring jumped from the Class A Carolina League to Class AAA Pawtucket, where he became a team leader. And while many of his strengths are intangible, he is starting to hold his own at the plate.

Hitting Tendencies
Naehring is a pesky line-drive hitter who makes contact. He'll battle a pitcher when he's behind in the count and doesn't strike out much despite his youth. Naehring has a little power into the alleys and could start to drive the ball when he gets older and gains experience. He hit .301 for Lynchburg before being promoted to Pawtucket, where his average dropped only to .275. He had pretty good run-producing ability, finishing with a combined 68 runs batted in.

Fielding/Baserunning
Naehring's limited range will keep him from being labeled a great shortstop, but he does catch what he gets to. When the Red Sox look at his good arm, they wonder how he'd look at third base. Naehring has good hands, and he's the type of player who grows on you as you watch him over a full season. He runs the bases well but seldom attempts to steal.

Projection
Naehring likely will return to Class AAA Pawtucket to begin the 1990 season. A hot start could earn him a stint in Boston before year's end.

Personal
Height: 6-2 Weight: 190
Bats right, throws right
Born: February 1, 1967

School: Miami of Ohio

Ratings

	Present	Future
Hitting	4	5
Power	3	4
Baserunning	4	5
Speed	5	5
Fielding	4	5
Arm	5	5
Range	4	4

Rating Key
7 Outstanding
6 Major League Caliber, High
5 Major League Caliber
4 Minor League Caliber, High
3 Minor League Caliber
2 Below Average
1 Poor

Career Statistics and Peak Projection

	G	AB	R	H	2B	3B	HR	RBI	BB	SO	AVG
1988 Winter Haven (Florida State League-Class A)	42	141	17	32	7	0	0	10	19	24	.227
1988 Elmira (New York-Penn League-Class A)	19	59	6	18	3	0	1	13	8	11	.305
1989 Lynchburg (Carolina League-Class A)	56	209	24	63	7	1	4	37	23	30	.301
1989 Pawtucket (International League-Class AAA)	79	273	32	75	16	1	3	31	27	41	.275
1989 Major League Equivalency	79	269	29	71	17	1	3	28	24	43	.264
Peak Projection	154	524	74	157	34	2	9	61	58		.299

Interpretation
It's clear Naehring will never be a power hitter, but his walk totals will have to rise, according to his Major League Equivalency. Since his strikeout total is low, he can afford to let a few go by without burying himself.

TOM REDINGTON

Atlanta Braves
Third Baseman
Braves' Third-Round Pick, June 1987 Draft

Personal
Height: 6-1 Weight: 190
Bats right, throws right
Born: February 13, 1969

School: Ezperanza High
in Anaheim, Calif.

Ratings

	Present	Future
Hitting	4	5
Power	4	5
Baserunning	3	4
Speed	4	4
Fielding	4	5
Arm	5	5
Range	3	4

Rating Key
7 Outstanding
6 Major League Caliber, High
5 Major League Caliber
4 Minor League Caliber, High
3 Minor League Caliber
2 Below Average
1 Poor

General
After an inconsistent 1988 season, Redington's potential surfaced in 1989 at Class A Burlington. Voted the Midwest League's "Prospect of the Year," Redington led the league with 17 home runs and a .490 slugging average—despite being promoted to the Class AA Southern League before the end of June. He left behind enough of an impression to receive the Midwest League's Most Valuable Player award and earn All-Star honors at third base. He added the "Star of Stars" award in the midseason all-star game.

Hitting Tendencies
There aren't many questions about Redington's power potential. He ranked second in the Braves' farm system with 20 homers at the Class A and AA levels last season. He is primarily a pull hitter who sits on fastballs, a fondness that major league pitchers can exploit. Redington hasn't learned to go the opposite way with breaking balls and outside pitches, an adjustment he'll need to make for his success to continue. That's part of the reason his average fell from .299 at Burlington to .245 at Class AA Greenville. Redington has displayed a good eye at the plate and isn't afraid to take a walk. If he makes adjustments to better pitching, he'll provide a good RBI bat in the lineup.

Fielding/Baserunning
Some scouts wonder whether Redington will remain a third baseman. His range is limited but he catches whatever he can reach and has a strong arm. He doesn't have speed on the basepaths and rarely attempts a stolen base.

Projection
Redington likely will return to Class AA Greenville to start the 1990 season. If he keeps improving, he'll join Atlanta in two years.

Career Statistics and Peak Projection

	G	AB	R	H	2B	3B	HR	RBI	BB	SO	AVG
1987 Sumter (South Atlantic League-Class A)	18	56	9	18	2	0	0	5	13	14	.321
1988 Sumter (South Atlantic League-Class A)	129	429	45	84	13	1	11	60	75	71	.196
1989 Burlington (Midwest League-Class A)	85	298	49	89	14	0	17	52	53	47	.299
1989 Greenville (Southern League-Class AA)	33	110	9	27	4	0	3	13	7	22	.245
1989 Major League Equivalency	33	107	8	24	4	0	2	11	6	22	.224
Peak Projection	154	508	66	145	24	0	17	69	41		.285

Interpretation
The peak projection system builds a decent line out of a data sample that is next to nothing. You have to keep in mind that Redington's peak season figures to be seven years away.

LUIS SOJO

Toronto Blue Jays
Shortstop
Signed by Blue Jays as a Non-Drafted Free Agent, January 1986

Personal
Height: 5-11   Weight: 174
Bats right, throws right
Born: March 1, 1966

School: Barquisimeto, Venezuela

Ratings

	Present	Future
Hitting	4	5
Power	2	3
Baserunning	4	5
Speed	5	5
Fielding	5	5
Arm	5	5
Range	5	5

Rating Key
7 Outstanding
6 Major League Caliber, High
5 Major League Caliber
4 Minor League Caliber, High
3 Minor League Caliber
2 Below Average
1 Poor

General
After playing two years at the Class A level, Sojo jumped to Class AAA Syracuse in 1989 and met all expectations for the first two-thirds of the season. Down the stretch, he tailed off slightly both offensively and defensively, perhaps due to fatigue. Still, Sojo finished with a .276 batting average and led the International League in fielding at shortstop. Some observers speculated he was worn down by the lengthy schedule following a season of winter ball. He had played in 135 games in 1988, fourth most in the South Atlantic League. He was an All-Star selection that year, leading the league in hits, ranking third in runs scored and sixth in batting.

Hitting Tendencies
Sojo is most effective when he's hitting line drives and hard ground balls toward the infield holes. He doesn't have the muscle to get many fly-ball hits, but he's earned praise for making good contact. Batting second for Syracuse much of last season, he delivered a number of key hits and finished with 54 runs batted in. He doesn't strike out much but seldom walks, either (42 strikeouts, 21 walks in 482 at-bats last season). His weakness for high fastballs is well known, but he's taking steps to be more selective.

Fielding/Baserunning
Sojo has all the tools to be a good defensive shortstop but could move to second base if necessary. He has good range, a good arm and turns the double play well. As a baserunner, he has average speed but was thrown out 14 times in 23 steal attempts in 1989.

Projection
Sojo likely will need another season at Class AAA Syracuse. He could be competing for a major league job in 1991.

Career Statistics and Peak Projection

	G	AB	R	H	2B	3B	HR	RBI	BB	SO	AVG
1987 Myrtle Beach (South Atlantic League-Class A)	72	223	23	47	5	4	2	15	17	18	.211
1988 Myrtle Beach (South Atlantic League-Class A)	135	536	83	155	22	5	5	56	35	35	.289
1989 Syracuse (International League-Class AAA)	121	482	54	133	20	5	3	54	21	42	.276
1989 Major League Equivalency	121	467	45	118	18	4	3	45	19	42	.253
Peak Projection	154	578	74	166	25	5	6	57	34		.286

Interpretation
The data sample, although small, shows a true contact hitter who neither walks nor strikes out much. The thing major league teams like to see from contact hitters—a .300 average—isn't in Sojo's peak line, however.

JERALD CLARK

San Diego Padres
Outfielder
Padres' 12th-Round Pick, June 1985 Draft

Personal
Height: 6-4 Weight: 190
Bats right, throws right
Born: August 10, 1963

School: Lamar

Ratings

	Present	Future
Hitting	5	5
Power	4	5
Baserunning	4	4
Speed	4	4
Fielding	5	5
Arm	5	5
Range	5	5

Rating Key
7 Outstanding
6 Major League Caliber, High
5 Major League Caliber
4 Minor League Caliber, High
3 Minor League Caliber
2 Below Average
1 Poor

General
Clark has hit better than .300 in each of his five minor league seasons, the last two at the Class AAA level. He was a 1989 All-Star in the Pacific Coast League, where he led Las Vegas with a .313 average and ranked third in the league in both runs batted in and total bases. He was a quiet leader for Las Vegas, and at age 26 is at the point where he must stick in the major leagues if he's ever going to become more than a part-time player. He earned his second career promotion to San Diego last September, offsetting a .195 average for the Padres with seven RBIs in 17 games. Scouts say Clark is an aggressive, hustling player who has the tools to become a well-rounded major leaguer.

Hitting Tendencies
Clark is noted for his ability to make contact, but he flourished as a power threat in 1989, belting 22 homers at Las Vegas. While that total might be slightly inflated due to the Pacific Coast's reputation as a hitter's playground, Clark still ranked fifth among PCL hitters with a ratio of one homer for every 19 at-bats. He can hit the ball to all fields and should have good gap power in the major leagues. He has excellent bat speed, which generates his power, and he's aggressive in the box. Instructors say Clark could have a little more discipline at times, but he has become a better two-strike hitter.

Fielding/Baserunning
Clark probably is best suited to play left field in the majors because of below-average arm strength. He is an average baserunner who has stolen five to six bases a year.

Projection
Clark is prepared to compete for a regular job in the major leagues in 1990.

Career Statistics and Peak Projection

	G	AB	R	H	2B	3B	HR	RBI	BB	SO	AVG
1985 Spokane (Northwest League-Class A)	73	283	45	92	24	3	2	50	34	38	.325
1986 Reno (California League-Class A)	95	389	76	118	34	3	7	58	29	46	.303
1986 Beaumont (Texas League-Class AA)	16	56	9	18	4	1	0	6	5	9	.321
1986 Major League Equivalency	16	52	6	14	3	1	0	4	3	10	.269
1987 Wichita (Texas League-Class AA)	132	531	86	165	36	8	18	95	40	82	.311
1987 Major League Equivalency	132	490	53	124	27	4	13	59	25	87	.253
1988 Las Vegas (Pacific Coast League-Class AAA)	107	408	65	123	27	7	9	67	17	66	.301
1988 San Diego (National League)	6	15	0	3	1	0	0	3	0	4	.200
1988 Major League Equivalency	113	390	38	93	21	3	6	42	10	74	.238
1989 Las Vegas (Pacific Coast League-Class AAA)	107	419	84	131	27	4	22	83	38	81	.313
1989 San Diego (National League)	17	41	5	8	2	0	1	7	3	9	.195
1989 Major League Equivalency	124	429	58	108	22	2	18	60	28	95	.252
Peak Projection	154	569	82	153	32	3	21	81	36		.268

Interpretation
According to the Major League Equivalencies, Clark hasn't progressed much since 1987. That weighs heavily in his projected peak season, which shows some good power but not a lot of on-base ability.

JUAN BELL

Baltimore Orioles
Shortstop
Signed by Los Angeles as a Non-Drafted Free Agent, September 1984

Personal
Height: 5-11 Weight: 157
Bats left and right, throws right
Born: March 29, 1968

School: Gastone F. Deligne
High in Dominican Republic

Ratings

	Present	Future
Hitting	4	5
Power	2	3
Baserunning	4	5
Speed	6	6
Fielding	5	5
Arm	6	6
Range	5	5

Rating Key
7 Outstanding
6 Major League Caliber, High
5 Major League Caliber
4 Minor League Caliber, High
3 Minor League Caliber
2 Below Average
1 Poor

General
Bell, the younger brother of Toronto Blue Jays outfielder George Bell, was acquired by Baltimore as part of the Eddie Murray deal following the 1988 season. He is another middle infielder from San Pedro de Macoris in the Dominican Republic, and like most of those players, he has a lot of raw, natural ability that needs to be refined. He'll turn just 22 in spring training this year but already has put in five seasons in the minor leagues. He will not be a power hitter like his brother, but he has some of his moodiness, which he must keep suppressed to realize his potential. Bell made his major league debut with Baltimore last September.

Hitting Tendencies
Bell, whose natural side is righthanded, has been switch-hitting for nearly 10 years. He is a line-drive hitter without much power, but he should be able to drive the ball for more hits once he completely matures. Scouts say he'll also be a better hitter when he improves the mental part of his game and learns the strike zone. Bell has averaged 97 strikeouts per year over the last three seasons and only 38 walks. His stock likely would rise if he took advantage of his speed to become more of an on-base threat.

Fielding/Baserunning
Bell has all the tools scouts value in a shortstop. He has the reflexes and speed to pick off shots in the hole and a rifle-like arm to complete the play. He runs the bases well and holds promise as a stealing threat in the major leagues.

Projection
Bell figures to be groomed another season at Class AAA Rochester in 1990 and advance to the major leagues in 1991.

Career Statistics and Peak Projection

	G	AB	R	H	2B	3B	HR	RBI	BB	SO	AVG
1985 Bradenton Dodgers (Gulf Coast League-Rookie)	42	106	11	17	0	0	0	8	12	20	.160
1986 Sarasota Dodgers (Gulf Coast League-Rookie)	59	217	38	52	6	2	0	26	29	28	.240
1987 Bakersfield (California League-Class A)	134	473	54	116	15	3	4	58	43	91	.245
1988 San Antonio (Texas League-Class AA)	61	215	37	60	4	2	5	21	16	37	.279
1988 Albuquerque (Pacific Coast League-Class AAA)	73	257	42	77	9	3	8	45	16	70	.300
1988 Major League Equivalency	134	453	59	118	11	3	10	48	25	116	.260
1989 Rochester (International League-Class AAA)	146	408	50	107	15	6	2	32	39	92	.262
1989 Baltimore (American League)	8	4	2	0	0	0	0	0	0	1	.000
1989 Major League Equivalency	154	404	45	99	13	4	2	28	35	101	.245
Peak Projection	154	522	89	154	19	4	10	60	52		.295

Interpretation
The calculations make about the same assessment of Bell in his 1988 and 1989 Major League Equivalencies. If he can regain the power of 1988, he'll project as a balanced hitter, particularly for a middle infielder.

TODD HUNDLEY

New York Mets
Catcher
Mets' Second-Round Pick, June 1987 Draft

Personal
Height: 5-11 Weight: 170
Bats left and right, throws right
Born: May 27, 1969

School: South Torrance
High in Torrance, Calif.

Ratings

	Present	Future
Hitting	3	4
Power	3	4
Baserunning	3	4
Speed	2	2
Fielding	4	5
Arm	5	6
Range	4	5

Rating Key
7 Outstanding
6 Major League Caliber, High
5 Major League Caliber
4 Minor League Caliber, High
3 Minor League Caliber
2 Below Average
1 Poor

General
The son of former major league catcher Randy Hundley, Todd Hundley stamped himself as the best catching prospect in the Mets' organization with a fine 1989 season at Class A Columbia. He showed offensive promise with his finest year to date, earning South Atlantic League All-Star honors as much for his newfound hitting success as his solid defense. He was drafted in 1987 as compensation for the loss of free agent Ray Knight.

Hitting Tendencies
Hundley is a switch-hitter but probably has a better stroke batting lefthanded. He struggled badly in each of his first two seasons in the minors, posting back-to-back sub-.200 seasons in the New York-Penn League. The Mets say his improvement in 1989 was legitimate. They believe it's a sign he'll hit for extra-base power and drive in runs. As Hundley grows older, he is getting stronger and learning more. He has a good understanding of the strike zone, which should only help if he's to prove 1989 was no fluke.

Fielding/Baserunning
Hundley has an above-average arm and blocks the ball well. He'll call a better game as he acquires experience, although he already looks confident handling a pitching staff. He caught in 120 of Columbia's 140 games last season, showing the kind of durability that was a trademark of his father (who established a standing major league record in 1968 by catching in 160 games). As a baserunner, he's never been a stealing threat.

Projection
The Mets likely will send Hundley to Class AA Jackson to begin the 1990 season. He is probably at least two years away from the majors.

Career Statistics

	G	AB	R	H	2B	3B	HR	RBI	BB	SO	AVG
1987—Little Falls (New York-Penn League-Class A)	34	103	12	15	4	0	1	10	12	27	.146
1988—Little Falls (New York-Penn League-Class A)	52	176	23	33	8	0	2	18	16	31	.188
1988—St. Lucie (Florida State League-Class A)	1	1	0	0	0	0	0	0	2	1	.000
1989—Columbia (South Atlantic League-Class A)	125	439	67	118	23	4	11	66	54	67	.269

(Projections unavailable because player has not competed at Class AA or Class AAA levels)

BRIAN HUNTER

Atlanta Braves
First Baseman/Outfielder
Braves' Eighth-Round Pick, June 1987 Draft

Personal
Height: 6-0 Weight: 195
Bats right, throws left
Born: March 4, 1968

School: Cerritos Community College in Norwalk, Calif.

Ratings

	Present	Future
Hitting	4	5
Power	4	5
Baserunning	4	5
Speed	4	4
Fielding	4	5
Arm	4	4
Range	4	5

Rating Key
7 Outstanding
6 Major League Caliber, High
5 Major League Caliber
4 Minor League Caliber, High
3 Minor League Caliber
2 Below Average
1 Poor

General
Some observers believe Hunter is the best all-around player in the Atlanta farm system. He's capable of hitting for power and a good average, and he plays excellent defense at first base. The Braves moved him to left field at Class AA Greenville in 1989, but they consider first base his best position. Adjusting to the outfield, Hunter hit with power nonetheless, ranking fifth in the Southern League with 82 runs batted in and sixth with a club-high 19 home runs. In 1988, he tied for the lead in the Class A Midwest League with 22 home runs and led the Braves' Burlington outpost with 71 RBIs.

Hitting Tendencies
Hunter has flashed signs of his long-ball potential in three minor league campaigns. Instructors predict he'll also hit for a higher average as he gains experience and acquires a better knowledge of the strike zone. Granted, there will be occasional strikeouts with his power stroke, but Hunter did reduce his strikeout total to 61 last season after fanning 98 times in 1988. The Braves are teaching him to lay off bad balls in hopes he can draw more walks. He walked only 33 times in 451 at-bats at Greenville last year.

Fielding/Baserunning
Hunter is a smooth-fielding first baseman who could step into the position in the major leagues. The Braves are testing his versatility by playing him in left field, where he gets a good jump on the ball but has only an average arm. He will not steal many bases but has good baserunning instincts.

Projection
Hunter is on schedule to play at Class AAA Richmond in 1990 and could compete for a spot on the Braves' roster in 1991.

Career Statistics and Peak Projection

	G	AB	R	H	2B	3B	HR	RBI	BB	SO	AVG
1987 Pulaski (Appalachian League-Rookie)	65	251	38	58	10	2	8	30	18	47	.231
1988 Burlington (Midwest League-Class A)	117	417	58	108	17	0	22	71	45	90	.259
1988 Durham (Carolina League-Class A)	13	49	13	17	3	0	3	9	7	8	.347
1989 Greenville (Southern League-Class AA)	124	451	57	114	19	2	19	82	33	61	.253
1989 Major League Equivalency	124	440	48	103	19	2	15	69	27	62	.234
Peak Projection	154	536	94	150	27	2	31	96	46		.281

Interpretation
In his peak season, Hunter will thrive as a home run threat in Atlanta's Fulton County Stadium. That assumption is based on just one season in the Class AA Southern League.

BRIAN LANE

Cincinnati Reds
Third Baseman
Reds' Third-Round Pick, June 1987 Draft

Personal
Height: 6-3   Weight: 190
Bats right, throws right
Born: June 15, 1969

School: Midway High
in Waco, Tex.

Ratings

	Present	Future
Hitting	4	5
Power	4	5
Baserunning	4	4
Speed	3	3
Fielding	3	5
Arm	5	5
Range	4	5

Rating Key
7 Outstanding
6 Major League Caliber, High
5 Major League Caliber
4 Minor League Caliber, High
3 Minor League Caliber
2 Below Average
1 Poor

General
Robin Ventura arrived in the Southern League amid considerable fanfare and created enough of a stir to receive league All-Star honors at third base. But it was Chattanooga third baseman Brian Lane who emerged as the more productive hitter over the long haul. Very mature for his age, Lane started the season as the league's youngest player (19) and went on to build a reputation as a dangerous hitter with runners on base. His 89 runs batted in ranked fourth in the league and he outhomered Ventura, 11-3. Fighting off the effect of twice being hit in the hand by pitches, he skidded down the stretch and finished with a batting mark below his contemporary's, .252 to .278.

Hitting Tendencies
Lane's strong suit as a hitter is his ability to deliver the RBI. Among prospects in the Reds' system, he ranked second in 1989 with 89 RBIs. Lane pounds line drives into the gaps, and he'll hit his share of home runs when he gets under the ball. He needs to cut down on his strikeout total (95 last season) and have the discipline to take a walk when there's nothing good to hit.

Fielding/Baserunning
Lane has the arm to gun the ball across the diamond but still needs to polish his fielding. Nevertheless, to compare his 1989 numbers with Ventura's, Lane made 27 errors in 344 total chances and posted a .922 fielding average; Ventura led the league's third basemen with a .930 average, committing 26 errors in 371 chances. On the bases, Lane doesn't rate as a stealing threat.

Projection
The Reds figure to groom Lane at the Class AAA level in 1990 and could have him ready for the major leagues in 1991.

Career Statistics and Peak Projection

	G	AB	R	H	2B	3B	HR	RBI	BB	SO	AVG
1987 Billings (Pioneer League-Rookie)	56	175	19	35	6	1	3	16	18	73	.200
1988 Greensboro (South Atlantic League-Class A)	115	451	55	127	17	3	3	52	32	68	.282
1989 Chattanooga (Southern League-Class AA)	130	464	59	117	19	4	11	89	46	95	.252
1989 Major League Equivalency	130	447	44	100	18	2	8	66	34	97	.224
Peak Projection	154	521	80	142	25	2	16	68	53		.272

Interpretation
Any 20-year-old who drives in 89 runs and bats at least .250 in the Southern League is a legitimate prospect. The peak system gives him numbers similar to Buddy Bell's in his final year in Cincinnati.

KELLY MANN

Atlanta Braves
Catcher
Chicago Cubs' 20th-Round Pick, June 1985 Draft

Personal
Height: 6-3 Weight: 215
Bats right, throws right
Born: August 17, 1967

School: Santa Monica High
in Santa Monica, Calif.

Ratings

	Present	Future
Hitting	3	5
Power	2	4
Baserunning	2	3
Speed	2	2
Fielding	5	5
Arm	6	6
Range	5	5

Rating Key
7 Outstanding
6 Major League Caliber, High
5 Major League Caliber
4 Minor League Caliber, High
3 Minor League Caliber
2 Below Average
1 Poor

General
Drafted by the Chicago Cubs four rounds ahead of Mark Grace, Mann still qualifies as a bargain 20th-round pick. He got his first major league experience with the Braves last September after coming to Atlanta in the Paul Assenmacher deal. The trade could wind up a godsend in Mann's career, given Atlanta's lack of depth at catcher and the Cubs' backlog of prospects there. Last season, his fifth in the Chicago organization, he had a career-high 56 runs batted in playing his first full year at the Class AA level. It was a positive sign, considering there are questions about Mann's bat. His defense has always earned raves.

Hitting Tendencies
At 6-3, 215 pounds, Mann has the build of a power hitter. In his case, it's not completely a blessing. Far too often, Mann tries to crank the ball out of the park when he should be trying to make contact. In each of his last two seasons, Mann has hit eight home runs, a number scouts say he'd probably match (especially in Atlanta's friendly quarters) if he'd let the long ball fly naturally. For now, he needs to show more discipline and tame his swing.

Fielding/Baserunning
Mann has established himself as one of the top defensive catchers in the minor leagues. He is a good receiver with a great arm, posting an outstanding caught-stealing percentage throughout his career. Last season, he threw out 54.6 percent of the runners attempting to steal to lead Southern League regulars. He's not a stealing threat himself, with only 10 stolen bases in five seasons.

Projection
Mann figures to start the 1990 season at Class AA Greenville or Class AAA Richmond. If he hits, he could stick with the Braves in 1991.

Career Statistics and Peak Projection

	G	AB	R	H	2B	3B	HR	RBI	BB	SO	AVG
1985 Wytheville (Appalachian League-Rookie)	26	75	6	15	3	0	1	10	6	21	.200
1986 Geneva (New York-Penn League-Class A)	60	191	17	37	1	0	2	15	18	38	.194
1986 Peoria (Midwest League-Class A)	3	13	4	6	2	0	0	4	0	1	.462
1987 Peoria (Midwest League-Class A)	95	287	24	73	16	1	4	45	23	66	.254
1988 Winston-Salem (Carolina League-Class A)	94	307	32	84	11	0	8	40	24	46	.274
1988 Pittsfield (Eastern League-Class AA)	22	51	7	10	3	0	0	3	3	14	.196
1988 Major League Equivalency	22	50	6	9	3	0	0	3	3	14	.180
1989 Charlotte (Southern League-Class AA)	117	345	37	85	14	1	8	56	33	60	.246
1989 Atlanta (National League)	7	24	1	5	2	0	0	1	0	6	.208
1989 Major League Equivalency	124	353	26	74	15	1	5	39	22	67	.210
Peak Projection	154	464	51	116	23	1	10	50	40		.251

Interpretation
Mann has been playing minor league baseball since he graduated from high school yet hasn't developed offensively. His stint in Atlanta last season was discouragingly consistent with his 1988 Major League Equivalency. His projected peak isn't bad for a catcher, at least by current standards.

DERRICK MAY

Chicago Cubs
Outfielder
Cubs' First-Round Pick, June 1986 Draft

Personal
Height: 6-4 Weight: 210
Bats left, throws right
Born: July 14, 1968

School: Newark High
in Newark, Del.

Ratings

	Present	Future
Hitting	4	5
Power	3	5
Baserunning	4	4
Speed	4	4
Fielding	4	4
Arm	4	4
Range	5	5

Rating Key
7 Outstanding
6 Major League Caliber, High
5 Major League Caliber
4 Minor League Caliber, High
3 Minor League Caliber
2 Below Average
1 Poor

General
May, the son of former major league outfielder Dave May, has the potential to be a legitimate power hitter but hasn't produced the kind of home run numbers the Cubs anticipated when they selected him ninth overall in the 1986 draft. Chicago isn't about to give up on the big youngster, however. May has posted a career .302 batting average over four minor league seasons and made steady progress through the organization despite being one of the youngest players at each level (he was just 17 when he joined the rookie Appalachian League in 1986). Making the jump to Class AA Charlotte in 1989, May was a Southern League All-Star pick in the outfield.

Hitting Tendencies
May reminds some Cubs officials of a young Darryl Strawberry, but he hasn't displayed that kind of home run stroke. What he does do is put the ball in play consistently, whatever level of pitching he faces. He ranked second in hits in the Class AA Southern League in 1989 and tied for the lead in the Class A Carolina League in 1988. Despite the fact that May hits near .300 each season and drives in his share of runs, his big-league destiny—regular or reserve—may hinge upon his reaching his power potential.

Fielding/Baserunning
May probably is best suited for left field in the major leagues. His arm rates slightly below average, and he'll catch what he can get to—but he's no flier. He is a decent baserunner with decent speed for a man his size.

Projection
May figures to play at either Class AA Charlotte or Class AAA Iowa in 1990 and probably is two years away from the majors.

Career Statistics and Peak Projection

	G	AB	R	H	2B	3B	HR	RBI	BB	SO	AVG
1986 Wytheville (Appalachian League-Rookie)	54	178	25	57	6	1	0	23	16	17	.320
1987 Peoria (Midwest League-Class A)	128	439	60	131	19	8	9	52	42	106	.298
1988 Winston-Salem (Carolina League-Class A)	130	485	76	148	29	9	8	65	37	82	.305
1989 Charlotte (Southern League-Class AA)	136	491	72	145	26	5	9	70	33	76	.295
1989 Major League Equivalency	136	466	52	120	21	3	7	51	22	80	.258
Peak Projection	154	521	84	157	27	3	13	67	37		.300

Interpretation
May gets a little environmental assistance, what with his numbers adjusted for Wrigley Field. Still, the peak projection likes what the 21-year-old did at the Class AA level in 1989. The Cubs likely would want better power production from a player at his peak.

TIM McINTOSH

Milwaukee Brewers
Catcher
Brewers' Third-Round Pick, June 1986 Draft

Personal
Height: 5-11　Weight: 195
Bats right, throws right
Born: March 21, 1965

School: Minnesota

Ratings

	Present	Future
Hitting	4	5
Power	4	6
Baserunning	3	4
Speed	3	3
Fielding	3	5
Arm	4	5
Range	3	5

Rating Key
7 Outstanding
6 Major League Caliber, High
5 Major League Caliber
4 Minor League Caliber, High
3 Minor League Caliber
2 Below Average
1 Poor

General
The Brewers appear committed to develop McIntosh behind the plate after shifting him between catcher and the outfield during his first four seasons in the minors. He played 34 games in the outfield for Class AA El Paso in 1989, but McIntosh received Texas League All-Star honors at catcher, primarily for the big bat he's always carried. A very strong player who enjoys weight lifting, he topped the Brewer farm system with 93 runs batted in last season, tying for third in the Texas League. He led El Paso with 17 home runs and ranked in the league's top five in total bases and doubles. McIntosh also received All-Star recognition in the Class A California League in 1988.

Hitting Tendencies
Offense is the best part of McIntosh's game. He has promising power, particularly when he pulls the ball to left and left-center field, and a home run swing that showed fewer holes in 1989. McIntosh reduced his strikeout total to 72 last season after fanning 96 times in each of his previous two years. Because he drives the ball a long way, he's been a good doubles and RBI man. He has the potential to hit for average in the majors (he's a career .291 batter in the minors) if he cuts back on his swing and learns to take outside pitches to the opposite field.

Fielding/Baserunning
McIntosh has worked hard to improve as a catcher. He has a strong, accurate arm but needs to learn more about the mechanics and fundamentals of receiving and calling a game. The Brewers are encouraged by his development. He has below-average speed, with 22 career steals.

Projection
McIntosh likely will move up to Class AAA Denver in 1990. If he continues to develop, he could play in the majors sometime in 1991.

Career Statistics and Peak Projection

	G	AB	R	H	2B	3B	HR	RBI	BB	SO	AVG
1986 Beloit (Midwest League-Class A)	49	173	26	45	3	2	4	21	18	33	.260
1987 Beloit (Midwest League-Class A)	130	461	83	139	30	3	20	85	49	96	.302
1988 Stockton (California League-Class A)	138	519	81	147	32	6	15	92	57	96	.283
1989 El Paso (Texas League-Class AA)	120	463	72	139	30	3	17	93	29	72	.300
1989 Major League Equivalency	120	433	45	109	23	1	11	59	19	81	.252
Peak Projection	154	549	75	153	31	1	20	78	34		.279

Interpretation
McIntosh's impressive 1989 totals at Class AA El Paso rate only about average on the Major League Equivalency scale. His average rises only slightly on the peak line, primarily because he was 24 and still playing Double-A ball last year.

BERT HEFFERNAN

Milwaukee Brewers
Catcher
Brewers' Ninth-Round Pick, June 1988 Draft

Personal
Height: 5-10 Weight: 185
Bats left, throws right
Born: March 3, 1965

School: Clemson

Ratings

	Present	Future
Hitting	3	5
Power	3	5
Baserunning	4	4
Speed	4	4
Fielding	5	6
Arm	5	6
Range	4	5

Rating Key
7 Outstanding
6 Major League Caliber, High
5 Major League Caliber
4 Minor League Caliber, High
3 Minor League Caliber
2 Below Average
1 Poor

General
When it comes to hustle, Heffernan takes a back seat to no one. He is very much a leader who gets the most out of his ability by putting forth 100 percent, whatever the score. Heffernan made quite an impression in 1989, earning All-Star honors in the Class A Midwest League. He led the league's catchers in fielding and paced the Beloit offense with a team-high .296 average (third best in the league). He reminds some scouts of a young Mike Scioscia at this stage of his career. Drafted out of Clemson, Heffernan also was an All-Star pick at Helena in the rookie Pioneer League in 1988.

Hitting Tendencies
Heffernan is a good contact hitter who doesn't swing at many bad pitches (136 career walks, 97 strikeouts). He has only eight home runs over two seasons, but he is expected to develop a better power stroke as he gains some at-bats. He currently has good gap power and should knock in a better-than-average number of runs for a catcher. He hangs in well against lefthanded pitching, and he's an eager student who should improve in all areas.

Fielding/Baserunning
Heffernan's defense gets high marks in all departments. He moves well behind the plate and has a strong, accurate arm. Because he's always thinking, pitchers go to work with an added measure of confidence. He led all regular catchers in the Midwest League last season by throwing out 46.5 percent of the runners attempting to steal. His own speed afoot is only average, but he runs the bases hard.

Projection
Heffernan likely will begin the 1990 season at Class AA El Paso and appears destined to compete for a major league job in 1992.

Career Statistics

	G	AB	R	H	2B	3B	HR	RBI	BB	SO	AVG
1988—Beloit (Midwest League-Class A)	5	14	1	3	0	0	0	0	5	0	.214
1988—Helena (Pioneer League-Rookie)	65	196	47	55	13	0	4	31	61	40	.281
1989—Beloit (Midwest League-Class A)	127	425	53	126	20	1	4	59	70	57	.296

(Projections unavailable because player has not competed at Class AA or Class AAA levels)

JEFF HUSON

Montreal Expos
Shortstop
Signed by Expos as a Non-Drafted Free Agent, August 1985

General
Huson is the player who comes to mind when scouts talk of prospects who "come to play the game." A scrapper who gets the most out of his ability, Huson has great presence on the field, looking and acting like a major leaguer. In the last two seasons, he's been up with the Expos three times. Huson was a jack rabbit leadoff man at Class AAA Indianapolis last season and a league All-Star pick at shortstop. He's a versatile player who is willing to learn to better himself, having played short, second base and center field in the minors.

Hitting Tendencies
Huson is a good contact hitter who chokes up on the bat and sprays the ball around. He doesn't strike out much (once every 12 at-bats playing Class AA and AAA ball), draws a lot of walks and has a good on-base percentage. He won't be a power threat, but he improved his hitting effectiveness by muscling up in an off-season weight program after the 1988 season. With more upper-body strength, Huson batted .304 at Indianapolis last year and finished second in the American Association batting race.

Fielding/Baserunning
Usually a good fielder, Huson had a rocky spell with the Expos last season, committing eight errors in 20 games. Some of those miscues can be traced to his adjusting to artificial turf. Whether playing short or second, he usually gives his club solid defense up the middle. On the bases, he is an aggressive, daring runner who creates scoring opportunities. In 1988, he led the Southern League with 56 thefts.

Projection
Huson likely will stick in the majors in 1990 although probably in a reserve role.

Personal
Height: 6-3 Weight: 185
Bats left, throws right
Born: August 15, 1964

School: Wyoming

Ratings

	Present	Future
Hitting	4	5
Power	3	3
Baserunning	5	6
Speed	5	5
Fielding	4	5
Arm	4	4
Range	4	5

Rating Key
7 Outstanding
6 Major League Caliber, High
5 Major League Caliber
4 Minor League Caliber, High
3 Minor League Caliber
2 Below Average
1 Poor

Career Statistics and Peak Projection

	G	AB	R	H	2B	3B	HR	RBI	BB	SO	AVG
1986 Burlington (Midwest League-Class A)	133	457	85	132	19	1	16	72	76	68	.289
1986 Jacksonville (Southern League-Class AA)	1	4	0	0	0	0	0	0	0	0	.000
1986 Major League Equivalency	1	4	0	0	0	0	0	0	0	0	.000
1987 West Palm Beach (Florida State League-Class A)	131	455	54	130	15	4	1	53	50	30	.286
1988 Jacksonville (Southern League-Class AA)	128	471	72	117	18	1	0	34	59	45	.248
1988 Montreal (National League)	20	42	7	13	2	0	0	3	4	3	.310
1988 Major League Equivalency	148	498	63	115	19	1	0	30	48	52	.231
1989 Indianapolis (American Association-Class AAA)	102	378	70	115	17	4	3	35	50	26	.304
1989 Montreal (National League)	32	74	1	12	5	0	0	2	6	6	.162
1989 Major League Equivalency	134	443	62	118	22	3	3	32	47	35	.266
Peak Projection	154	570	81	153	27	3	3	50	68		.268

Interpretation
Huson moved up the ladder at normal speed for a college product. He didn't look quite ready in his trial with Montreal last season, but the system puts him only two years away from his peak. On that line, there is nothing that really stands out.

GREG COLBRUNN

Montreal Expos
Catcher
Expos' Sixth-Round Pick, June 1987 Draft

Personal
Height: 6-0 Weight: 190
Bats right, throws right
Born: July 26, 1969

School: Fontana High
in Fontana, Calif.

Ratings

	Present	Future
Hitting	3	5
Power	3	5
Baserunning	3	4
Speed	2	2
Fielding	3	5
Arm	4	5
Range	3	5

Rating Key
7 Outstanding
6 Major League Caliber, High
5 Major League Caliber
4 Minor League Caliber, High
3 Minor League Caliber
2 Below Average
1 Poor

General
Colbrunn is a converted third baseman who has been catching only since he joined the Expos' system. Now, just two seasons later, he's regarded as their top catching prospect. Colbrunn made the jump to the Class AA level midway through 1989 and finished on a strong note offensively, batting .275 at Jacksonville. A high school draftee who turned down a scholarship offer from Stanford to sign with Montreal, he is a hard, determined worker who has progressed rapidly at his new position.

Hitting Tendencies
Colbrunn has very good bat speed and is an aggressive hitter, although he must learn to be more selective at this stage. Only 20 years old, he has a lot of natural strength and is expected to hit the occasional long ball as he matures physically. He is a line-drive hitter whose intangibles (intelligence, a desire to succeed and love for the game) will help him as he develops. Colbrunn hit better following his promotion to Jacksonville in 1989, rebounding from a .237 start at Class A West Palm Beach.

Fielding/Baserunning
Overall, Colbrunn has adapted well to catching. He has good instincts and is the type of catcher a pitcher likes to throw to—a leader. He's a good receiver who will call a better game as he gains experience. He has a strong arm but needs to concentrate on releasing the ball quickly. On the basepaths, he has below-average speed.

Projection
Because of his youth and lack of catching experience, Colbrunn likely will return to Class AA Jacksonville to start the 1990 season. He is probably two or three years away from Montreal.

Career Statistics and Peak Projection

	G	AB	R	H	2B	3B	HR	RBI	BB	SO	AVG
1988 Rockford (Midwest League-Class A)	115	417	55	111	18	2	7	46	22	60	.266
1989 West Palm Beach (Florida State League-Class A)	59	228	20	54	8	0	0	25	6	29	.237
1989 Jacksonville (Southern League-Class AA)	55	178	21	49	11	1	3	18	13	33	.275
1989 Major League Equivalency	55	174	18	45	11	1	3	16	11	36	.259
Peak Projection	154	494	74	150	33	3	14	68	44		.303

Interpretation
The peak system likes the fact that Colbrunn batted .275 against Class AA pitching at age 20. Although the sample size is small, it shows a prospect with good line-drive power.

GREG SMITH

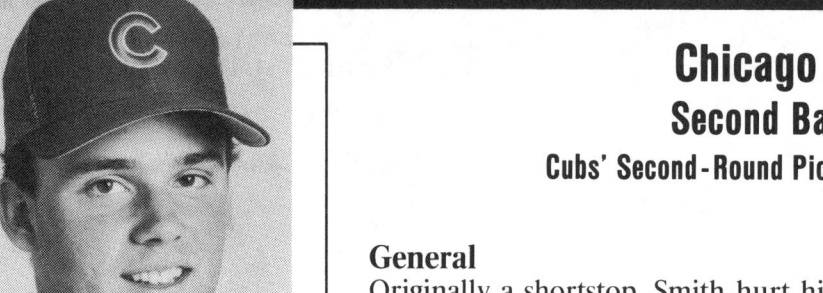

Chicago Cubs
Second Baseman
Cubs' Second-Round Pick, June 1985 Draft

Personal
Height: 5-11 Weight: 170
Bats left and right, throws right
Born: April 5, 1967

School: Glenelg High
in Glenelg, Md.

Ratings

	Present	Future
Hitting	4	5
Power	3	4
Baserunning	5	5
Speed	5	5
Fielding	5	5
Arm	4	4
Range	4	5

Rating Key
7 Outstanding
6 Major League Caliber, High
5 Major League Caliber
4 Minor League Caliber, High
3 Minor League Caliber
2 Below Average
1 Poor

General
Originally a shortstop, Smith hurt his arm in a tryout camp and has played second base since the start of the 1988 season. He's drawn raves ever since, earning All-Star honors at the position in two leagues. Playing his first season at the Class AA level in 1989, Smith batted a career-high .296 for Charlotte (the fourth-best mark in the Southern League) and was called up by the Cubs in September. At Class A Winston-Salem in 1988, his .280 mark was tops for a switch-hitter among batting qualifiers in the Carolina League. The Cubs may be loaded for bear with middle infielders, but Smith has warranted attention with his steady hitting and good glove.

Hitting Tendencies
Smith is a switch-hitter who can run, and he makes good contact from both sides of the plate. A selective hitter, his patience paid off in 1989 as he rapped 138 hits to rank among the Southern League leaders. With his knowledge of the strike zone, he's able to work a pitcher for a walk when his club needs a man on base. He's displayed some pop in his bat at times, but he'll be more valuable hitting for average than for power.

Fielding/Baserunning
The Cubs believe Smith might be the best fielding second baseman in the minor leagues. He has good range and good hands, but his arm speed may be a weakness. He is an outstanding runner and basestealer who should get even better with experience. Despite missing 45 games in 1988, most due to a knee injury, he tied for third in the Carolina League with 52 stolen bases in 64 attempts.

Projection
Smith likely will be the starting second baseman at Class AAA Iowa in 1990 and is on target to reach the majors later in the season or in 1991.

Career Statistics and Peak Projection

	G	AB	R	H	2B	3B	HR	RBI	BB	SO	AVG
1985 Wytheville (Appalachian League-Rookie)	51	179	28	42	6	2	0	15	20	27	.235
1986 Peoria (Midwest League-Class A)	53	170	24	43	6	3	2	26	19	45	.253
1987 Peoria (Midwest League-Class A)	124	444	69	120	23	5	6	56	62	96	.270
1988 Winston-Salem (Carolina League-Class A)	95	361	62	101	12	2	4	29	46	50	.280
1989 Charlotte (Southern League-Class AA)	126	467	59	138	23	6	5	64	42	52	.296
1989 Chicago (National League)	4	5	1	2	0	0	0	2	0	0	.400
1989 Major League Equivalency	130	448	44	116	18	3	4	49	28	55	.259
Peak Projection	154	538	71	159	25	3	7	57	45		.294

Interpretation
Smith's power won't propel him to Wrigley Field, but the peak calculations indicate he'll hit .294 there. His Major League Equivalency doesn't show a lot of on-base ability just yet.

RUBEN GONZALEZ

Personal
Height: 6-0 Weight: 205
Bats right, throws right
Born: November 3, 1966

School: Pepperdine

Ratings

	Present	Future
Hitting	4	5
Power	4	5
Baserunning	3	4
Speed	4	4
Fielding	3	4
Arm	4	4
Range	3	4

Rating Key
7 Outstanding
6 Major League Caliber, High
5 Major League Caliber
4 Minor League Caliber, High
3 Minor League Caliber
2 Below Average
1 Poor

Seattle Mariners
First Baseman
Mariners' 51st-Round Pick, June 1987 Draft

General
Gonzalez, the 1,179th player selected in the 1987 amateur draft, made an impression in 1989 the Mariners aren't likely to soon forget. Playing for Class A San Bernardino, he became the first player since Jose Vidal in 1963 to win the Triple Crown in the California League, batting .308 with 27 home runs and 101 runs batted in. Gonzalez had bulked up in an off-season workout program after winning the 1988 Midwest League batting title with a .314 mark at Wausau. He saw the California League's Most Valuable Player award go to Stockton's John Jaha last season, but he received league All-Star honors at designated hitter.

Hitting Tendencies
Gonzalez is a guess hitter who guessed right most of the time in 1989. He is a good breaking-ball hitter who also can sit on a fastball when he's expecting it. His stock as a power threat soared after he attacked the weights in the off-season, yet he remained a pure, patient hitter who wasn't tempted to flail at bad balls. A tough strikeout, Gonzalez hits the ball well to both alleys and holds promise as a doubles and RBI man. His biggest difficulty has been handling the inside pitch. A promotion to the Class AA level will help determine whether he can thrive—or survive—as a guess hitter.

Fielding/Baserunning
Gonzalez has an adequate arm but needs to work on his overall defense. His footwork and agility around the bag are lacking at this stage. Similarly, he is a below-average runner who is not considered a stealing threat.

Projection
Gonzalez is ticketed to play at Class AA Williamsport in 1990 and is on schedule to reach the major leagues in 1992.

Career Statistics

	G	AB	R	H	2B	3B	HR	RBI	BB	SO	AVG
1987 Bellingham (Northwest League-Class A)	40	125	24	38	10	0	7	29	17	12	.304
1988 Wausau (Midwest League-Class A)	115	430	56	135	32	2	9	59	35	50	.314
1989 San Bernardino (California League-Class A)	135	507	74	156	34	0	27	101	56	64	.308

(Projections unavailable because player has not competed at Class AA or Class AAA levels)

IVAN RODRIGUEZ

Texas Rangers
Catcher
Signed by Rangers as a Non-Drafted Free Agent, July 1988

Personal
Height: 5-9 Weight: 165
Bats right, throws right
Born: November 30, 1971

School: Vega Baja, Puerto Rico

Ratings

	Present	Future
Hitting	3	5
Power	3	5
Baserunning	4	4
Speed	3	3
Fielding	3	5
Arm	4	5
Range	3	5

Rating Key
7 Outstanding
6 Major League Caliber, High
5 Major League Caliber
4 Minor League Caliber, High
3 Minor League Caliber
2 Below Average
1 Poor

General
Just 17 years old last season, Rodriguez played well beyond the Rangers' expectations in his first year of pro ball. Skipping the rookie level to join the full-season South Atlantic League, he was the regular catcher at Class A Gastonia, which set a single-season record for a Texas farm club by winning 92 games. Rodriguez did make mistakes due to his inexperience, but that didn't worry the Rangers, who regard him as their best catching prospect in years. He is a hard worker who is destined to improve.

Hitting Tendencies
Rodriguez had a better season than expected with the bat. He surprised scouts with some long-ball punch, belting seven home runs in 386 at-bats, and he'll doubtlessly get stronger as he physically matures. Rodriguez made good, hard contact and, despite his inexperience, struck out only 58 times. He has the potential to be a gap-type hitter who will deliver his share of doubles and runs batted in.

Fielding/Baserunning
Rodriguez's lack of maturity hurt his defense at times last season. He'd sometimes dwell on a disappointing at-bat when he got behind the plate and, consequently, commit a defensive mistake (i.e., a league-high 34 passed balls in 96 games). Overall, however, he has a take-charge attitude and excellent tools. He'll call a good game when he matures and he can throw people out (44 of 133 runners attempting to steal in 1989). He won't be a stealing threat himself.

Projection
Rodriguez would benefit from another season at the Class A level, either at Charlotte in the Florida State League or Gastonia in 1990. He is at least three years away from the major leagues.

Career Statistics

	G	AB	R	H	2B	3B	HR	RBI	BB	SO	AVG
1989—Gastonia (South Atlantic League-Class A)	112	386	38	92	22	1	7	42	21	58	.238

(Projections unavailable because player has not competed at Class AA or Class AAA levels)

JOHN JAHA

Milwaukee Brewers
First Baseman
Brewers' 14th-Round Pick, June 1984 Draft

Personal
Height: 6-1   Weight: 195
Bats right, throws right
Born: May 27, 1966

School: David Douglas High
in Portland, Ore.

Ratings

	Present	Future
Hitting	3	5
Power	4	5
Baserunning	3	4
Speed	4	4
Fielding	4	5
Arm	4	4
Range	4	5

Rating Key
7 Outstanding
6 Major League Caliber, High
5 Major League Caliber
4 Minor League Caliber, High
3 Minor League Caliber
2 Below Average
1 Poor

General
Jaha made slow, if steady, progress through the lower levels of the Brewers' farm system for four seasons. Last year, his fifth as a pro, he made up for lost time, wielding a smoking bat that carried him to Most Valuable Player honors in the Class A California League. Some observers wonder whether that performance was a glitch or indicative of his evolving as an impact-type offensive player. It was his second tour through the league with Stockton, although he missed a good part of the 1988 campaign with a rib injury. Jaha, drafted out of high school in 1984, has maintained good work habits and remained upbeat.

Hitting Tendencies
Jaha's 1989 numbers suggest he's finding his stroke as a power hitter. He has the muscle to hit the long ball to any field and move runners across the plate. Last season, his 25 homers and 91 runs batted in both ranked second in the California League, and he topped the circuit with 13 sacrifice flies. Unlike many big hitters, Jaha has the discipline to get on base via charity. He has drawn more than 100 walks twice in his career and last season managed a league-leading .422 on-base percentage. When he's swinging he isn't always hitting, however, as evidenced by his 115 strikeouts in 1989.

Fielding/Baserunning
Jaha has good instincts at first base and plays a steady game. He's not a lumbering runner on the bases but has never stolen more than 10 bases in a season.

Projection
Jaha finally will move up a grade in 1990, most likely to Class AA El Paso. If his bat stays hot, he could reach the major leagues sometime in 1991.

Career Statistics

	G	AB	R	H	2B	3B	HR	RBI	BB	SO	AVG
1985—Helena (Pioneer League-Rookie)	24	68	13	18	3	0	2	14	14	23	.265
1986—Tri-Cities (Northwest League-Class A)	73	258	65	82	13	2	15	67	70	75	.318
1987—Beloit (Midwest League-Class A)	122	377	68	101	22	0	7	47	102	86	.268
1988—Stockton (California League-Class A)	99	302	58	77	14	6	8	54	69	85	.255
1989—Stockton (California League-Class A)	140	479	83	140	26	5	25	91	112	115	.292

(Projections unavailable because player has not competed at Class AA or Class AAA levels)

TYLER HOUSTON

Atlanta Braves
Catcher
Braves' First-Round Pick, June 1989 Draft

Personal
Height: 6-2   Weight: 205
Bats left, throws right
Born: January 17, 1971

School: Valley High
in Las Vegas, Nev.

Ratings

	Present	Future
Hitting	2	5
Power	2	5
Baserunning	2	4
Speed	2	3
Fielding	3	5
Arm	3	5
Range	3	5

Rating Key
7 Outstanding
6 Major League Caliber, High
5 Major League Caliber
4 Minor League Caliber, High
3 Minor League Caliber
2 Below Average
1 Poor

General
Some observers (specifically, his detractors on opposing teams) would like to believe that Houston moved from prospect to suspect after one season of rookie ball. Of course, they deny Houston's aggressive playing style, his overly confident manner or big signing bonus colored their assessments. His numbers did not meet expectations for a player drafted No. 2 overall: a .244 batting average, four home runs and 24 runs batted in at Idaho Falls in the Pioneer League. Then again, Houston was just 18 years old, drafted fresh out of high school and playing in a league heavily populated by players with collegiate experience. Most everyone concedes he has talent and confidence. What he needs is time to refine his very raw skills.

Hitting Tendencies
Houston's biggest problem in his first pro season was a lack of discipline at the plate. He showed little patience, swinging instead at too many bad pitches. He also struggled with breaking balls. Still, he has power potential and a line-drive swing that will allow him to hit for average if he's selective. Pioneer League pitchers worked him carefully last season; swinging against high schoolers with limited repertoires, he fared better, batting .485 as a senior. That, the Braves believe, is indicative of his ability.

Fielding/Baserunning
Houston has a very good arm and will learn to handle pitchers effectively with experience. He did allow a league-high 14 passed balls in 1989. On the bases, he will not be a stealing threat.

Projection
Houston is ticketed to play for a full-season Class A team in 1990, either at Sumter or Durham. Atlanta is probably three seasons away.

Career Statistics

	G	AB	R	H	2B	3B	HR	RBI	BB	SO	AVG
1989—Idaho Falls (Pioneer League-Rookie)	50	176	30	43	11	0	4	24	25	41	.244

(Projections unavailable because player has not competed at Class AA or Class AAA levels)

The Pitchers

Righthander Ben McDonald

Two years ago, the minor leagues' current top pitching prospect was still attending John F. Kennedy High School in Taylor, Mich. Steve Avery has come a long way since the spring of 1988, and his next stop likely will be the major leagues.

"We knew right away he would be our pick, period," Atlanta Braves General Manager Bobby Cox said. "He was very impressive."

In the collective opinion of scouts, minor league managers, farm directors, coaches and instructors, the lefthanded Avery tops the list of prospects who comprise the major leagues' next wave of pitching talent. He is what is often referred to as a "can't miss" prospect, and while some of those players do in fact fail to achieve big-league stardom, the consensus is that Avery is destined for a long and distinguished career.

"He has come fast, but everybody knew he would," Cox said. "When you take one look at him, you can visualize him making the All-Star team 10 years in a row."

Avery, the third overall pick in the June 1988 draft behind Andy Benes (San Diego) and Mark Lewis (Cleveland), quickly established himself as the best in a very good crop of young pitchers in the Atlanta organization. In his first professional stop, Avery was 7-1 with a 1.50 earned-run average in the rookie-level Appalachian League. Midway through last season, he advanced to Class AA Greenville after posting a sparkling 1.45 ERA to start the year at Class A

Righthander Curt Schilling

Lefthander Steve Avery

HOW THEY RANK

Pitchers

1. Steve Avery, Atlanta Braves, lefthander
2. Ben McDonald, Baltimore, righthander
3. Mike Harkey, Chicago Cubs, righthander
4. Pat Combs, Philadelphia Phillies, lefthander
5. Darryl Kile, Houston Astros, righthander
6. Charles Nagy, Cleveland Indians, righthander
7. Kevin Morton, Boston Red Sox, lefthander
8. Kent Mercker, Atlanta Braves, lefthander
9. Wilson Alvarez, Chi. White Sox, lefthander
10. Alex Sanchez, Toronto Blue Jays, righthander
11. Howard Farmer, Montreal Expos, righthander
12. Roger Salkeld, Seattle Mariners, righthander
13. Curt Schilling, Baltimore Orioles, righthander
14. Kiki Jones, Los Angeles Dodgers, righthander
15. Rafael Valdez, San Diego Padres, righthander
16. Jose DeJesus, Kansas City Royals, righthander
17. Willie Banks, Minnesota Twins, righthander
18. Jason Grimsley, Philadelphia, righthander
19. Tommy Greene, Atlanta Braves, righthander
20. John Ericks, St. Louis Cardinals, righthander
21. Mel Rojas, Montreal Expos, righthander
22. Robb Nen, Texas Rangers, righthander
23. Kevin Appier, Kansas City Royals, righthander
24. Mike Linskey, Baltimore Orioles, lefthander
25. Mark Gardner, Montreal Expos, righthander
26. Scott Aldred, Detroit Tigers, lefthander
27. Julio Valera, New York Mets, righthander
28. Steve Adkins, New York Yankees, lefthander
29. Mike Milchin, St. Louis Cardinals, lefthander
30. David Proctor, New York Mets, righthander
31. Stan Belinda, Pittsburgh Pirates, righthander
32. Luis Vasquez, Cincinnati Reds, righthander
33. Kevin Tapani, Minnesota Twins, righthander
34. Chris Hammond, Cincinnati Reds, lefthander
35. Jamie McAndrew, L.A. Dodgers, righthander
36. Rudy Seanez, Cleveland Indians, righthander
37. Rodney Imes, Cincinnati Reds, righthander
38. Nate Cromwell, Toronto Blue Jays, lefthander
39. Paul Abbott, Minnesota Twins, righthander
40. Eric McCray, Texas Rangers, lefthander
41. Mike Fetters, California Angels, righthander
42. Johnny Ard, Minnesota Twins, righthander
43. Glenn Carter, California Angels, righthander
44. Blaine Beatty, New York Mets, lefthander
45. Rheal Cormier, St. Louis Cardinals, lefthander
46. Mike Stanton, Atlanta Braves, lefthander
47. Keith Richardson, Pittsburgh, righthander
48. Frank Castillo, Chicago Cubs, righthander
49. Josias Manzanillo, Boston, righthander
50. Pat Mahomes, Minnesota Twins, righthander
51. Wayne Edwards, Chi. White Sox, lefthander
52. Mark Clark, St. Louis Cardinals, righthander
53. Joe Ausanio, Pittsburgh Pirates, righthander
54. Roger Smithberg, S.D. Padres, righthander
55. Shawn Boskie, Chicago Cubs, righthander
56. Richie Lewis, Montreal Expos, righthander
57. Narciso Elvira, Milwaukee Brewers, lefthander
58. Pat Gomez, Atlanta Braves, lefthander
59. Scott Radinsky, Chicago White Sox, lefthander
60. Eric Gunderson, S.F. Giants, lefthander
61. Willie Smith, New York Yankees, righthander
62. Terry Bross, New York Mets, righthander

Lefthander Kent Mercker

Righthander Charles Nagy

Durham.

Avery has all the tools a scout looks for in a pitcher: a hard fastball to go with a good curve and changeup, good physical size and an advanced knowledge of pitching. Avery turns just 20 years old as the 1990 season unfolds.

The Braves will have the young lefthander in spring camp to compete for a spot on their major league roster, but many within the organization will be satisfied if he starts the year at Class AAA Richmond. Despite Avery's glowing statistics and reviews, the club has resisted the temptation to rush him, allowing him to first enjoy success at the various minor league levels.

The pitcher judged the No. 2 prospect spent all of two games in the minor leagues before joining the Baltimore Orioles last September. Ben McDonald, the first overall pick in the 1989 draft, joined Baltimore for a six-game trial after lengthy contract negotiations limited him to two tuneup appearances in the Class A Carolina League. Orioles officials are counting on "Big Ben" to become their pitching ace through the 1990s.

Mike Harkey figured to be one of the top rookie pitchers a year ago. Instead, Harkey spent an injury-plagued 1989 season in the minor leagues. The Chicago Cubs' top prospect appeared to be fully recovered as winter gave way to spring and is expected to enjoy the success in 1990 that he was supposed to have last year.

The Phillies' Pat Combs rose from the Class A level to the Philadelphia starting rotation in 1989. Joining the big club in September, he turned in a 4-0 record with a 2.09 ERA to establish himself as a solid bet to make the Phillies' rotation in 1990.

Houston's Darryl Kile was another pitcher who quickly sprung to the forefront in 1989. Kile, whose first pro season in 1988 was limited to the rookie-league level, advanced all the way to Class AAA Tucson last year and is a candidate to join the Astros' rotation sometime in 1990.

Charles Nagy of the Cleveland Indians is one of several members of the 1988 U.S. Olympic team who made his pro debut in 1989. Like most of the others, the big righthander was able to make a quick adjustment from amateur to professional baseball.

Kevin Morton was drafted in 1989 by the Boston Red Sox with one of the compensation picks they received for losing Bruce Hurst to free agency. While he isn't yet ready to make Boston fans forget Hurst, Morton is already a top prospect.

The Braves' Kent Mercker follows Avery on the list of outstanding young pitchers being developed by the club. Like Avery, he's a lefthanded starter, but he's two years older. Atlanta is expecting big things from Mercker, perhaps beginning in 1990.

Wilson Alvarez was among the Texas Rangers' most valued prospects at the start of 1989, but Harold Baines' services do not come cheaply. The Rangers parted with Alvarez to acquire Baines from the Chi-

Righthander Kevin Appier

cago White Sox midway through the 1989 season. Chicago was a little more patient with the hard-throwing lefthander and left him at the Class AA level to finish the season.

The Top 10 concludes with Alex Sanchez, who has pitched the last year and a half at Class AAA Syracuse. The Blue Jays believe he will soon be taking up residence in Toronto.

In all, 62 pitchers were included in the Top 150 prospects, covering all levels of the minor leagues. Twenty-five of the 26 organizations are represented on the pitching list, with the Braves and Minnesota Twins having a high of five prospects each. Following Avery and Mercker for the Braves are Tommy Greene, Mike Stanton and Pat Gomez. The Twins' list is composed of Willie Banks, Kevin Tapani, Paul Abbott, Johnny Ard and Pat Mahomes.

The lone team not represented is the one that, arguably, needs the least help—the World Series champion Oakland Athletics.

STEVE AVERY

Atlanta Braves
Pitcher
Braves' First-Round Pick, June 1988 Draft

Personal
Height: 6-4   Weight: 180
Throws left, bats left
Born: April 14, 1970

School: John F. Kennedy
High in Taylor, Mich.

Ratings

	Present	Future
Fastball	4	5
Curve	5	6
Changeup	5	6
Control	5	6
Stamina	4	5
Poise	4	6
Fielding	4	5

Rating Key
7 Outstanding
6 Major League Caliber, High
5 Major League Caliber
4 Minor League Caliber, High
3 Minor League Caliber
2 Below Average
1 Poor

General
The major leagues beckon for Avery, a dominating lefthander who was blowing away high school hitters as recently as 1988. Picked third overall in the June 1988 draft, he was a formidable 19-year-old talent pitching against older players for Class A Durham and Class AA Greenville in 1989. Some within the Braves' organization believe he could have been successful in the major leagues. As a high school phenom in Michigan, he was named his state's Mr. Baseball as the top prep player. His transition to the pro ranks was nothing short of sensational: a 7-1 record and 1.50 earned-run average in the rookie Appalachian League in 1988.

Pitching Tendencies
Avery is a strikeout pitcher who has command of three major league pitches. His best pitch is the live, moving fastball he throws between 88 and 92 mph. Mix in a big overhand curve and outstanding changeup and you have a hurler with the classic strikeout repertoire. In 1989, Avery fanned 90 in 86⅔ innings at Durham, then added 75 strikeouts in 84⅓ innings for Greenville. In Avery's three minor league stops, hitters have scraped together an average of only 6.3 hits per nine innings. Scouts marvel over the confidence and composure that belie his youth.

Fielding/Holding Runners
Avery is a good athlete who helps himself in all areas. He fields his position well and keeps runners close—at least when he has runners to worry about.

Projection
The Braves would like to nurture Avery a mite longer, probably at the Class AAA level at least for the start of the 1990 season. He'll likely reach the majors before the end of the year.

Career Statistics and Major League Equivalencies

	G	IP	W	L	R	ER	H	HR	SO	BB	ERA
1988 Pulaski (Appalachian League-Rookie)	10	66	7	1	16	11	38	2	80	19	1.50
1989 Durham (Carolina League-Class A)	13	86⅔	6	4	22	14	59	5	90	20	1.45
1989 Greenville (Southern League-Class AA)	13	84⅓	6	3	32	26	68	3	75	34	2.77
1989 Major League Equivalency	13	84⅓			38	31	76	4	71	41	3.31

Interpretation
Avery's Major League Equivalency line shows a pitcher who is poised to make the jump to the major leagues. Although the Class AA sample is rather small, it reveals in the MLE that Avery doesn't have the control problems that keep pitchers down and he does not surrender a lot of hits.

BEN McDONALD

Baltimore Orioles
Pitcher
Orioles' First-Round Pick, June 1989 Draft

Personal
Height: 6-7 Weight: 215
Throws right, bats right
Born: November 24, 1967

School: Louisiana State

Ratings

	Present	Future
Fastball	6	6
Curve	5	6
Changeup	4	5
Control	5	5
Stamina	5	6
Poise	5	5
Fielding	5	5

Rating Key
7 Outstanding
6 Major League Caliber, High
5 Major League Caliber
4 Minor League Caliber, High
3 Minor League Caliber
2 Below Average
1 Poor

General
Regarded by many scouts as the crown jewel of the pitching prospects, McDonald was the first overall pick in the 1989 draft after starring with Louisiana State and the 1988 U.S. Olympic team. His lengthy contract negotiations with the Orioles limited his 1989 season to just two games in the Class A Carolina League and six games with Baltimore in September. McDonald capped his amateur career by winning the 1989 Golden Spikes Award, given annually to the nation's top amateur player. With Team USA in 1988, he was 8-2 over the summer schedule and pitched two complete-game victories in the Seoul Olympics. For a young pitcher with limited experience, "Big Ben" has tremendous poise and a great mound presence.

Pitching Tendencies
McDonald overpowered hitters at the amateur level with a fastball that is consistently clocked in the 90s. He has very good command of the fastball and his curve, both of which he spots effectively. The pitches have good movement, which prevents hitters from making solid contact. McDonald is working on a changeup and forkball to round out his arsenal. He is an aggressive pitcher who won't hesitate to go inside or challenge hitters. His size alone can intimidate opponents, and he's capable of throwing a lot of innings per season.

Fielding/Holding Runners
McDonald is a good athlete who also was a rugged forward on the LSU basketball squad. He fields his position well but does need to refine his move to first.

Projection
McDonald will compete for a spot in Baltimore's starting rotation in 1990.

Career Statistics and Major League Equivalencies

	G	IP	W	L	R	ER	H	HR	SO	BB	ERA
1989 Frederick (Carolina League-Class A)	2	9	0	0	2	2	10	0	9	0	2.00
1989 Baltimore (American League)	6	7⅓	1	0	7	7	8	2	3	4	8.59
1989 Major League Equivalency	6	7⅓	1	0	7	7	8	2	3	4	8.59

Interpretation
There's nothing to interpret here. McDonald has no minor league career to speak of—nor is he likely to acquire one. He most likely will jump right into the major leagues in 1990.

MIKE HARKEY

Chicago Cubs
Pitcher
Cubs' First-Round Pick, June 1987 Draft

Personal
Height: 6-5 Weight: 220
Throws right, bats right
Born: October 25, 1966

School: Cal State Fullerton

Ratings

	Present	Future
Fastball	6	6
Curve	6	6
Changeup	5	6
Control	5	5
Stamina	4	5
Poise	5	5
Fielding	5	5

Rating Key
7 Outstanding
6 Major League Caliber, High
5 Major League Caliber
4 Minor League Caliber, High
3 Minor League Caliber
2 Below Average
1 Poor

General
Who would have thought Harkey, a preseason favorite to contend for National League Rookie of the Year honors in 1989, would bomb in spring training? Well, Harkey didn't make it out of camp with the Chicago Cubs. Assigned to Class AAA Iowa instead, he fell victim to both knee and shoulder injuries and pitched in only 12 games all season. Only the year before, Harkey had devastated hitters in the minor leagues. He was a combined 16-4 at the Class AA and AAA levels and showed good stuff in five late-season starts for Chicago. "He may not have won any games for us," Cubs Manager Don Zimmer said of Harkey's hard-luck 0-3 record, "but he'll win plenty next year." Harkey won but two decisions—and none where he was expected to, in Chicago. The Cubs expect him to be fully recovered in time for the 1990 season.

Pitching Tendencies
Harkey has listened to Cub coaches and become an aggressive pitcher who challenges hitters. As a collegian, he supposedly shied away from that kind of confrontation, something pitchers with 95-mph fastballs don't usually do. Harkey has a repertoire of four pitches—fastball, slider, curve and changeup—and has learned the importance of using them all. He has good control, but his fastball will run in menacingly on righthanded hitters.

Fielding/Holding Runners
Harkey is a good fielder who won't beat himself. He holds runners well, especially for a pitcher his size.

Projection
If he is healthy, Harkey will bid for a spot in the Cubs' starting rotation in 1990.

Career Statistics and Major League Equivalencies

	G	IP	W	L	R	ER	H	HR	SO	BB	ERA
1987 Peoria (Midwest League-Class A)	12	76	2	3	45	30	81	3	48	28	3.55
1987 Pittsfield (Eastern League-Class AA)	1	2	0	0	0	0	1	0	2	0	0.00
1987 Major League Equivalency	1	2			0	0	1	0	2	0	0.00
1988 Pittsfield (Eastern League-Class AA)	13	85⅔	9	2	29	13	66	1	73	35	1.37
1988 Iowa (American Association-Class AAA)	12	78⅔	7	2	36	31	55	6	62	33	3.55
1988 Chicago (National League)	5	34⅔	0	3	14	10	33	0	18	15	2.60
1988 Major League Equivalency	30	199			87	58	165	7	147	92	2.62
1989 Iowa (American Association-Class AAA)	12	63	2	7	37	31	67	7	37	25	4.43
1989 Major League Equivalency	12	63			41	35	72	8	35	28	5.00

Interpretation
Harkey's injuries hampered his 1989 season, but his 1988 Major League Equivalency showed a pitcher ready to step into the Cubs' rotation. His strikeout total is misleadingly low in his 1989 MLE.

PAT COMBS

Philadelphia Phillies
Pitcher
Phillies' First-Round Pick, June 1988 Draft

Personal
Height: 6-4   Weight: 205
Throws left, bats left
Born: October 29, 1966

School: Baylor

Ratings

	Present	Future
Fastball	5	5
Curve	5	5
Changeup	5	5
Control	5	6
Stamina	5	6
Poise	5	6
Fielding	4	5

Rating Key
7 Outstanding
6 Major League Caliber, High
5 Major League Caliber
4 Minor League Caliber, High
3 Minor League Caliber
2 Below Average
1 Poor

General
Combs, the final player cut from the 1988 U.S. Olympic team, climbed all the way from Class A Clearwater to Philadelphia in 1989, his first season in pro ball. He improved every step of the way and finished a combined 17-8, including a 4-0 record with the Phillies in September. Among his victories were a four-hit, complete-game shutout against St. Louis and a four-hit, seven-inning effort against New York at Shea Stadium. "He has an excellent shot to make our staff next spring," Phillies Manager Nick Leyva remarked at the time. "He's pitched more than 200 innings and he's still pitching with power and command." The 11th player picked in the 1988 draft, Combs set single-season and career strikeout marks at Baylor, where he was 16-7 in two seasons.

Pitching Tendencies
Combs has tremendous poise on the mound. He has command of four major league-caliber pitches—fastball, curve, straight change, split-finger—and throws them all for strikes. His ball has good movement, especially when he keeps it down, but he gets hit when his fastball is up in the strike zone. Combs is not overpowering but knows how to execute a game plan and work hitters intelligently. Whenever he had problems in 1989, it was due to his tendency to get into too many long counts. He had fewer of those as the year progressed, however.

Fielding/Holding Runners
Combs is an average fielder. He has a quick delivery to the plate, but his move to first base is slow. The Phillies are teaching him the slide step, which he appears to be picking up.

Projection
Based on his stellar September in Philadelphia, Combs is a leading candidate to land a job in the Phillies' rotation in 1990.

Career Statistics and Major League Equivalencies

	G	IP	W	L	R	ER	H	HR	SO	BB	ERA
1989 Clearwater (Florida State League-Class A)	6	41⅔	2	1	8	6	35	0	24	11	1.30
1989 Reading (Eastern League-Class AA)	19	125	8	7	57	47	104	16	77	40	3.38
1989 Scranton/Wilkes-Barre (International-Class AAA)	3	24⅓	3	0	4	1	15	0	20	7	0.37
1989 Philadelphia (National League)	6	38⅔	4	0	10	9	36	2	30	6	2.09
1989 Major League Equivalency	28	188			79	64	165	20	122	59	3.06

Interpretation
The Major League Equivalency indicates Combs is ready for the majors, and his Philadelphia line agrees. His 5-1 strikeouts-to-walks ratio with the Phillies can't be overlooked, although the MLE adjusts that down over a full season.

DARRYL KILE

Houston Astros
Pitcher
Astros' 30th-Round Pick, June 1987 Draft

Personal
Height: 6-5   Weight: 185
Throws right, bats right
Born: December 2, 1968

School: Chaffey College
in Alta Loma, Calif.

Ratings

	Present	Future
Fastball	5	6
Curve	5	6
Changeup	3	5
Control	4	5
Stamina	4	5
Poise	4	5
Fielding	4	5

Rating Key
7 Outstanding
6 Major League Caliber, High
5 Major League Caliber
4 Minor League Caliber, High
3 Minor League Caliber
2 Below Average
1 Poor

General
Kile has rocketed through the Astros' system, rising from the rookie-class Gulf Coast League to the Class AAA level in two seasons. Pitching mostly at Class AA Columbus in 1989, the junior college product anchored the Mudcats' starting staff and was named to the Southern League All-Star team. Kile held opponents to a .173 batting average, the lowest among the league's starting pitchers, and fired a two-hit gem and three-hitter among his 11 victories. He ranked fourth in the league with a 2.58 earned-run average and second with six complete games. Kile was promoted to Class AAA Tucson for the final month of the season but managed only a 5.96 ERA in six starts.

Pitching Tendencies
Kile makes the most of his two best pitches, a fastball he throws in the low 90s and a hard slider. If he develops a good off-speed pitch, he'll be even more imposing. Like many young strikeout pitchers, Kile does have occasional control problems. His career strikeouts-to-walks ratio thus far is not even close to 2-1. Still, the strikeout totals are impressive: 126 in 151⅓ innings last season and 54 strikeouts in 59⅔ innings in rookie ball. He has room to improve his overall knowledge of pitching, which should come with experience. And at 6-foot-5, he has the size to be durable and intimidating.

Fielding/Holding Runners
Kile is a good athlete and fields his position well. He needs to develop a better move to first, but runners didn't enjoy too many liberties in 1989, getting thrown out 10 times in 32 steal attempts.

Projection
Kile likely will open 1990 at Class AAA Tucson and could be in the Houston rotation before the end of the season.

Career Statistics and Major League Equivalencies

	G	IP	W	L	R	ER	H	HR	SO	BB	ERA
1988 Sarasota Astros (Gulf Coast League-Rookie)	12	59⅔	5	3	34	21	48	1	54	33	3.17
1989 Columbus (Southern League-Class AA)	20	125⅔	11	6	47	36	74	5	108	68	2.58
1989 Tucson (Pacific Coast League-Class AAA)	6	25⅔	2	1	20	17	33	1	18	13	5.96
1989 Major League Equivalency	28	160⅔			108	97	194	10	113	64	5.43

Interpretation
According to his Major League Equivalency, Kile isn't close to being ready for Houston. His hits-allowed total in the equation is frightful. The deep center-field fence in Columbus apparently worked in Kile's favor since the adjustment is more severe than usual.

CHARLES NAGY

Cleveland Indians
Pitcher
Indians' First-Round Pick, June 1988 Draft

Personal
Height: 6-3 Weight: 200
Throws right, bats left
Born: May 5, 1967

School: Connecticut

Ratings

	Present	Future
Fastball	5	6
Curve	4	5
Changeup	4	5
Control	5	6
Stamina	4	5
Poise	4	5
Fielding	4	5

Rating Key
7 Outstanding
6 Major League Caliber, High
5 Major League Caliber
4 Minor League Caliber, High
3 Minor League Caliber
2 Below Average
1 Poor

General
Nagy was honored as the Carolina League's 1989 Pitcher of the Year in just his first minor league campaign. Assigned to Class A Kinston, he pitched four shutouts and six complete games in 13 starts to earn a promotion to Canton-Akron in the Class AA Eastern League. The 17th player chosen in the 1988 draft (and Cleveland's second first-round pick that year), Nagy delayed the start of his minor league career to participate in the 1988 Olympic Games. He led Team USA with a 1.05 earned-run average over its summer schedule, posting a 3-1 record and six saves as a reliever-starter. He is a quick learner with the drive to succeed, the type who can quietly lead by example.

Pitching Tendencies
Nagy's moving fastball and above-average slider grade out a level higher due to a good changeup that keeps hitters off-balance. The big righthander has excellent command of his repertoire, particularly his breaking pitches. He can throw them for strikes anywhere in the count and seldom gives up careless walks. Nagy allowed only 9.16 baserunners per nine innings at Kinston last season, best among Carolina League starters, and held opponents to a .202 batting average, also the top mark. He is a strikeout pitcher, averaging close to one per inning in 1989.

Fielding/Holding Runners
Nagy is an adept athlete who fields his position well. Although some instructors believe he could speed up his delivery to the plate, opponents were successful on only 18 of 38 stolen base attempts in 1989.

Projection
Nagy likely will pitch at the Class AAA level in 1990 and could see major league duty before season's end.

Career Statistics and Major League Equivalencies

	G	IP	W	L	R	ER	H	HR	SO	BB	ERA
1989 Kinston (Carolina League-Class A)	13	95⅓	8	4	22	16	69	0	99	24	1.51
1989 Canton-Akron (Eastern League-Class AA)	15	94	4	5	44	35	102	4	65	32	3.35
1989 Major League Equivalency	15	94			54	43	116	5	62	39	4.12

Interpretation
Nagy's career sample is too small to make any hard evaluations just yet.

KEVIN MORTON

Boston Red Sox
Pitcher
Red Sox's Supplemental Pick Following First Round, June 1989 Draft

Personal
Height: 6-1 Weight: 175
Throws left, bats right
Born: August 3, 1968

School: Seton Hall

Ratings

	Present	Future
Fastball	4	5
Curve	4	6
Changeup	4	5
Control	5	6
Stamina	4	5
Poise	5	6
Fielding	4	5

Rating Key
7 Outstanding
6 Major League Caliber, High
5 Major League Caliber
4 Minor League Caliber, High
3 Minor League Caliber
2 Below Average
1 Poor

General
Drafted by Boston as compensation for the loss of Bruce Hurst through free agency, Morton made a sterling impression in 1989 at three minor league stops. His 6-6 record was not due to mediocre ability. On the contrary, the slender lefthander fashioned a cumulative 2.08 earned-run average and allowed just 5.2 hits per nine innings pitched. He advanced to Lynchburg, the Red Sox's top Class A affiliate, where he pitched four complete games and two shutouts in nine starts. Morton was drafted 29th overall after his junior season at Seton Hall, where he was 11-2 with a 1.67 ERA in 1989 and 26-5 in three seasons.

Pitching Tendencies
Morton is a crafty rather than overpowering pitcher. He's able to handcuff hitters without major heat by throwing several variations of an outstanding curve. The curve and a good changeup make his fastball that much better (he's sneaky fast, hitters say) and his knowledge of pitching is very advanced. Morton has command of every pitch and the numbers didn't lie in 1989: only 24 walks with 111 strikeouts in 95 innings. He gets very high marks for his poise and presence on the mound, and scouts expect he'll rise through the Boston system in a hurry.

Fielding/Holding Runners
Morton has been described as a complete player who helps himself. He fielded his position well last season, but opponents were able to take a few liberties on the bases, stealing 14 times in 17 attempts.

Projection
Morton likely will move up to Class AA New Britain to start the season but could jump to Class AAA Pawtucket before season's end. Don't be surprised if he's in Boston within two years.

Career Statistics

	G	IP	W	L	R	ER	H	HR	SO	BB	ERA
1989 Winter Haven Red Sox (Gulf Coast League-Rookie)	2	6	1	0	0	0	2	0	11	1	0.00
1989 Elmira (New York-Penn League-Class A)	3	24	1	1	6	5	11	0	32	6	1.88
1989 Lynchburg (Carolina League-Class A)	9	65	4	5	20	17	42	2	68	17	2.35

(Projections unavailable because player has not competed at Class AA or Class AAA levels)

KENT MERCKER

Atlanta Braves
Pitcher
Braves' First-Round Pick, June 1986 Draft

Personal
Height: 6-1 Weight: 195
Throws left, bats left
Born: February 1, 1968

School: Dublin High
in Dublin, Ohio

Ratings

	Present	Future
Fastball	6	6
Curve	5	5
Changeup	5	5
Control	4	5
Stamina	4	5
Poise	5	6
Fielding	4	5

Rating Key
7 Outstanding
6 Major League Caliber, High
5 Major League Caliber
4 Minor League Caliber, High
3 Minor League Caliber
2 Below Average
1 Poor

General
Mercker has a bulldog makeup for a pitcher, with outstanding ability and a competitive nature. He is a hard-nosed player who wants the ball in the big game. The Braves tabbed him as their outstanding minor league pitcher back in 1988, when he shared Pitcher of the Year honors in the Carolina League and earned a promotion to Class AA Greenville. It was an extra-satisfying season for Mercker, considering he missed nearly all of 1987 after undergoing elbow surgery. He continued his climb at Class AAA Richmond in 1989, leading the staff in starts, innings pitched and strikeouts to earn a stint with Atlanta at the end of the season. Mercker was the fifth player chosen overall in the June 1986 draft.

Pitching Tendencies
Mercker has a major league fastball that seems to explode across the plate. He has an excellent changeup and a good curveball, but he's had problems throwing the breaking pitch for strikes. When he does have all of his pitches working, Mercker is tough to beat. Over his last two seasons, he struck out 367 batters in 349 innings. At the Class AAA level in 1989, he allowed only 5.7 hits per every nine innings pitched. He's making his mark as a workhorse starter who keeps improving his consistency. That, scouts say, will be the key to whether he's successful at the major league level.

Fielding/Holding Runners
Mercker is a good athlete who does all the little things he needs to do to help himself.

Projection
Mercker figures to be competing for a spot in the Braves' starting rotation in 1990.

Career Statistics and Major League Equivalencies

	G	IP	W	L	R	ER	H	HR	SO	BB	ERA
1986 Bradenton Braves (Gulf Coast League-Rookie)	9	47⅓	4	3	21	13	37	1	42	16	2.47
1987 Durham (Carolina League-Class A)	3	11⅔	0	1	8	7	11	1	14	6	5.40
1988 Durham (Carolina League-Class A)	19	127⅔	11	4	44	39	102	5	159	47	2.75
1988 Greenville (Southern League-Class AA)	9	48⅓	3	1	20	18	36	2	60	26	3.35
1988 Major League Equivalency	9	48⅓			22	20	39	2	57	29	3.72
1989 Richmond (International League-Class AAA)	27	168⅔	9	12	66	60	107	17	144	95	3.20
1989 Atlanta (National League)	2	4⅓	0	0	6	6	8	0	4	6	12.46
1989 Major League Equivalency	29	173			92	84	133	22	141	130	4.37

Interpretation
Mercker was roughed up in two major league appearances last season, and his Major League Equivalency doesn't indicate he's ready to face that kind of competition. His MLE walk total is alarmingly high-nearly seven hitters per nine innings.

WILSON ALVAREZ

Chicago White Sox
Pitcher
Signed by Texas Rangers as a Non-Drafted Free Agent, September 1986

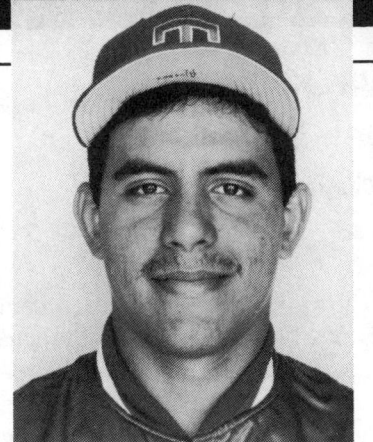

Personal
Height: 6-1 Weight: 175
Throws left, bats left
Born: March 24, 1970

School: Maracaibo, Venezuela

Ratings

	Present	Future
Fastball	5	6
Curve	4	6
Changeup	3	5
Control	4	5
Stamina	4	5
Poise	4	5
Fielding	4	5

Rating Key
7 Outstanding
6 Major League Caliber, High
5 Major League Caliber
4 Minor League Caliber, High
3 Minor League Caliber
2 Below Average
1 Poor

General
The White Sox are very high on Alvarez, one of three players they acquired in the Harold Baines trade with Texas. Only 19 years old last season, Alvarez pitched at Port Charlotte, Tulsa and Texas before concluding the year at Class AA Birmingham for the White Sox. All the movement could have undone the young lefthander, but he was pitching well at the end of the season, helping Birmingham to the Southern League championship with a two-hit complete game shutout in the final game of the Western Division playoffs. For the season, he was a combined 11-8. Alvarez was born and raised in Maracaibo, Venezuela, the hometown of Luis Aparicio.

Pitching Tendencies
Alvarez's best pitch is his hard fastball in the 90-plus mph range. He throws a good curveball as well, but the key to his success could be the development of his changeup. If he comes up with a nasty one to complement his fastball and curve, the White Sox believe he'll cause headaches all through the American League. He has good command of his pitches and an air of confidence on the mound. Alvarez has achieved some notoriety as a strikeout pitcher, leading the Rangers' organization with 143 strikeouts in 143⅔ innings in 1988. Last season, his total dipped to 98 in 164⅔ innings.

Fielding/Holding Runners
A very confident player, Alvarez isn't hesitant to go after a ball hit his way. His move to the bases is sound.

Projection
Alvarez will report to the White Sox's spring camp with a legitimate shot at a starting job. Considering his age, an assignment to Class AAA Vancouver wouldn't be a setback.

Career Statistics and Major League Equivalencies

	G	IP	W	L	R	ER	H	HR	SO	BB	ERA
1987 Gastonia (South Atlantic League-Class A)	8	32	1	5	24	23	39	5	19	23	6.47
1987 Sarasota Rangers (Gulf Coast League-Rookie)	10	44⅔	2	5	29	26	41	6	46	21	5.24
1988 Gastonia (South Atlantic League-Class A)	23	127	4	11	63	42	113	5	134	49	2.98
1988 Oklahoma City (American Association-Class AAA)	5	16⅔	1	1	8	7	17	2	9	6	3.78
1988 Major League Equivalency	5	16⅔			10	8	19	2	9	7	4.32
1989 Charlotte (Florida State League-Class A)	13	81	7	4	29	19	68	2	51	21	2.11
1989 Tulsa (Texas League-Class AA)	7	48	2	2	14	11	40	1	29	16	2.06
1989 Texas (American League)	1	0	0	1	3	3	3	2	0	2	
1989 Birmingham (Southern League-Class AA)	6	35⅔	2	1	12	12	32	2	18	16	3.03
1989 Major League Equivalency	13	83⅔			29	26	78	3	45	36	2.80

Interpretation
The 1989 Major League Equivalency gives Alvarez a lower hits-allowed total than innings pitched, an exceptional mark for someone who pitched last season at age 19. The steady decline in strikeouts also is reflected in the MLEs.

ALEX SANCHEZ

Toronto Blue Jays
Pitcher
Blue Jays' First-Round Pick, June 1987 Draft

Personal
Height: 6-2   Weight: 190
Throws right, bats right
Born: April 8, 1966

School: UCLA

Ratings

	Present	Future
Fastball	5	6
Curve	5	6
Changeup	3	5
Control	4	5
Stamina	4	5
Poise	4	5
Fielding	4	5

Rating Key
7 Outstanding
6 Major League Caliber, High
5 Major League Caliber
4 Minor League Caliber, High
3 Minor League Caliber
2 Below Average
1 Poor

General
Sanchez has met the challenge at each minor league level after being drafted 17th overall in 1987. Pitching mostly at Class AAA Syracuse last season, he received All-Star recognition for the third straight year and was voted the International League's Most Valuable Pitcher. He tied for the league lead with 13 victories, ranked second with 141 strikeouts and earned his first promotion to the big leagues. Sanchez has a desirable makeup for a starting pitcher, with a positive attitude and a good work ethic. He has ranked among his league's departmental leaders wherever he's pitched and won strikeout crowns in the Class A New York-Penn League (1987) and Class AA Southern League (1988).

Pitching Tendencies
Sanchez has overmatched minor league hitters with two major league-caliber pitches. His fastball is well respected, but it's his curveball that creates the most headaches. He is working diligently to add a changeup to his attack, but he hasn't learned to throw the pitch consistently for strikes. Sanchez has allowed only 6.6 hits per nine innings in his minor league career and last season limited International League hitters to a .200 batting average. Scouts say he got away with some mistakes that he wouldn't have in the majors, but experience should make him smarter.

Fielding/Holding Runners
Runners have taken liberties against Sanchez (16 of 22 steals against him in 1989) but he's developing a quicker move. He is an adequate fielder.

Projection
Sanchez likely will return to Syracuse to start the 1990 season and appears destined to compete for a spot in the Blue Jays' starting rotation in 1991.

Career Statistics and Major League Equivalencies

	G	IP	W	L	R	ER	H	HR	SO	BB	ERA
1987 St. Catharines (New York-Penn League-Class A)	17	95⅓	8	3	33	28	92	3	116	38	2.64
1987 Myrtle Beach (South Atlantic League-Class A)	1	3	0	0	1	1	2	1	4	0	3.00
1988 Knoxville (Southern League-Class AA)	24	149⅓	12	5	56	42	100	8	166	74	2.53
1988 Syracuse (International League-Class AAA)	10	57⅔	4	3	26	23	47	8	57	43	3.59
1988 Major League Equivalency	34	207			102	81	166	20	204	160	3.52
1989 Syracuse (International League-Class AAA)	28	169⅔	13	7	68	59	125	14	141	74	3.13
1989 Toronto (American League)	4	11⅓	0	1	13	13	16	1	4	14	10.03
1989 Major League Equivalency	32	181⅓			93	82	153	18	133	112	4.07

Interpretation
The system doesn't believe Sanchez is quite ready to break into the Blue Jays' rotation. His walk totals in the Major League Equivalencies are high. When the MLE adjusts for his 1989 Toronto line, it fears much the same will happen.

HOWARD FARMER

Montreal Expos
Pitcher
Expos' Seventh-Round Pick, June 1987 Draft

General
Farmer has an outstanding arm, throwing a fastball and curve that already are major league caliber. Pitching virtually the entire season at Class AA Jacksonville in 1989, he ranked third in the Southern League in earned-run average, strikeouts and innings pitched. That earned him a promotion to Class AAA Indianapolis, where he won his only start and didn't allow an earned run. Had it not been for Farmer's good spring camp last season, the Expos would have sent him to A ball for a third year. He already had proved himself at that level in 1988, pitching nearly as well as Tom Gordon in the Midwest League. Farmer, however, who was 15-7, was left off the league's All-Star team in favor of Gordon, a hard-luck 7-5 pitcher. Scouts say Farmer just needs seasoning to be ready to pitch in the majors.

Pitching Tendencies
Farmer can throw his bread-and-butter pitches, a curveball and 90-plus mph fastball, for strikes. Last season, he started throwing a slider the organization wants him to develop as his out pitch. He has good control, with a strikeouts-to-walks ratio of nearly 3-1 the last two seasons, and doesn't surrender a lot of hits (fewer than six hits per nine innings at Jacksonville in 1989). Farmer has the size and stamina to be a dominant starter, having hurled nearly 200 innings in each of his last two years.

Fielding/Holding Runners
Farmer is an excellent fielder who turned seven double plays in 1988 to lead Midwest League pitchers. He does a good job of holding runners.

Projection
Farmer has an outside shot at a major league job in 1990 but likely will pitch at Class AAA Indianapolis. Look for him in Montreal in 1991.

Personal
Height: 6-2 Weight: 185
Throws right, bats right
Born: January 18, 1966

School: Jackson State in Jackson, Miss.

Ratings

	Present	Future
Fastball	4	5
Curve	4	5
Changeup	3	5
Control	5	6
Stamina	5	5
Poise	4	5
Fielding	5	6

Rating Key
7 Outstanding
6 Major League Caliber, High
5 Major League Caliber
4 Minor League Caliber, High
3 Minor League Caliber
2 Below Average
1 Poor

Career Statistics and Major League Equivalencies

	G	IP	W	L	R	ER	H	HR	SO	BB	ERA
1987 Jamestown (New York-Penn League-Class A)	15	96⅓	0	0	42	35	93	4	63	30	15.43
1988 Rockford (Midwest League-Class A)	27	193⅔	15	7	70	54	153	10	145	58	2.51
1989 Jacksonville (Southern League-Class AA)	26	184	12	9	59	45	122	5	151	50	2.20
1989 Indianapolis (American Association-Class AAA)	1	7	1	0	1	0	3	0	3	3	0.00
1989 Major League Equivalency	26	184			73	55	138	6	144	62	2.69

Interpretation
Farmer was too much for the Class AA Southern League hitters last season, and the Major League Equivalency translates that into success at the big-league level. He has a good, balanced statistical profile the Expos will take note of, especially after losing three starters to free agency.

ROGER SALKELD

Seattle Mariners
Pitcher
Mariners' First-Round Pick, June 1989 Draft

Personal
Height: 6-5 Weight: 215
Throws right, bats right
Born: March 6, 1971

School: Saugus High
in Saugus, Calif.

Ratings

	Present	Future
Fastball	5	6
Curve	3	5
Changeup	3	5
Control	4	5
Stamina	4	6
Poise	4	5
Fielding	4	5

Rating Key
7 Outstanding
6 Major League Caliber, High
5 Major League Caliber
4 Minor League Caliber, High
3 Minor League Caliber
2 Below Average
1 Poor

General
He has pitched just 42 innings for a short-season Class A team, but Salkeld already is considered to have the best arm in the Seattle organization. The third pick overall in the 1989 draft, Salkeld blew away Northwest League hitters after joining the Mariners' Bellingham affiliate almost midway through the season. In eight games, the big right-hander posted a 1.29 earned-run average and fanned 55 batters. Still a teen-ager, he is expected to become only more overpowering as he physically and mentally matures.

Pitching Tendencies
Salkeld is a hard-throwing strikeout pitcher with excellent control. His best pitch is a fastball clocked in the low 90s, and he keeps hitters off-balance with a good curveball and decent changeup. Although his fastball is plenty hard, it's also fairly straight, which wasn't a problem at the high school level. The Mariners want him to get more movement on the pitch and to overcome a tendency to overthrow his changeup. When he becomes more adept at moving the ball around the strike zone (part of the learning process for a hurler his age), he'll be tough to hit even when he doesn't have his best velocity. With the good control he's shown so far (168 batters faced, 10 walks in 1989), that adjustment should come easily.

Fielding/Holding Runners
Salkeld is a good athlete who helps himself in the field. Considering that a minimum of runners have reached base, he has displayed a rather quick pickoff move to first base.

Projection
Salkeld is on schedule to pitch at Class A San Bernardino in 1990 and probably is three years away from the majors.

Career Statistics

	G	IP	W	L	R	ER	H	HR	SO	BB	ERA
1989 Bellingham (Northwest League-Class A)	8	42	2	2	17	6	27	0	55	10	1.29

(Projections unavailable because player has not competed at Class AA or Class AAA levels)

CURT SCHILLING

Baltimore Orioles
Pitcher
Boston Red Sox's Second-Round Pick, January 1986 Draft

General
Schilling has nothing left to prove at the minor league level. In each of his last three seasons, he has pitched more than 165 innings. He tied for the lead in victories, shutouts and complete games in the Class AAA International League in 1989 and led the circuit in innings pitched. Now comes crunch time. Schilling has pitched with Baltimore in each of the last two seasons, including a valuable five-game stint during the divisional dogfight with Toronto in 1989. The Orioles like his stamina and durability, and he'll likely pitch under considerable scrutiny this spring. He was acquired from the Boston Red Sox as part of the Mike Boddicker deal in 1988.

Pitching Tendencies
Schilling's reputation as an aggressive power pitcher is well-founded. He comes right at hitters from his three-quarters motion, challenging them with his hard stuff. He's hardly a one-pitch wonder, however. Schilling is working to become the complete pitcher, developing a slider and changeup he'll mix up with a forkball. He has fairly good command of his pitches, although he needs to throw his breaking ball and changeup more consistently for strikes. Careless walks have not been a problem. With his size, durability and makeup, he could be a front-line starter.

Fielding/Holding Runners
Schilling is a good fielder with an exceptionally quick move to both home plate and first base. At Rochester last season, opponents stole only four bases against him in 18 attempts.

Projection
Schilling will be pitching for a spot in the Orioles' starting rotation in 1990.

Personal
Height: 6-4   Weight: 205
Throws right, bats right
Born: November 14, 1966

School: Yavapai Junior College in Prescott, Ariz.

Ratings

	Present	Future
Fastball	5	5
Curve	4	5
Changeup	4	5
Control	4	5
Stamina	5	5
Poise	5	5
Fielding	5	5

Rating Key
7 Outstanding
6 Major League Caliber, High
5 Major League Caliber
4 Minor League Caliber, High
3 Minor League Caliber
2 Below Average
1 Poor

Career Statistics and Major League Equivalencies

	G	IP	W	L	R	ER	H	HR	SO	BB	ERA
1986 Elmira (New York-Penn League-Class A)	16	93⅔	7	3	34	27	92	3	75	30	2.59
1987 Greensboro (South Atlantic League-Class A)	29	184	8	15	96	78	179	10	189	65	3.82
1988 New Britain (Eastern League-Class AA)	17	106	8	5	44	35	91	3	62	40	2.97
1988 Charlotte (Southern League-Class AA)	7	45⅓	5	2	19	16	36	3	30	23	3.18
1988 Baltimore (American League)	4	14⅔	0	3	19	16	22	3	4	10	9.82
1988 Major League Equivalency	28	166			103	84	176	11	95	97	4.55
1989 Rochester (International League-Class AAA)	27	185⅓	13	11	76	66	176	11	109	59	3.21
1989 Baltimore (American League)	5	8⅔	0	1	6	6	10	2	6	3	6.23
1989 Major League Equivalency	32	194			100	88	214	15	114	79	4.08

Interpretation
Schilling's Major League Equivalency improves from 1988 to 1989, reflecting his progress through the minors. He's still surrendering too many hits, however, and in Baltimore he was victimized by the home run as well.

KIKI JONES

Los Angeles Dodgers
Pitcher
Dodgers' First-Round Pick, June 1989 Draft

Personal
Height: 5-11   Weight: 170
Throws right, bats right
Born: June 8, 1970

School: Hillsborough High
in Tampa, Fla.

Ratings

	Present	Future
Fastball	5	6
Curve	4	5
Changeup	3	5
Control	4	5
Stamina	4	5
Poise	4	5
Fielding	4	5

Rating Key
7 Outstanding
6 Major League Caliber, High
5 Major League Caliber
4 Minor League Caliber, High
3 Minor League Caliber
2 Below Average
1 Poor

General
As scouts followed Jones before the 1989 amateur draft, they couldn't believe a player his size could throw as hard as he did. The list of believers now includes the entire Pioneer League. Playing for the Dodgers' Great Falls rookie club, Jones overmatched the league on his way to an 8-0 record, 1.58 earned-run average and league All-Star honors. The live-wire righthander was drafted 15th overall out of Tampa's Hillsborough High, a school that produced such major leaguers as Dwight Gooden, Gary Sheffield and Floyd Youmans. He is an outstanding athlete who starred at the prep level as both a pitcher (22-6 over three seasons) and hard-hitting shortstop (.437 as a senior).

Pitching Tendencies
Jones' pitches have excellent velocity and his fastball explodes across the plate—perhaps because hitters don't expect the short righthander to be throwing Gooden-like gas. He has a good curveball, but his changeup needed special attention in the winter instructional league. The 19-year-old Jones needs to improve his knowledge of pitching, but the Dodgers believe that will come through experience.

Fielding/Holding Runners
Jones is athletically gifted and takes advantage of his high school experience at shortstop to make good plays coming off the mound. He needs to work on his pickoff move to first, primarily because he hasn't allowed many runners to reach base. Opponents did, however, steal only five bases in nine attempts last season.

Projection
Jones would benefit in 1990 playing for a full-season Class A club, most likely at Bakersfield. At most, he is three years away from the major leagues.

Career Statistics

	G	IP	W	L	R	ER	H	HR	SO	BB	ERA
1989 Great Falls (Pioneer League-Rookie)	12	62⅔	8	0	15	11	40	2	63	21	1.58

(Projections unavailable because player has not competed at Class AA or Class AAA levels)

RAFAEL VALDEZ

San Diego Padres
Pitcher
Padres' Second-Round Pick, March 1985 Dominican Draft

Personal
Height: 5-11 Weight: 165
Bats right, throws right
Born: December 17, 1967

Ratings

	Present	Future
Fastball	5	6
Curve	3	5
Changeup	3	5
Control	3	5
Stamina	4	5
Poise	4	5
Fielding	5	5

Rating Key
7 Outstanding
6 Major League Caliber, High
5 Major League Caliber
4 Minor League Caliber, High
3 Minor League Caliber
2 Below Average
1 Poor

General
Valdez is a converted infielder who has been pitching only for two seasons. Nevertheless, he was named the Padres' minor league Pitcher of the Year in 1989 after posting a combined 15-5 record and 2.19 earned-run average at the Class A and AA levels. At Class A Riverside, Valdez simply overmatched California League hitters, hurling a perfect game, two two-hitters and a three-hitter all before August. Promoted to Class AA Wichita, he posted a perfect record and 1.94 ERA in six starts and won one game in the Texas League championship series. He could arrive in the big leagues way ahead of schedule if he continues his astonishing development.

Pitching Tendencies
Valdez has an outstanding arm, throwing a 90-mph fastball that has good movement and location. While he learns the proper pitching mechanics, he is developing the curveball and changeup he didn't need when he dominated hitters with heat at the Class A level. If he refines those pitches, he could post numbers in the majors similar to his 1989 figures: 117 hits allowed and 163 strikeouts in 185 innings. He has twice as many career strikeouts as walks, a positive sign given his limited pitching experience.

Fielding/Holding Runners
Originally signed as a shortstop, Valdez the pitcher displays the same kind of handiwork with a glove that made him a solid defensive prospect at short. His pickoff move is improving but still needs work.

Projection
Some within the Padres' organization believe Valdez could start the 1990 season in the majors. Another year of seasoning could only help his development, however, and he'd get that at Class AAA Las Vegas.

Career Statistics and Major League Equivalencies

	G	IP	W	L	R	ER	H	HR	SO	BB	ERA
1988 Charleston (South Atlantic League-Class A)	28	152⅓	11	4	42	38	117	6	100	46	2.25
1989 Riverside (California League-Class A)	21	143⅓	10	5	40	36	89	6	137	58	2.26
1989 Wichita (Texas League-Class AA)	6	41⅔	5	0	10	9	28	1	26	24	1.94
1989 Major League Equivalency	6	41⅔			10	9	29	1	25	25	1.94

Interpretation
Since Wichita is a hitters' park, Valdez's Major League Equivalency line is virtually identical to his Class AA totals. Valdez has held the upper hand in every league he's pitched in thus far, although his sample size of innings is quite small when applied to the MLE.

JOSE DeJESUS

Kansas City Royals
Pitcher
Signed by Royals as a Non-Drafted Free Agent, May 1983

Personal
Height: 6-5   Weight: 175
Throws right, bats right
Born: January 6, 1965

School: Luis Munoz Iglesias High in Puerto Rico

Ratings

	Present	Future
Fastball	5	6
Curve	4	5
Changeup	4	5
Control	3	5
Stamina	4	5
Poise	4	5
Fielding	4	5

Rating Key
7 Outstanding
6 Major League Caliber, High
5 Major League Caliber
4 Minor League Caliber, High
3 Minor League Caliber
2 Below Average
1 Poor

General
At least one scout rated DeJesus the top pitching prospect in the American Association in 1989. He has the best fastball in the Kansas City organization, and the Royals have considered moving him from the starting rotation to the bullpen. He'd open a lot of eyes as a closer, partly because his pitches sometimes have a mind of their own. DeJesus pitched both ways at Class AAA Omaha in 1989 and appeared in three games with Kansas City down the stretch. He prefers pitching as a starter and has the arm to go a full nine innings. Since the start of his minor league career in 1983, he has allowed fewer hits than innings pitched each season.

Pitching Tendencies
Although he has pitched in the minors for seven seasons, DeJesus is still classified by most scouts as a thrower instead of a pitcher. He has a blistering fastball of 90-plus mph but doesn't always know where it's going. Ditto for his hard, moving slider. DeJesus walked a league-high 98 batters in 145⅓ innings last season at Omaha, which partly explains his 8-11 record. Once he finds his groove, he can be overpowering. He fanned 158 at Omaha to rank second in the league and led all American Association starters with an average of 9.75 strikeouts per nine innings. Opponents managed only a .214 batting average. If DeJesus matures and acquires better command of his pitches, scouts say he'll advance to the major league ranks.

Fielding/Holding Runners
DeJesus is adequate defensively and has an average move to the bases.

Projection
DeJesus likely will be competing for a spot in the major leagues in 1990—if he throws strikes consistently.

Career Statistics and Major League Equivalencies

	G	IP	W	L	R	ER	H	HR	SO	BB	ERA
1983 Sarasota (Gulf Coast League-Rookie)	10	24	1	2	18	11	17	0	10	17	4.13
1984 Charleston (South Atlantic League-Class A)	27	163	11	2	98	80	152	8	85	69	4.42
1985 Fort Myers (Florida State League-Class A)	27	129⅔	8	10	70	62	119	9	94	59	4.30
1986 Fort Myers (Florida State League-Class A)	22	110	4	9	64	42	87	4	97	82	3.44
1987 Memphis (Southern League-Class AA)	25	130⅓	4	11	78	65	106	8	79	99	4.49
1987 Major League Equivalency	25	130⅓			76	64	107	8	75	97	4.42
1988 Memphis (Southern League-Class AA)	20	116	9	9	56	50	88	5	149	70	3.88
1988 Omaha (American Association-Class AAA)	7	49⅔	2	3	22	19	44	1	57	14	3.44
1988 Kansas City (American League)	2	2⅔	0	1	10	8	6	0	2	5	27.00
1988 Major League Equivalency	29	168⅓			105	92	155	7	198	107	4.92
1989 Omaha (American Association-Class AAA)	31	145⅓	8	11	78	61	112	9	158	98	3.78
1989 Kansas City (American League)	3	8	0	0	4	4	7	1	2	8	4.50
1989 Major League Equivalency	34	153⅓			101	80	134	12	152	129	4.70

Interpretation
DeJesus' Major League Equivalencies do not reflect any reasonable progression. His strikeout and walk totals indicate that his fastball, while overpowering, has yet to be harnessed.

WILLIE BANKS

Minnesota Twins
Pitcher
Twins' First-Round Pick, June 1987 Draft

Personal
Height: 6-1 Weight: 190
Throws right, bats right
Born: February 27, 1969

School: St. Anthony's High in Jersey City, N.J.

Ratings

	Present	Future
Fastball	5	6
Curve	4	5
Changeup	3	5
Control	2	5
Stamina	4	5
Poise	4	5
Fielding	4	5

Rating Key
7 Outstanding
6 Major League Caliber, High
5 Major League Caliber
4 Minor League Caliber, High
3 Minor League Caliber
2 Below Average
1 Poor

General
Banks is scheduled to reach Minnesota after the first wave of young pitching talent that is just beginning to arrive from the farm. No other arrival is more eagerly anticipated, however. The third player selected in the 1987 draft, Banks showed better control of his pitches and his immediate future as he began making the transition last season from thrower to pitcher. He made steady progress at Class A Visalia in the California League, pitching a no-hitter, one-hitter and two-hitter among his 12 victories. He captured the league strikeout crown, tied for the lead with four shutouts and ranked fourth with seven complete games. With older prospects ahead of Banks, the Twins will allow him time to refine his skills.

Pitching Tendencies
Banks' consistent 90-plus mph fastball is reason enough for the Twins to be excited, but he rounds out a promising three-pitch arsenal with a good curve and a changeup that is steadily improving. Another good sign: Banks is learning that pitch selection, command and the other nuances are vital to his developing to full potential. He still has control problems associated with youth (24 wild pitches in 1989) but walked far fewer batters in 1989 while retaining a strikeout-per-inning ratio. California League hitters batted just .197 against him.

Fielding/Holding Runners
Banks is a good athlete but is prone to commit errors in the field (23 errors in three seasons). He is tough to run against, with California League opponents stealing only 13 bases in 28 attempts against him.

Projection
Banks is ticketed to pitch for Class AA Orlando in 1990 and likely is two years away from Minnesota.

Career Statistics

	G	IP	W	L	R	ER	H	HR	SO	BB	ERA
1987 Elizabethton (Appalachian League-Rookie)	13	65⅔	1	8	71	51	73	3	71	62	6.99
1988 Kenosha (Midwest League-Class A)	24	125⅔	10	10	73	52	109	3	113	107	3.72
1989 Visalia (California League-Class A)	27	174	12	9	70	50	122	5	173	85	2.59
1989 Orlando (Southern League-Class AA)	1	7	1	0	4	4	10	0	9	0	5.14

(Projections unavailable due to player's limited experience at Class AA level)

JASON GRIMSLEY

Philadelphia Phillies
Pitcher
Phillies' 11th-Round Pick, June 1985 Draft

Personal
Height: 6-3 Weight: 180
Throws right, bats right
Born: August 7, 1967

School: Tarkington High in Cleveland, Tex.

Ratings

	Present	Future
Fastball	4	6
Curve	4	6
Changeup	3	5
Control	2	5
Stamina	4	5
Poise	4	5
Fielding	4	5

Rating Key
7 Outstanding
6 Major League Caliber, High
5 Major League Caliber
4 Minor League Caliber, High
3 Minor League Caliber
2 Below Average
1 Poor

General
Grimsley throws major league heat but has struggled with his control at five minor league stops and a September 1989 tour with the Phillies. In four starts for Philadelphia, he walked 19 batters in 18⅓ innings and was 1-3 with a 5.89 earned-run average. Prior to his promotion, Grimsley had shown signs of settling down. In his last month at Class AA Reading, he went 5-0 with a 1.91 ERA in six starts. Overall, he ranked among the Eastern League leaders in victories, ERA, strikeouts, innings pitched and complete games. He was selected the Phillies' 1989 minor league Pitcher of the Year.

Pitching Tendencies
Grimsley has an above-average curveball to complement a fastball he throws in the low 90s. He is sometimes guilty of trying to overthrow, and that's when he encounters control difficulties (315 walks in 458⅔ minor league innings). Scouts say he doesn't bend his back leg as much as he should, which, once corrected, would allow him to hit his spots—and throw even harder. He needs to find the right release point in his delivery and go from there. When he's on, Grimsley is tough to hit. At Reading in 1989, he pitched a no-hitter against Harrisburg and a two-hitter against the Albany Yankees, the Eastern League champions. The Phillies are excited about his stuff; it's just a matter of the big right-hander learning to throw it over the plate.

Fielding/Holding Baserunners
A former high school shortstop, Grimsley is an adept fielder. His move to first base is average.

Projection
Grimsley likely will begin the 1990 season at Class AAA Scranton and has a chance to return to the major leagues before year's end.

Career Statistics and Major League Equivalencies

	G	IP	W	L	R	ER	H	HR	SO	BB	ERA
1985 Bend (Northwest League-Class A)	6	11⅓	0	1	21	17	12	0	10	25	13.50
1986 Utica (New York-Penn League-Class A)	14	64⅔	1	10	61	46	63	3	46	77	6.40
1987 Spartanburg (South Atlantic League-Class A)	23	88⅓	7	4	48	31	59	4	98	54	3.16
1988 Clearwater (Florida State League-Class A)	16	101⅓	4	7	48	42	80	2	90	37	3.73
1988 Reading (Eastern League-Class AA)	5	21⅓	1	3	19	17	20	1	14	13	7.17
1988 Major League Equivalency	5	21⅓			21	19	22	1	13	15	8.02
1989 Reading (Eastern League-Class AA)	26	172	11	8	65	57	121	8	134	109	2.98
1989 Philadelphia (National League)	4	18⅓	1	3	13	12	19	2	7	19	5.89
1989 Major League Equivalency	30	190⅓			87	77	150	17	135	143	3.64

Interpretation
The strikeouts are there, but few pitchers would succeed at the major league level with a walk total like the one Grimsley shows in his 1989 Major League Equivalency.

TOMMY GREENE

Atlanta Braves
Pitcher
Braves' First-Round Pick, June 1985 Draft

Personal
Height: 6-5 Weight: 225
Throws right, bats right
Born: April 6, 1967

School: Whiteville High in Whiteville, N.C.

Ratings

	Present	Future
Fastball	4	5
Curve	4	5
Changeup	4	5
Control	4	5
Stamina	4	5
Poise	4	5
Fielding	4	5

Rating Key
7 Outstanding
6 Major League Caliber, High
5 Major League Caliber
4 Minor League Caliber, High
3 Minor League Caliber
2 Below Average
1 Poor

General
Greene's progress has been held up by his inconsistency through five minor league campaigns. On some nights, the big righthander is virtually unhittable. When he doesn't have his best stuff, he's susceptible to a beating. Greene hasn't matured as quickly as the Braves had hoped, although he did appear more focused in his second season at Class AAA Richmond in 1989. His record was below .500 for the second straight year, but he showed enough overall improvement to earn four starts in a September trial with the Braves. He had his good stuff on September 21, pitching a three-hit complete-game shutout over Houston. Greene was named Atlanta's minor league Pitcher of the Year in 1986 and was the 14th player chosen overall in the June 1985 draft.

Pitching Tendencies
Greene has a quality fastball, curve and changeup, but has problems at times with command of all three. When he gets into a jam, he sometimes has difficulty pitching his way out. Scouts predict he'll shake those troubles when he sharpens his mental approach and improves his overall knowledge of pitching. On pure ability, Greene rates among the best prospects. He doesn't walk an excessive number of hitters and has averaged nearly 130 strikeouts in his last two seasons. At 6-5, 225 pounds, he has the size to be a durable starter.

Fielding/Holding Runners
Greene is a good athlete who was errorless in 26 games at Richmond in 1989. His move to the bases is only adequate (International League opponents stole 20 bases in 23 attempts last season).

Projection
Greene will get the opportunity in spring training to win a spot on the Braves' 1990 opening-day roster.

Career Statistics and Major League Equivalencies

	G	IP	W	L	R	ER	H	HR	SO	BB	ERA
1985 Pulaski (Appalachian League-Rookie)	12	50⅔	2	5	45	43	49	7	32	27	7.64
1986 Sumter (South Atlantic League-Class A)	28	174⅔	11	7	95	91	162	17	169	82	4.89
1987 Greenville (Southern League-Class AA)	23	142⅓	11	8	60	52	103	13	101	66	3.29
1987 Major League Equivalency	23	142⅓			66	57	110	14	96	72	3.60
1988 Richmond (International League-Class AAA)	29	177⅓	7	17	98	94	169	10	130	70	4.77
1988 Major League Equivalency	29	177⅓			122	117	192	12	124	87	5.94
1989 Richmond (International League-Class AAA)	26	152	9	12	74	61	136	9	125	50	3.61
1989 Atlanta (National League)	4	26⅓	1	2	12	12	22	5	17	6	4.10
1989 Major League Equivalency	30	178⅓			109	92	181	17	136	71	4.64

Interpretation
Greene's Major League Equivalencies show he hasn't kept his hits allowed under control since his 1987 season in the Class AA Southern League. His strikeouts-to-walks ratio has improved, however. In a brief trial with the Braves at the end of the 1989 season, Greene exceeded expectations set down by his Richmond MLE. He kept the hits down, a sign that he may have broken through the barrier during the course of his Class AAA season.

JOHN ERICKS

St. Louis Cardinals
Pitcher
Cardinals' First-Round Pick, June 1988 Draft

General
Ericks is the top pitching prospect in the Cardinals' system but has been kept in the low minors because of erratic control (128 walks in 208⅓ minor league innings). He pitched all year at Class A Savannah in 1989, but if he learns to throw strikes consistently, he'll rise quickly through the organization.

Pitching Tendencies
Ericks is a classic strikeout pitcher, averaging more than one strikeout per inning in his career. As a collegian at Illinois, he set a single-season school record by fanning 108 batters (in only 87⅓ innings) and tied a single-game mark with 18 strikeouts. At Savannah in 1989, he topped all minor league pitchers with 211 strikeouts and ranked among the leaders with a 2.04 earned-run average. Ericks has a blazing fastball that tops out the radar guns, but he hasn't completely mastered the curve or changeup. No matter. If he's throwing strikes, all he needs is his fastball. Scouts believe few batters will hit it, even at the major league level. To go with that smoke, he has the size and durability to be a dominant pitcher. The key to his success will be his ability to throw his fastball for strikes. The Cardinals have no doubts he'll be able to do that—eventually.

Fielding/Holding Runners
Ericks is a fairly good fielder, especially for a pitcher his size. He does need to work on holding runners and on his pickoff move to first. At times, he suffers from a lack of concentration.

Projection
Ericks likely will open the 1990 season at a high-level Class A club, such as St. Petersburg, or at Class AA Arkansas. He is probably two years away from the major leagues.

Personal
Height: 6-7   Weight: 220
Throws right, bats right
Born: September 16, 1967

School: Illinois

Ratings

	Present	Future
Fastball	5	6
Curve	4	5
Changeup	4	5
Control	3	5
Stamina	4	5
Poise	4	5
Fielding	4	5

Rating Key
7 Outstanding
6 Major League Caliber, High
5 Major League Caliber
4 Minor League Caliber, High
3 Minor League Caliber
2 Below Average
1 Poor

Career Statistics

	G	IP	W	L	R	ER	H	HR	SO	BB	ERA
1988 Johnson City (Appalachian League-Rookie)	9	41	3	2	20	17	27	1	41	27	3.73
1989 Savannah (South Atlantic League-Class A)	28	167⅓	11	10	59	38	90	4	211	101	2.04

(Projections unavailable because player has not competed at Class AA or Class AAA levels)

MEL ROJAS

Montreal Expos
Pitcher
Signed by Expos as a Non-Drafted Free Agent, November 1985

Personal
Height: 5-11   Weight: 165
Throws right, bats right
Born: December 10, 1966

School: Santo Domingo, Dominican Republic

Ratings

	Present	Future
Fastball	5	6
Curve	3	5
Changeup	3	5
Control	4	5
Stamina	4	5
Poise	4	5
Fielding	3	5

Rating Key
7 Outstanding
6 Major League Caliber, High
5 Major League Caliber
4 Minor League Caliber, High
3 Minor League Caliber
2 Below Average
1 Poor

General
Rojas pitched as a starter and reliever in 1989 after working strictly as a starter in his first three seasons in the Montreal farm system. The Expos aren't pressuring him to fill one role or the other, allowing him time to find his niche. At Class AA Jacksonville last season, he allowed only 62 hits in 112 innings (an exceptional average of under five hits every nine innings) while striking out 104 batters. He started 12 games and relieved in 22, notching five saves with 17 games finished. Rojas has displayed poise under pressure and doesn't get rattled when things don't go his way. He is a nephew of the Alou brothers and was signed by his uncle Jesus.

Pitching Tendencies
Rojas has an outstanding fastball, which is his primary strikeout pitch. He has a good forkball and is developing a slider, but he needs better command and consistency with the forkball and his hard stuff. Rojas did pitch with better control at times last season but still averaged 4.5 walks every nine innings. At 5-11, 165 pounds, he is not physically overpowering or intimidating, so his velocity surprises hitters. His big-league timetable hinges upon how quickly he refines his breaking pitches.

Fielding/Holding Runners
Rojas needs some seasoning in most phases of his game. He has shown some defensive skills and does an adequate job of holding runners, but there is room for improvement in both areas.

Projection
Rojas seems destined to begin the 1990 season at Class AAA Indianapolis, where he likely will pitch as a starter and reliever. If the Expos like him in one particular role, he could join them before year's end.

Career Statistics and Major League Equivalencies

	G	IP	W	L	R	ER	H	HR	SO	BB	ERA
1986 Bradenton Expos (Gulf Coast League-Rookie)	13	55⅓	4	5	39	30	63	0	34	37	4.88
1987 Burlington (Midwest League-Class A)	25	158⅔	8	9	84	67	146	10	100	67	3.80
1988 Rockford (Midwest League-Class A)	12	81	6	4	38	28	88	5	63	21	2.45
1988 West Palm Beach (Florida State League-Class A)	2	5	1	0	2	2	4	1	4	1	3.60
1989 Jacksonville (Southern League-Class AA)	34	112	10	7	39	31	62	1	104	57	2.49
1989 Major League Equivalency	34	112			49	39	71	1	103	69	3.13

Interpretation
Rojas' Major League Equivalency is particularly kind. It shows a pitcher who walks far too many batters yet still manages to control the game by limiting the number of hits he allows.

ROBB NEN

Texas Rangers
Pitcher
Rangers' 32nd-Round Pick, June 1987 Draft

Personal
Height: 6-3 Weight: 175
Throws right, bats right
Born: November 28, 1969

School: Los Alamitos High
in Los Alamitos, Calif.

Ratings

	Present	Future
Fastball	4	6
Curve	3	5
Changeup	4	5
Control	3	5
Stamina	4	5
Poise	4	5
Fielding	4	5

Rating Key
7 Outstanding
6 Major League Caliber, High
5 Major League Caliber
4 Minor League Caliber, High
3 Minor League Caliber
2 Below Average
1 Poor

General
His 1988 season had been nearly disastrous: a 4-10 record, 8.11 earned-run average and 90 walks in 96⅔ innings. But to Robb Nen, that was ancient history in 1989. He was a changed man at Class A Gastonia, pitching with confidence and poise that was noticed league-wide. His fastball was something that wasn't easily detected—by hitters, that is. Nen struck out 146 batters (tops in the Rangers' farm system) and bounced back with a 7-4 record. Already physically intimidating, Nen, just turned 20, could get even bigger. He has excellent work habits and is a competitor. He is the son of Dick Nen, the former big-league first baseman who played mostly with the Washington Senators.

Pitching Tendencies
Nen is the hardest thrower in the Rangers' organization. His fastball has good movement and pushes the radar gun into the mid-90s. What he needs is a breaking pitch to keep hitters off-balance. Other than the fastball, which he throws close to 90 percent of the time, Nen's only other good pitch is his changeup. He needs to polish his breaking pitch, which will have a bearing on his success at higher levels. If he can throw it for strikes, his fastball will be devastating. Last season, South Atlantic League hitters batted only .195 against Nen, whose 2.41 ERA ranked fourth in the league.

Fielding/Holding Runners
Nen is considered a good athlete, but he challenged for the league high by committing six errors in 1989. Runners were successful on 37 of 46 steals.

Projection
Nen likely will begin the 1990 season at the Rangers' top Class A team, Port Charlotte. He is two to three years away from Texas.

Career Statistics

	G	IP	W	L	R	ER	H	HR	SO	BB	ERA
1987 Sarasota Rangers (Gulf Coast League-Rookie)	2	2⅓	0	0	2	2	4	0	4	3	7.71
1988 Butte (Pioneer League-Rookie)	14	48⅓	4	5	55	47	65	4	30	45	8.75
1988 Gastonia (South Atlantic League-Class A)	14	48⅓	0	5	57	40	69	5	36	45	7.45
1989 Gastonia (South Atlantic League-Class A)	24	138⅓	7	4	47	37	96	7	146	76	2.41

(Projections unavailable because player has not competed at Class AA or Class AAA levels)

KEVIN APPIER

Kansas City Royals
Pitcher
Royals' First-Round Pick, June 1987 Draft

Personal
Height: 6-2 Weight: 180
Throws right, bats right
Born: December 6, 1967

School: Antelope Valley High in Lancaster, Calif.

Ratings

	Present	Future
Fastball	4	5
Curve	4	5
Changeup	4	5
Control	4	5
Stamina	4	5
Poise	4	5
Fielding	4	5

Rating Key
7 Outstanding
6 Major League Caliber, High
5 Major League Caliber
4 Minor League Caliber, High
3 Minor League Caliber
2 Below Average
1 Poor

General
He wasn't an instant success in the major leagues in 1989, but at the minor league level, Appier has consistently shown the promise associated with first-round draft picks. He was hardly the force some envisioned when summoned to Kansas City last June to fill in as a fifth starter. After five starts and one relief appearance, Appier was 1-4 with a 9.14 earned-run average and headed back to Class AAA Omaha on the Fourth of July. Clearly, many observers say, the call came too early. Appier had spent virtually the entire 1988 season at Class A Baseball City and has pitched in just 64 games in his minor league career. Scouts agree that he needs to acquire some innings before results can meet expectations.

Pitching Tendencies
Appier is a smooth-working righthander with excellent command of three quality pitches. He has a fastball that sinks, a hard slider and a split-fingered pitch with good movement. Appier's ability to pitch around the strike zone shows up annually in his low walk totals. He has averaged only 2.9 walks per nine innings in his career and is showing some promise as a strikeout pitcher. He'll likely get stronger by the time he completely matures and have the arm to add a little juice to his fastball.

Fielding/Holding Runners
Appier is a good athlete who fields his position well and has a decent move to the bases.

Projection
Some predict Appier will compete for a spot on the Royals' 1990 roster, but an extra year of seasoning at the Class AAA level wouldn't hurt his development.

Career Statistics and Major League Equivalencies

	G	IP	W	L	R	ER	H	HR	SO	BB	ERA
1987 Eugene (Northwest League-Class A)	15	77	8	2	43	26	81	2	72	29	3.04
1988 Baseball City (Florida State League-Class A)	24	147⅓	10	9	58	45	134	1	112	39	2.75
1988 Memphis (Southern League-Class AA)	3	19⅔	2	0	5	4	11	0	18	7	1.83
1988 Major League Equivalency	3	19⅔			6	5	12	0	17	8	2.29
1989 Omaha (American Association-Class AAA)	22	139	8	8	70	61	141	6	109	42	3.95
1989 Kansas City (American League)	6	21⅔	1	4	22	22	34	3	10	12	9.14
1989 Major League Equivalency	28	160⅔			108	97	194	10	113	64	5.43

Interpretation
Appier's rocky trial with the Royals in 1989 causes his Major League Equivalency to balloon. He's had enough stuff and control to taste success in the minors, although he still figures to give up close to one hit per inning.

MIKE LINSKEY

Baltimore Orioles
Pitcher
Orioles' Ninth-Round Pick, June 1988 Draft

Personal
Height: 6-5 Weight: 215
Throws left, bats left
Born: June 18, 1966

School: James Madison

Ratings

	Present	Future
Fastball	4	5
Curve	4	5
Changeup	4	5
Control	5	5
Stamina	5	5
Poise	5	6
Fielding	4	5

Rating Key
7 Outstanding
6 Major League Caliber, High
5 Major League Caliber
4 Minor League Caliber, High
3 Minor League Caliber
2 Below Average
1 Poor

General
Linskey continued the local-boy-makes-good script, earning honors last season as the Orioles' minor league Pitcher of the Year. A hometown favorite who was born and raised in Baltimore and still resides there, he has moved quickly through the Orioles' farm system, reaching Class AA Hagerstown less than a year after being drafted. After starting nine games for Class A Frederick to begin the season, Linskey finished up strong in the Eastern League, ranking third in shutouts, fourth (tie) in complete games and fifth (tie) in earned-run average. Overall, his combined 2.19 ERA was the best in the Orioles' farm system and he ranked second with 136 strikeouts.

Pitching Tendencies
Linskey has excellent command of a four-pitch repertoire: fastball, curve, knuckle curve and changeup. He's consistently around the strike zone, and last season ranked fifth among starters in the Eastern League with just 10.3 baserunners allowed per nine innings. He's the kind of big lefthander who takes command of a game, and he's already pitched a one-hitter and two three-hitters in just 1½ seasons. With all of his ability and stamina (10 complete games and 189⅓ innings pitched in 1989), Linskey could arrive in Baltimore in a hurry.

Fielding/Holding Runners
Linskey is a well-conditioned athlete who has good skills in the field. He has a quick delivery to the plate, particularly for his size, and a good move to first. Paired with excellent catching at Frederick, he had only one base stolen against him in eight attempts.

Projection
Linskey is ready to advance to Class AAA Rochester in 1990 and could be pitching in the majors before the season ends.

Career Statistics and Major League Equivalencies

	G	IP	W	L	R	ER	H	HR	SO	BB	ERA
1988 Erie (New York-Penn League-Class A)	10	55	3	3	24	19	46	3	50	18	3.11
1989 Frederick (Carolina League-Class A)	9	61⅓	2	2	7	6	47	0	46	16	0.88
1989 Hagerstown (Eastern League-Class AA)	18	128	10	6	45	40	108	6	90	35	2.81
1989 Major League Equivalency	18	128			59	52	126	8	86	46	3.66

Interpretation
Linskey's Major League Equivalency suggests he could pitch in the majors now. He has a balanced statistical profile, and his Class AA sample, although limited to one season, is large enough to be useful.

MARK GARDNER

Montreal Expos
Pitcher
Expos' Eighth-Round Pick, June 1985 Draft

Personal
Height: 6-1 Weight: 190
Throws right, bats right
Born: March 1, 1962

School: Fresno State

Ratings

	Present	Future
Fastball	5	5
Curve	5	6
Changeup	3	4
Control	5	6
Stamina	5	5
Poise	5	5
Fielding	4	5

Rating Key
7 Outstanding
6 Major League Caliber, High
5 Major League Caliber
4 Minor League Caliber, High
3 Minor League Caliber
2 Below Average
1 Poor

General
Pitching his first full season at the Class AAA level, Gardner was named the 1989 Most Valuable Pitcher in the American Association. He will play next year at 28, however, not exactly the ideal age to still be toiling in the minor leagues. Gardner's future with Montreal probably is in the bullpen, although he's worked strictly as a starter (save for two games) in five minor league campaigns. The Expos took a hard look in 1988, when he led all pitchers within the organization with 201 strikeouts while pitching at the Class AA and AAA levels. He topped the farm system again in 1989 with 175 strikeouts (the most by an American Association hurler in 15 years) and was called up twice by Montreal.

Pitching Tendencies
There is little doubt that Gardner is a strikeout pitcher. He has an outstanding overhand curveball and a fastball that rates slightly above average. Expos scouts say he is especially tough against righthanded hitters and has good control. He has quietly established himself as one of the toughest pitchers at the minor league level the last two years, surrendering an average of only 6.5 hits every nine innings and posting a combined 2.23 earned-run average. The fact that he's pitched consistently well and hasn't squawked about not getting a shot in Montreal speaks well for his composure.

Fielding/Holding Runners
Gardner has shown he's about average as a fielder. He has a good pickoff move to first base.

Projection
The Expos will give Gardner a serious look in spring training, most likely testing him as a reliever.

Career Statistics and Major League Equivalencies

	G	IP	W	L	R	ER	H	HR	SO	BB	ERA
1985 Jamestown (New York-Penn League-Class A)	3	13	0	0	4	4	9	0	16	4	2.77
1985 West Palm Beach (Florida State League-Class A)	10	60⅔	5	4	24	16	54	4	44	18	2.37
1986 Jacksonville (Southern League-Class AA)	29	168⅔	10	11	88	72	144	8	140	90	3.84
1986 Major League Equivalency	29	168⅔			82	67	142	7	133	84	3.57
1987 Indianapolis (American Association-Class AAA)	9	46	3	3	32	29	48	8	41	28	5.67
1987 Jacksonville (Southern League-Class AA)	17	101	4	6	50	47	101	13	78	42	4.19
1987 Major League Equivalency	26	147			84	78	154	22	113	72	4.78
1988 Jacksonville (Southern League-Class AA)	15	112⅓	6	3	24	20	72	4	130	36	1.60
1988 Indianapolis (American Association-Class AAA)	13	84⅓	4	2	30	26	65	5	71	32	2.77
1988 Major League Equivalency	24	158⅓			64	56	130	14	163	72	3.18
1989 Indianapolis (American Association-Class AAA)	24	163⅓	12	4	51	43	122	3	175	59	2.37
1989 Montreal (National League)	7	26⅓	0	3	16	15	26	2	21	11	5.13
1989 Major League Equivalency	31	189⅔			79	68	164	6	188	83	3.23

Interpretation
Gardner's Major League Equivalencies say "Expos material," but he's never really adjusted quickly after any promotion during his career. At age 28, he's old for a prospect. If the peak performance system were applied to pitchers, it would show his 1989 season as the best he'd ever manage.

SCOTT ALDRED

Detroit Tigers
Pitcher
Tigers' 16th-Round Pick, June 1986 Draft

Personal
Height: 6-4   Weight: 195
Throws left, bats left
Born: June 12, 1968

School: Hill-McCloy High
in Montrose, Mich.

Ratings

	Present	Future
Fastball	5	5
Curve	4	5
Changeup	3	5
Control	4	5
Stamina	4	5
Poise	4	5
Fielding	4	5

Rating Key
7 Outstanding
6 Major League Caliber, High
5 Major League Caliber
4 Minor League Caliber, High
3 Minor League Caliber
2 Below Average
1 Poor

General
Aldred, one of Detroit Manager Sparky Anderson's favorite prospects, may not be far from paying dividends at the big-league level. Just turned 21 last season, he led the Tigers' London affiliate with 10 victories at the Class AA level. He's a talent the Tigers can wait for, but Aldred appears intent on arriving quickly. At 6-4, 195 pounds, he has an outstanding build plus the mental makeup to become a front-line starter. He was able to come back strong following a hand injury midway through last season. In three minor league campaigns, Aldred has a nine-inning average of only 7.9 hits allowed. Among his victories in 1989 was a one-hitter over New Britain.

Pitching Tendencies
Aldred gets his fastball up to 90 mph and has a good-looking curveball he throws with confidence. He hasn't developed any consistency with his changeup, however, but he isn't afraid to throw any of his pitches at any point. Aldred's control is occasionally lacking (he has a career average of 4.9 walks per nine innings) but he did show better command in 1989. He's gifted with a good knowledge of pitching, especially considering his limited experience. He worked just 122 innings in 1989 due to his hand injury.

Fielding/Holding Runners
Aldred can help himself with his glove but could stand to polish his move to the bases. Eastern League opponents stole 22 bases in 30 attempts last season.

Projection
Aldred is ticketed to begin the 1990 season at Class AAA Toledo. If he continues to progress, Detroit could call for his services before season's end.

Career Statistics and Major League Equivalencies

	G	IP	W	L	R	ER	H	HR	SO	BB	ERA
1987 Fayetteville (South Atlantic League-Class A)	21	110	4	9	56	44	101	5	91	69	3.57
1988 Lakeland (Florida State League-Class A)	25	131⅓	8	7	61	52	122	6	102	72	3.56
1989 London (Eastern League-Class AA)	20	122	10	6	55	52	98	11	97	59	3.84
1989 Major League Equivalency	20	122			66	63	110	13	92	71	4.65

Interpretation
Aldred's Major League Equivalency indicates that he is not quite yet Detroit caliber. His problem, like that of many other young pitchers, is a consistently high annual walk total.

JULIO VALERA

New York Mets
Pitcher
Signed by Mets as a Non-Drafted Free Agent, March 1986

Personal
Height: 6-2 Weight: 185
Throws right, bats right
Born: October 13, 1968

School: Manuel Mendez
Liciaga High in Puerto Rico

Ratings

	Present	Future
Fastball	5	6
Curve	4	5
Changeup	4	5
Control	4	5
Stamina	4	5
Poise	4	5
Fielding	4	5

Rating Key
7 Outstanding
6 Major League Caliber, High
5 Major League Caliber
4 Minor League Caliber, High
3 Minor League Caliber
2 Below Average
1 Poor

General
Valera was a man headed in the right direction in 1989. He started the season at Class A St. Lucie, quickly advanced to Class AA Jackson and earned a late-season promotion to Class AAA Tidewater. At each stop, the fourth-year pro sparkled. He was a Texas League All-Star pick at Jackson, where he tied for the league lead with a 2.49 earned-run average in 19 starts (including six complete games). His 15 wins overall tied a career high set in 1988, when he ranked second in victories in the South Atlantic League. The big concern about Valera had been his tendency to gain weight, but he seemed to take control of that problem last season.

Pitching Tendencies
Valera's pitches have plenty of velocity, with his hard stuff pushing the radar gun past 90 mph. He has a good, sinking fastball complemented by a split-fingered fastball, a curve and slider. He consistently pitches around the strike zone, with a strikeouts-to-walks ratio of 3-1 over his minor league career. He'll get those strikeouts every season, partly because of the sheer number of innings he gives his team. After ranking third in the South Atlantic League with 191 innings pitched in 1988, Valera worked 195⅓ innings last season, placing him among the leaders in all of the minor leagues.

Fielding/Holding Runners
A pitcher who keeps his cool, Valera is an excellent fielder who holds baserunners tight.

Projection
Valera is ticketed to begin the 1990 season at the Class AAA level. If he picks up at Tidewater where he left off in 1989, he's destined to pitch in the major leagues before the year ends.

Career Statistics and Major League Equivalencies

	G	IP	W	L	R	ER	H	HR	SO	BB	ERA
1986 Kingsport (Appalachian League-Rookie)	13	76⅓	3	10	58	44	91	5	64	29	5.19
1987 Columbia (South Atlantic League-Class A)	22	125⅓	8	7	53	39	114	7	97	31	2.80
1988 Columbia (South Atlantic League-Class A)	30	191	77	15	11	68	171	8	144	51	3.20
1989 St. Lucie (Florida State League-Class A)	6	45	4	2	5	5	34	1	45	6	1.00
1989 Jackson (Texas League-Class AA)	19	137⅓	10	6	47	38	123	4	107	36	2.49
1989 Tidewater (International League-Class AAA)	2	13	1	1	3	3	8	1	10	5	2.08
1989 Major League Equivalency	19	137⅓			58	47	140	5	102	45	3.08

Interpretation
Valera's Major League Equivalency shows a pretty solid earned-run average, but it's probably not good enough to put anyone in the Mets' deep rotation out of a job. Still, at age 22, he rates as a top prospect for the very near future. His hits-per-inning ratio could adjust down during the interim.

STEVE ADKINS

New York Yankees
Pitcher
Yankees' 15th-Round Pick, June 1986 Draft

Personal
Height: 6-6   Weight: 210
Throws left, bats right
Born: October 26, 1964

School: Pennsylvania

Ratings

	Present	Future
Fastball	4	5
Curve	6	6
Changeup	4	5
Control	4	5
Stamina	4	5
Poise	4	5
Fielding	4	5

Rating Key
7 Outstanding
6 Major League Caliber, High
5 Major League Caliber
4 Minor League Caliber, High
3 Minor League Caliber
2 Below Average
1 Poor

General
When is a 17-6 pitcher not the ace of his staff? When he's the Albany Yankees' Rodney Imes and a guy named Adkins gets promoted from Class A ball and finishes 12-1, throws five two-hitters (three in succession) and posts a league-low 2.07 earned-run average. Indeed, Adkins has the credentials, size and tricky repertoire that indicate he'll be a dominating pitcher. He's already 25 years old, having stayed in school to earn a degree in engineering, and pitched his first three seasons at the Class A level. He worked mostly as a reliever at Prince William in 1988 and for Ft. Lauderdale at the start of last season. He was named to the Eastern League's 1989 All-Star team.

Pitching Tendencies
Adkins' best pitch is a knuckle curve that some scouts say is the best they've ever seen. The pitch looks like a fastball but drops straight down. Even when batters know it's coming, they can't hit it. And when they worry about it, they get locked up by Adkins' other pitches, a fastball and changeup. When he has all three pitches working, he is nearly unhittable. At Albany in 1989, he averaged 10.1 strikeouts and only 5.1 hits allowed every nine innings. He pitched shutouts in five of his 16 starts and opponents batted only .165 against him. Scouts say he needs to gain a little more control, given his career average of 4.3 walks per nine innings. He is a quick worker.

Fielding/Holding Runners
Adkins is a good athlete and adequate fielder. Opponents stole only eight bases in 18 attempts against him last season.

Projection
Adkins figures to move up to Class AAA Columbus in 1990 but could make the climb all the way to the major leagues.

Career Statistics and Major League Equivalencies

	G	IP	W	L	R	ER	H	HR	SO	BB	ERA
1986 Oneonta (New York-Penn League-Class A)	14	80⅓	8	2	23	15	59	1	74	36	1.68
1987 Fort Lauderdale (Florida State League-Class A)	5	21⅓	1	1	11	11	26	2	7	8	4.64
1987 Prince William (Carolina League-Class A)	21	115⅔	9	8	72	62	120	11	84	70	4.82
1988 Prince William (Carolina League-Class A)	31	94⅓	6	4	44	35	88	6	92	40	3.34
1989 Fort Lauderdale (Florida State League-Class A)	11	45⅔	3	3	15	12	40	2	48	14	2.36
1989 Albany (Eastern League-Class AA)	16	117⅔	12	1	31	27	67	5	132	58	2.07
1989 Major League Equivalency	16	117⅔			40	35	78	6	126	75	2.68

Interpretation
Adkins had Class AA hitters at his mercy in 1989. In this case, the Major League Equivalency may not fully adjust for a player who apparently was too strong for his league. Hence, Adkins may not be completely ready, contrary to what his MLE suggests.

MIKE MILCHIN

St. Louis Cardinals
Pitcher
Cardinals' Second-Round Pick, June 1989 Draft

Personal
Height: 6-3 Weight: 195
Throws left, bats left
Born: February 28, 1968

School: Clemson

Ratings

	Present	Future
Fastball	4	5
Curve	4	5
Changeup	5	6
Control	4	5
Stamina	4	5
Poise	4	5
Fielding	4	5

Rating Key
7 Outstanding
6 Major League Caliber, High
5 Major League Caliber
4 Minor League Caliber, High
3 Minor League Caliber
2 Below Average
1 Poor

General
Milchin broke in at Hamilton in the New York-Penn League in 1989 but quickly moved up to Class A Springfield. He may progress to the major league level quicker than other pitchers in the Cardinal farm system, given his ability to throw strikes. That's saying something, considering he only recently became a full-time pitcher. As a collegiate star at Clemson, Milchin gained just as much acclaim as a slugging first baseman. He batted .370 with 11 homers and 68 runs batted in as a junior and .285 with 53 RBIs his senior season. On the mound, he was sensational as a closer in 1988, notching eight saves, a 3-0 record and a 1.09 earned-run average. On the 1988 U.S. Olympic squad, he was 4-1 with a 1.93 ERA. The Cardinals will use him in a starting role.

Pitching Tendencies
Milchin has a good understanding of pitching and good control of all three of his pitches. He has a fastball, a curve and an excellent change-up, and knows how to mix them up. The Cardinals expect his fastball to gain velocity as he pitches more and builds up his arm strength. The lefthander gets high marks for his delivery, which is extremely smooth. Even at this stage, he has been compared with Joe Magrane. Milchin still makes mistakes due to his inexperience, but scouts believe a few years of seasoning will remedy that.

Fielding/Holding Runners
The former first baseman is a good fielder but needs to work on his move to first.

Projection
Milchin likely will open 1990 at either Class A St. Petersburg or Class AA Arkansas. He appears destined to reach the majors late in 1991 or in 1992.

Career Statistics

	G	IP	W	L	R	ER	H	HR	SO	BB	ERA
1989 Hamilton (New York-Penn League-Class A)	8	41⅓	1	2	11	10	35	2	46	9	2.18
1989 Springfield (Midwest League-Class A)	6	42	3	2	14	10	30	3	44	10	2.14

(Projections unavailable because player has not competed at Class AA or Class AAA levels)

DAVID PROCTOR

New York Mets
Pitcher
Mets' First-Round Pick, June 1988 Draft

Personal
Height: 6-3 Weight: 195
Throws right, bats left
Born: March 17, 1968

School: Allen County
Community College in Kansas

Ratings

	Present	Future
Fastball	5	6
Curve	4	5
Changeup	4	5
Control	2	5
Stamina	4	5
Poise	4	5
Fielding	4	5

Rating Key
7 Outstanding
6 Major League Caliber, High
5 Major League Caliber
4 Minor League Caliber, High
3 Minor League Caliber
2 Below Average
1 Poor

General
Proctor, the nephew of former major league pitcher Mike Torrez, pitched at Class A St. Lucie in 1989, his first full minor league season. He is a hard thrower who the Mets believe has the potential to become a dominant strikeout-type pitcher. After a slow start at St. Lucie, Proctor regrouped to finish with a 2.36 earned-run average, placing him fifth among Florida State League pitchers. His 7-6 record was due partly to a lack of offensive support, not from lack of ability. Proctor, the 21st player selected in the 1988 draft, was 12-4 in two seasons at the junior college level.

Pitching Tendencies
Proctor has strictly major league heat, with a fastball that has been clocked as high as 96 mph. He had a lot of success in college with his slider and a split-fingered pitch, but he needs better command of his curveball at this stage. He's a pitcher who is accustomed to throwing regularly, which helps him maintain a groove. If he isn't allowed to get his work on the sidelines, his control may not be sharp in games. In two minor league campaigns, he has totaled nearly as many walks as strikeouts (118 walks, 138 strikeouts). Proctor has been tough to hit, however, allowing an average of only 7.2 hits per nine innings in the minors.

Fielding/Holding Runners
Proctor improved his fielding in 1989, committing three errors in 22 games after totaling five errors in 12 games in 1988. He is working to polish his pickoff move.

Projection
Proctor is on schedule to make the jump to Class AA Jackson in 1990 and probably is two years away from New York.

Career Statistics

	G	IP	W	L	R	ER	H	HR	SO	BB	ERA
1988 Little Falls (New York-Penn League-Class A)	12	68⅓	5	3	43	32	57	4	53	45	4.21
1989 St. Lucie (Florida State League-Class A)	22	133⅓	7	6	50	35	104	7	85	73	2.36

(Projections unavailable because player has not competed at Class AA or Class AAA levels)

STAN BELINDA

Pittsburgh Pirates
Pitcher
Pirates' 10th-Round Pick, June 1986 Draft

Personal
Height: 6-3 Weight: 195
Throws right, bats right
Born: August 6, 1966

School: Allegany Community College in Cumberland, Md.

Ratings

	Present	Future
Fastball	4	5
Curve	3	5
Changeup	3	5
Control	5	6
Stamina	4	5
Poise	4	6
Fielding	3	5

Rating Key
7 Outstanding
6 Major League Caliber, High
5 Major League Caliber
4 Minor League Caliber, High
3 Minor League Caliber
2 Below Average
1 Poor

General
Belinda is a submarine-style reliever who has the utmost confidence in his ability to get hitters out. He has an outstanding competitive makeup and has grown physically since being drafted four seasons ago. Called up by the Pirates last September, he wasn't awed by the major leagues and was 0-1 in eight appearances. He pitched at both Class AA Harrisburg and Class AAA Buffalo before his promotion, posting a combined 3-6 record with 22 saves. He has totaled 52 saves over the last three seasons.

Pitching Tendencies
Belinda has surprising velocity for his delivery, which varies from side-arm to submarine. He has an above-average fastball that seems to sneak up on hitters, mainly because he unloads from a different angle. He also throws a breaking ball and a forkball, but neither is as good as his fastball. If he learns to throw those pitches consistently for strikes, he'll become a more effective pitcher. Because of his motion, he manages to keep his pitches down and put a lot of sinking movement on the ball. Consequently, he throws a lot of groundball pitches, an important requisite for a reliever. Last season, he limited opponents to a .190 batting average.

Fielding/Holding Runners
Because of his unconventional delivery, Belinda sometimes winds up in awkward fielding position when he follows through. If he gets to the ball, however, he'll usually make the play. His motion to the plate is slow, which allows runners to get a good jump on stolen base attempts.

Projection
The Pirates will have Belinda in their major league camp to compete for a spot on the 1990 roster.

Career Statistics and Major League Equivalencies

	G	IP	W	L	R	ER	H	HR	SO	BB	ERA
1986 Bradenton Pirates (Gulf Coast League-Rookie)	17	20⅓	3	2	12	6	23	1	17	2	2.66
1986 Watertown (New York-Penn League-Class A)	5	8	0	0	3	3	5	1	5	2	3.38
1987 Macon (South Atlantic League-Class A)	50	82	6	4	26	19	59	4	75	27	2.09
1988 Salem (Carolina League-Class A)	53	71⅔	6	4	33	22	54	9	63	32	2.76
1989 Harrisburg (Eastern League-Class AA)	32	38⅔	1	4	13	10	32	1	33	25	2.33
1989 Buffalo (American Association-Class AAA)	19	28⅓	2	2	5	3	13	1	28	13	0.95
1989 Pittsburgh (National League)	8	10⅓	0	1	8	7	13	0	10	2	6.10
1989 Major League Equivalency	59	77⅓			29	22	62	2	68	47	2.56

Interpretation
It's easy to see why Pittsburgh called up Belinda after what he did to hitters at the Class AA and AAA levels in 1989. His Major League Equivalency draws more on his minor league successes than what he did with the Pirates.

LUIS VASQUEZ

Personal
Height: 6-1 Weight: 170
Throws right, bats right
Born: March 23, 1967

School: Estrada Bolivar, Venezuela

Ratings

	Present	Future
Fastball	4	5
Curve	5	6
Changeup	3	5
Control	3	5
Stamina	4	5
Poise	4	5
Fielding	4	5

Rating Key
7 Outstanding
6 Major League Caliber, High
5 Major League Caliber
4 Minor League Caliber, High
3 Minor League Caliber
2 Below Average
1 Poor

Cincinnati Reds
Pitcher
Signed by Boston Red Sox as a Non-Drafted Free Agent, January 1985

General
Vasquez still has much to learn about pitching, but the Reds believe he has the basic tools necessary to become a quality pitcher in the major leagues. Acquired in the Todd Benzinger-Nick Esasky trade after the 1988 season, the Venezuela native originally was signed by Boston at age 17. He advanced to the Class AAA level in 1988, his fourth season in the Red Sox's chain, after missing much of 1987 due to elbow surgery. He brought to the Reds a reputation of being a hot-tempered sort, but coaches were able to convince him last season that his energies would be better spent learning the fundamentals and nuances of his profession. His arm is as strong as anyone's, and he led the American Association last season with 29 starts at Nashville.

Pitching Tendencies
Vasquez has an outstanding breaking ball and good fastball, both of which he used to become a strikeout pitcher of some renown the previous two seasons. He was especially tough in 1988, fanning 170 batters in 187⅔ innings, but struggled through stretches of wildness last season (84 walks in 162⅓ innings). He stopped throwing his breaking ball when his control suffered, a move that wasn't all bad. Vasquez opted instead for a changeup, a pitch coaches had been trying to develop all along. He has a way to go, but the hard-throwing righthander has the potential to be a consistent winner with a good repertoire.

Fielding/Holding Runners
Vasquez is a good athlete who can get off the mound to make a play. His move to first base is sound.

Projection
The Reds will give Vasquez a look in spring training, but he'll likely return to Class AAA Nashville to start the year.

Career Statistics and Major League Equivalencies

	G	IP	W	L	R	ER	H	HR	SO	BB	ERA
1985 Elmira (New York-Penn League-Class A)	18	57⅓	2	4	28	22	50	6	42	24	3.45
1986 Winter Haven (Florida State League-Class A)	31	159⅓	15	3	65	60	145	6	92	58	3.39
1987 New Britain (Eastern League-Class AA)	10	61	3	2	23	19	63	4	26	19	2.80
1987 Major League Equivalency	10	61			24	20	66	4	25	20	2.95
1988 New Britain (Eastern League-Class AA)	15	112⅓	3	9	46	31	87	8	97	28	2.48
1988 Pawtucket (International League-Class AAA)	12	75⅓	5	4	37	30	74	7	73	15	3.58
1988 Major League Equivalency	27	187⅔			106	78	186	19	162	56	3.74
1989 Nashville (American Association-Class AAA)	29	162⅓	11	13	91	83	170	11	115	84	4.60
1989 Major League Equivalency	29	162⅓			102	93	184	12	110	94	4.86

Interpretation
Oddly, Vasquez's won-lost record doesn't jibe with his decent earned-run average at several stops. It can be presumed he hasn't always had a bad defense behind him.

His low ERAs aside in the early projections, the Major League Equivalencies do not show him to be quite ready for the big leagues.

KEVIN TAPANI

Minnesota Twins
Pitcher
Oakland Athletics' Second-Round Pick, June 1986 Draft

Personal
Height: 6-0   Weight: 180
Throws right, bats right
Born: February 18, 1964

School: Central Michigan

Ratings

	Present	Future
Fastball	5	5
Curve	5	5
Changeup	5	5
Control	5	5
Stamina	5	5
Poise	5	5
Fielding	5	5

Rating Key
7 Outstanding
6 Major League Caliber, High
5 Major League Caliber
4 Minor League Caliber, High
3 Minor League Caliber
2 Below Average
1 Poor

General
The fact that Tapani has been traded twice in two years underscores his appeal, not a lack of value. Hardly a throw-in in a trade of little consequence, Tapani was a key acquisition for Minnesota in the five-for-one deal that sent one Frank Viola to the New York Mets in 1989. A heady and aggressive righthander, Tapani finished 13-9 overall last season in stops at Minnesota, New York and two Class AAA teams. He made a promising debut with the Twins in September, fashioning a 2-2 record and 3.86 earned-run average in five starts. He has started and relieved in his career, but the Twins are convinced his future is in their rotation. He was traded by Oakland to New York in a deal for Jesse Orosco after the 1987 season.

Pitching Tendencies
Save for an 0-1 record in a one-game stint with Tacoma in 1986, Tapani has been a winner wherever he's pitched. He can throw strikes anywhere in the count and has excellent command of every pitch in his repertoire. "Guys will play for you if they get the ball over the plate," Twins Manager Tom Kelly said after Tapani limited Texas to one walk and two runs in his first big-league start. His fastball isn't overpowering, but it is sneaky fast because of his nasty off-speed pitch. Tapani goes right after hitters by challenging them with strikes, an aggressive trait that helps keep the defense alert. The Twins expect glowing results once he settles down with one club for an entire season.

Fielding/Holding Runners
Tapani is a dependable fielder, but his move to first is suspect—minor league opponents stole 23 bases in 26 attempts against him in 1989.

Projection
The Twins expect Tapani to sew up a spot in their rotation in 1990.

Career Statistics and Major League Equivalencies

	G	IP	W	L	R	ER	H	HR	SO	BB	ERA
1986 Medford (Northwest League-Class A)	2	8⅓	1	0	3	0	6	0	9	3	0.00
1986 Modesto (California League-Class A)	11	69	6	1	26	19	74	2	44	22	2.48
1986 Huntsville (Southern League-Class AA)	1	6	1	0	4	4	8	0	2	1	6.00
1986 Tacoma (Pacific Coast League-Class AAA)	1	2⅓	0	1	6	4	5	1	1	1	15.43
1986 Major League Equivalency	2	8⅓			51	41	30	5	3	10	44.28
1987 Modesto (California League-Class A)	24	148⅓	10	7	74	62	122	14	121	60	3.76
1988 St. Lucie (Florida State League-Class A)	3	19	1	0	5	3	17	1	11	4	1.42
1988 Jackson (Texas League-Class AA)	24	62⅓	5	1	23	19	46	1	35	19	2.74
1988 Major League Equivalency	24	62⅓			29	24	53	1	33	24	3.47
1989 Tidewater (International League-Class AAA)	17	109	7	5	49	42	113	6	63	25	3.47
1989 New York Mets (National League)	3	7⅓	0	0	3	3	5	1	2	4	3.68
1989 Portland (Pacific Coast League-Class AAA)	6	41	4	2	15	10	38	4	30	12	2.20
1989 Minnesota (American League)	5	32⅔	2	2	15	14	16	2	21	8	3.86
1989 Major League Equivalency	23	137			67	58	123	10	86	40	3.81

Interpretation
Save for a 2.20 earned-run average he compiled at Class AAA Portland of the Pacific Coast League, Tapani's lines at his three other stops in 1989 are in line with his Major League Equivalency.

CHRIS HAMMOND

Cincinnati Reds
Pitcher
Reds' Sixth-Round Pick, June 1986 Draft

Personal
Height: 6-1 Weight: 190
Throws left, bats left
Born: January 21, 1966

School: Gulf Coast Community College in Panama City, Fla.

Ratings

	Present	Future
Fastball	5	6
Curve	4	5
Changeup	4	5
Control	3	5
Stamina	4	5
Poise	4	5
Fielding	4	5

Rating Key
7 Outstanding
6 Major League Caliber, High
5 Major League Caliber
4 Minor League Caliber, High
3 Minor League Caliber
2 Below Average
1 Poor

General
Hammond is one of the most promising pitchers in a Cincinnati farm system that is stocked with several good, young arms. The lefthander is a great competitor who reminds some Reds officials of Tom Browning. Hammond has a knack for winning games, even when he doesn't have his best stuff. After winning a team-high 11 decisions for Class A Tampa in 1987, he set a club record at Class AA Chattanooga in 1988 with 16 victories and led the Southern League with a 1.72 earned-run average. Both totals ranked first among pitchers at the Class AA level. Pitching in the shadow of Jack Armstrong at Class AAA Nashville in 1989, Hammond finished 11-7 as the lone lefthander on the staff.

Pitching Tendencies
Hammond has an above-average major league fastball, a good curve and an effective changeup. Ideally, he'd be devastating as a control-type pitcher, but he hasn't learned to throw all three pitches for strikes. At this stage, he walks too many batters (an average of 5.5 walks every nine innings at Nashville in 1989) and falls behind in the count too often. When he's on, he's difficult to hit. Opponents had only a .193 batting average in 1988, a .244 mark in 1989. Hammond can use his changeup to set up hitters for the strikeout. He averaged just over eight strikeouts per nine innings last season.

Fielding/Holding Runners
Hammond does all the little things to help himself in the field. The numbers show he needs to hold runners closer, however: opponents stole 29 bases in 34 attempts against him in 1989.

Projection
The Reds expect Hammond to be competing for a spot on their major league roster in 1990.

Career Statistics and Major League Equivalencies

	G	IP	W	L	R	ER	H	HR	SO	BB	ERA
1986 Sarasota Reds (Gulf Coast League-Rookie)	7	41⅔	3	2	21	13	27	0	53	17	2.81
1986 Tampa (Florida State League-Class A)	5	21⅔	0	2	8	8	25	0	5	13	3.32
1987 Tampa (Florida State League-Class A)	25	170	11	11	81	67	174	10	126	60	3.55
1988 Chattanooga (Southern League-Class AA)	26	182⅔	16	5	48	35	127	2	127	77	1.72
1988 Major League Equivalency	26	182			60	44	145	2	121	96	2.17
1989 Nashville (American Association-Class AAA)	24	157⅓	11	7	69	59	144	7	142	96	3.38
1989 Major League Equivalency	24	157⅓			77	66	155	8	135	107	3.77

Interpretation
Hammond is one of those pitchers who completely overmatched hitters at the Class AA level. The major league adjustment assumes that a player is properly matched to a particular level and, consequently, makes adjustments based on that level that it believes are sufficient for the player. Hammond's 1988 Chattanooga adventure throws the process completely off. Nevertheless, his 1989 season at Class AAA Nashville indicates he is in fact ready for a big-league trial.

JAMIE McANDREW

Los Angeles Dodgers
Pitcher
Dodgers' Supplemental Pick Following First Round, June 1989 Draft

Personal
Height: 6-2 Weight: 190
Throws right, bats right
Born: September 2, 1967

School: Florida

Ratings

	Present	Future
Fastball	4	5
Curve	4	5
Changeup	4	5
Control	4	5
Stamina	4	5
Poise	5	6
Fielding	4	5

Rating Key
7 Outstanding
6 Major League Caliber, High
5 Major League Caliber
4 Minor League Caliber, High
3 Minor League Caliber
2 Below Average
1 Poor

General
McAndrew, the son of former major league pitcher Jim McAndrew, was one of many gems on the Dodgers' rookie Great Falls team in 1989. Because of his college experience, he was a little more polished than other first-year players, although he still has room to refine his game. With a league-high 11 victories and a 1.65 earned-run average, the unbeaten righthander helped Great Falls to the Pioneer League championship and was an All-Star honoree. He started and relieved as a collegian at Florida, posting a 14-9 record with 17 saves and a 4.03 ERA over three seasons. McAndrew, the 28th player taken in the 1989 draft, was a supplemental pick awarded to Los Angeles for the loss of free-agent Steve Sax.

Pitching Tendencies
McAndrew has good velocity on his fastball and a good, slow curveball. The statistics show he made the most of both pitches: 72 strikeouts and 49 hits allowed in 76⅓ innings. In the off-season instructional leagues, Dodger coaches worked with him to quicken his delivery and improve his changeup. Otherwise, he has good command of his pitches and good control. Given his pitching experience at Florida (where former major league reliever Doug Corbett served as pitching coach), he could move quickly through the Dodgers' system.

Fielding/Holding Runners
McAndrew is a good athlete but had only a .769 fielding average in 1989, with three errors in 13 chances. He needs to work on his move to first and develop a quicker slide-step delivery.

Projection
McAndrew likely will begin 1990 at Bakersfield, a full-season Class A team. He is said to be two to three years away from the majors.

Career Statistics

	G	IP	W	L	R	ER	H	HR	SO	BB	ERA
1989 Great Falls (Pioneer League-Rookie)	13	76⅓	11	0	16	14	49	5	72	27	1.65

(Projections unavailable because player has not competed at Class AA or Class AAA levels)

RUDY SEANEZ

Cleveland Indians
Pitcher
Indians' Fourth-Round Pick, June 1986 Draft

Personal
Height: 5-10   Weight: 185
Throws right, bats right
Born: October 20, 1968

School: Brawley Union High
in Brawley, Calif.

Ratings

	Present	Future
Fastball	5	6
Curve	4	5
Changeup	4	5
Control	2	5
Stamina	4	5
Poise	4	5
Fielding	3	5

Rating Key
7 Outstanding
6 Major League Caliber, High
5 Major League Caliber
4 Minor League Caliber, High
3 Minor League Caliber
2 Below Average
1 Poor

General
Seanez has been a starter in each of his four seasons on the Cleveland farm, acquiring valuable innings that will help him fill a different role: relief closer. The Indians, impressed by the young righthander's explosive fastball, are grooming him to become a stopper in the mold of the Chicago Cubs' Mitch Williams. Seanez spent most of the 1989 season in the Class A Carolina League before relieving in five games for the Indians down the stretch. The fact he was still healthy in September was a victory in itself, what with his previous two seasons marked by injuries. Observers have noted his improved conditioning and flexibility.

Pitching Tendencies
Seanez pours pure gas at hitters. His fastball has been clocked as high as 98 mph on the fast radar gun—at least when the ball is in the vicinity of home plate. Seanez is still a very wild pitcher who walked 111 batters in 113 innings at Kinston last season. Nonetheless, that speed and wildness can work to his advantage. He's an intimidating thrower who stares down hitters from the mound, daring them to hit his fastball. Carolina League opponents batted only .223 against him last season, and he averaged nearly 12 strikeouts per nine innings. He hasn't shown the finesse to be a big-league starter and needs better command of his pitches to be consistently effective as a closer. If his control improves, the Indians believe he'll come quickly.

Fielding/Holding Runners
Seanez is a good fielder but needs a better move to first base. Carolina League opponents stole 50 bases in 58 attempts against him in 1989.

Projection
Seanez appears destined for Class AA Canton-Akron in 1990 and could stick in the majors within two seasons.

Career Statistics

	G	IP	W	L	R	ER	H	HR	SO	BB	ERA
1986 Burlington (Appalachian League-Rookie)	13	76	5	2	37	27	59	5	56	32	3.20
1987 Waterloo (Midwest League-Class A)	10	34⅔	0	4	29	26	35	6	23	23	6.75
1988 Waterloo (Midwest League-Class A)	22	113⅓	6	6	69	59	98	10	93	68	4.69
1989 Kinston (Carolina League-Class A)	25	113	8	10	66	52	94	0	149	111	4.14
1989 Colorado Springs (Pacific Coast League-Class AAA)	1	1	0	0	0	0	1	0	0	0	0.00
1989 Cleveland (American League)	5	5	0	0	2	2	1	0	7	4	3.60

(Projections unavailable due to player's limited experience at Class AAA and major league levels)

RODNEY IMES

Cincinnati Reds
Pitcher
New York Yankees' 16th-Round Pick, June 1987 Draft

Personal
Height: 6-5 Weight: 200
Throws right, bats right
Born: November 19, 1966

School: Old Dominion

Ratings

	Present	Future
Fastball	4	5
Curve	4	5
Changeup	5	6
Control	4	5
Stamina	4	5
Poise	4	5
Fielding	4	5

Rating Key
7 Outstanding
6 Major League Caliber, High
5 Major League Caliber
4 Minor League Caliber, High
3 Minor League Caliber
2 Below Average
1 Poor

General
Imes, a wiry 6-foot-5 righthander, was named the Eastern League's Pitcher of the Year in 1989, when he fashioned a 17-6 record for the Class AA Albany Yankees. His success can be traced directly to the development of his forkball, which he began throwing in his first minor league season in 1987. In 1988, his first full year, he won a total of 14 games at three different stops. The key to his effectiveness at the big-league level will depend on his ability to refine the rest of his repertoire. He was sent to Cincinnati along with prospect Hal Morris in a December trade for Tim Leary.

Pitching Tendencies
Imes specializes in nasty forkballs that have overmatched hitters through the Class AA level. Beyond that, he throws a fastball in the high 80-mph range, a split-fingered pitch and a slider. Imes usually has the upper hand because he's regularly pitching ahead in the count. He throws all of his pitches for strikes, which prevents hitters from sitting on the forkball. His forkball makes his fastball look harder than it is, which accounts for many of his strikeouts. In 171⅔ innings last season, Imes averaged just 1.9 walks and 9.9 baserunners allowed per nine innings. He's proved he has the stamina to be a dominant pitcher, working nine complete games in 1989 and seven in 1988, when he pitched 184 total innings.

Fielding/Holding Runners
Imes is a fluid athlete who can make a play in the field. His move to the bases isn't bad, considering opponents stole only 13 bases in 28 attempts last season.

Projection
Imes likely will begin the 1990 season at the AAA level.

Career Statistics and Major League Equivalencies

	G	IP	W	L	R	ER	H	HR	SO	BB	ERA
1987 Oneonta (New York-Penn League-Class A)	4	27⅔	4	0	1	1	16	1	10	5	0.33
1987 Prince William (Carolina League-Class A)	10	68⅓	2	3	35	30	68	4	49	20	3.95
1988 Albany (Eastern League-Class AA)	7	49⅓	4	1	21	15	46	2	24	16	2.74
1988 Prince William (Carolina League-Class A)	11	77	4	5	47	38	82	8	67	32	4.44
1988 Fort Lauderdale (Florida State League-Class A)	8	57⅔	6	2	18	11	48	3	47	17	1.72
1988 Major League Equivalency	7	49⅓			26	18	52	2	23	20	3.28
1989 Albany (Eastern League-Class AA)	24	171⅔	17	6	56	52	143	11	128	41	2.63
1989 Major League Equivalency	24	171⅔			73	67	166	14	122	53	3.51

Interpretation
Imes' Major League Equivalencies show he is ready to pitch in the majors. They are, however, based on stints in which he dominated Class AA hitters. Thus, the MLEs must be viewed with caution. If Imes were thrown into the starting rotation at this stage, major league hitters likely would find a weakness to exploit and punish him soundly until he adjusted.

NATE CROMWELL

Toronto Blue Jays
Pitcher
Blue Jays' 11th-Round Pick, June 1987 Draft

Personal
Height: 6-1   Weight: 175
Throws left, bats left
Born: August 23, 1968

School: Chaparral High
in Las Vegas, Nev.

Ratings

	Present	Future
Fastball	4	5
Curve	5	6
Changeup	4	5
Control	4	5
Stamina	4	5
Poise	4	5
Fielding	4	5

Rating Key
7 Outstanding
6 Major League Caliber, High
5 Major League Caliber
4 Minor League Caliber, High
3 Minor League Caliber
2 Below Average
1 Poor

General
Cromwell readopted the curveball he had abandoned early in his career and pitched himself into contention for a big-league job with a breakthrough 1989 season. The third-year pro led the Toronto farm system with 161 strikeouts, enough to claim the strikeout crown in the Florida State League, and topped the Jays' Class A Dunedin club with 12 victories. Although he was 12-14 over his first two seasons, Cromwell had started to turn things around in 1988. His record was an undistinguished 8-8, but he held South Atlantic League hitters to a .207 batting average and surrendered just 6.4 hits per nine innings. Last season, he led Florida State League pitchers with 30 starts.

Pitching Tendencies
For Cromwell to be effective, he has to throw his curveball for strikes. He mixes speeds well and has a good fastball and changeup, deliveries that look another grade better when his curve is on. When all three of his pitches are working, he can be dominating. He pitched with better control at times in 1989, although there were stretches where he struggled. He uncorked a league-high 25 wild pitches and averaged nearly five walks per nine innings. His strikeouts-to-walks ratio did improve to almost 2-1, although he previously wasn't regarded as a strikeout pitcher. Instructors say he must find ways to win on days he doesn't have his best stuff.

Fielding/Holding Runners
Cromwell is considered a good fielder and does a fairly good job of holding runners with a quick move to the bases.

Projection
Cromwell likely will begin the 1990 season at Class AA Knoxville and is on schedule to pitch in the major leagues by 1992.

Career Statistics

	G	IP	W	L	R	ER	H	HR	SO	BB	ERA
1987 Medicine Hat (Pioneer League-Rookie)	15	54⅓	4	6	36	26	54	1	47	37	4.31
1988 Myrtle Beach (South Atlantic League-Class A)	21	124⅓	8	8	47	40	88	6	86	67	2.90
1989 Dunedin (Florida State League-Class A)	31	151⅔	12	6	70	61	136	5	161	84	3.62

(Projections unavailable because player has not competed at Class AA or Class AAA levels)

PAUL ABBOTT

Minnesota Twins
Pitcher
Twins' Third-Round Pick, June 1985 Draft

Personal
Height: 6-3 Weight: 185
Throws right, bats right
Born: September 15, 1967

School: Sunny Hills High
in Fullerton, Calif.

Ratings

	Present	Future
Fastball	4	5
Curve	4	5
Changeup	4	5
Control	3	5
Stamina	4	5
Poise	4	5
Fielding	4	5

Rating Key
7 Outstanding
6 Major League Caliber, High
5 Major League Caliber
4 Minor League Caliber, High
3 Minor League Caliber
2 Below Average
1 Poor

General
A lack of control has slowed the development of Abbott. He is primarily a strikeout pitcher who doesn't surrender a lot of hits, but his success has been bittersweet. In 1988, he led the Class A California League with 205 strikeouts—and walked a league-high 143 batters. In 1989, he showed signs of conquering the control demons—until a tender elbow sidelined him the final six weeks of the season. He will be pitching at age 22 in 1990, his sixth year in the Minnesota system, but the Twins won't hurry him—not until he finds some confidence and command.

Pitching Tendencies
Before Abbott was sidelined with a sore arm in 1989, the Twins were heartened by his improved control. Over the previous two seasons, he had issued nearly seven walks per nine innings but escaped serious damage by limiting opponents to a shade under seven hits. Moving up to the Class AA level last season, he reduced his walks to 4.7 per nine innings without losing his strikeout prowess. He led Southern League starters with a strikeout ratio of 10.1 batters per nine innings and limited hitters to a .210 batting mark. Abbott has three quality pitches: a fastball, curveball and changeup. He is not overpowering, but his ball has good movement and he changes speeds well.

Fielding/Holding Runners
Abbott fields his position acceptably. Given his history of walks, he's had enough practice to develop a good pickoff move. He hasn't, however. Last season, opponents stole 29 bases against him in 32 attempts.

Projection
Abbott likely will move up to Class AAA Portland in 1990. If his arm is sound and he reacquaints himself with the strike zone, he could compete for a spot in the major leagues in 1991.

Career Statistics and Major League Equivalencies

	G	IP	W	L	R	ER	H	HR	SO	BB	ERA
1985 Elizabethton (Appalachian League-Rookie)	10	35	1	5	32	27	33	13	34	32	6.94
1986 Kenosha (Midwest League-Class A)	25	98	6	10	62	49	102	13	73	73	4.50
1987 Kenosha (Midwest League-Class A)	26	145⅓	13	6	76	59	102	11	138	103	3.65
1988 Visalia (California League-Class A)	28	172⅓	11	9	95	80	141	9	205	143	4.18
1989 Orlando (Southern League-Class AA)	17	90⅔	9	3	48	44	71	6	102	48	4.37
1989 Major League Equivalency	17	90⅔			51	46	74	6	97	51	4.57

Interpretation
Abbott's Major League Equivalency is based on a sample too small to be significant. For what it's worth, it supports the statistical image of a pitcher who is making steady progress.

ERIC McCRAY

Texas Rangers
Pitcher
Rangers' 10th-Round Pick, June 1988 Draft

Personal
Height: 5-10　Weight: 160
Throws left, bats left
Born: June 10, 1969

School: Farmerville High
in Farmerville, La.

Ratings

	Present	Future
Fastball	4	5
Curve	4	5
Changeup	4	5
Control	4	5
Stamina	4	5
Poise	5	6
Fielding	4	5

Rating Key
7 Outstanding
6 Major League Caliber, High
5 Major League Caliber
4 Minor League Caliber, High
3 Minor League Caliber
2 Below Average
1 Poor

General
McCray reminds some scouts of a young Vida Blue because of his motion and stature on the mound. He takes command with remarkable mound presence for his age. Just turned 20 last season, McCray is still growing and figures to become a stronger pitcher. Pitching at Class A Gastonia in 1989, his first full season in the minor leagues, he ranked sixth in the South Atlantic League and fourth among pitchers in the Texas organization with a 2.52 earned-run average. In 1988, his 1.44 mark ranked third among pitchers in the rookie-level Gulf Coast circuit.

Pitching Tendencies
McCray has three premium pitches in his repertoire: a fastball, curveball and changeup. He has good command of all three, but he needs to learn to mix them up more effectively. Like many young pitchers, McCray still isn't comfortable with the notion that he can win ball games without striking out the side every inning. The strikeouts surely will come (110 in 121⅔ innings last season) but he'll be a craftier pitcher when he doesn't try to blow his fastball past every hitter. McCray has very good control at this stage of his career. He's been tough to hit, surrendering just 6.8 hits per nine innings in his two minor league campaigns.

Fielding/Holding Runners
McCray is a good athlete who fields his position well. He has a decent move to the bases, with only 11 of 18 steal attempts successful against him in 1989.

Projection
McCray likely will be pitching for Class A Charlotte in 1990 and could make a run at the majors in two seasons.

Career Statistics

	G	IP	W	L	R	ER	H	HR	SO	BB	ERA
1988 Sarasota Rangers (Gulf Coast League-Rookie)	12	56⅓	3	2	15	9	39	1	42	27	1.44
1989 Gastonia (South Atlantic League-Class A)	22	121⅔	7	7	51	34	95	5	110	55	2.52

(Projections unavailable because player has not competed at Class AA or Class AAA levels)

MIKE FETTERS

Personal
Height: 6-4   Weight: 200
Throws right, bats right
Born: December 19, 1964

School: Pepperdine

Ratings

	Present	Future
Fastball	4	5
Curve	4	5
Changeup	4	5
Control	4	5
Stamina	4	5
Poise	4	5
Fielding	4	5

Rating Key
7 Outstanding
6 Major League Caliber, High
5 Major League Caliber
4 Minor League Caliber, High
3 Minor League Caliber
2 Below Average
1 Poor

California Angels
Pitcher
Angels' Supplemental Pick Following First Round, June 1986 Draft

General
One of the Angels' five opening-round picks in the June 1986 draft, Fetters asserted himself as a legitimate major league candidate with his best season to date in 1989. Pitching for Class AAA Edmonton, he led the Trappers' staff with a career-high 12 victories and claimed the Pacific Coast League strikeout crown with 144 strikeouts. Fetters' biggest problem has been his inconsistency, but he came close to overcoming that last year. He showed better work habits and was a coachable player who responded well to advice and instruction. Called up by the Angels in September, he was originally drafted as compensation for the loss of free-agent Juan Beniquez.

Pitching Tendencies
Fetters throws five pitches: a fastball, curveball, changeup, slider and forkball. And some people think five pitches are more than he needs. They believe that sizable repertoire is partly responsible for his inconsistency. Yet when Fetters has all of his pitches working, he can be dominating. His best pitch is probably his fastball, which sinks and slides. He had better control over his deliveries last season yet didn't lose any of his power. In four minor league seasons, he has averaged eight strikeouts per nine innings.

Fielding/Holding Runners
Fetters fields his position well and was able to speed up his delivery to the plate last season. With opponents getting a poorer jump, Edmonton catchers threw out nearly 42 percent of the runners (10 of 24) trying to steal on Fetters.

Projection
Fetters is on the brink of competing for a major league starting job in 1990.

Career Statistics and Major League Equivalencies

	G	IP	W	L	R	ER	H	HR	SO	BB	ERA
1986 Salem (Northwest League-Class A)	12	72	4	2	39	27	60	4	72	51	3.38
1987 Palm Springs (California League-Class A)	19	116	9	7	62	46	106	2	105	73	3.57
1988 Midland (Texas League-Class AA)	20	114	8	8	62	46	116	10	101	67	5.92
1988 Edmonton (Pacific Coast League-Class AAA)	2	14	2	0	3	3	8	0	11	10	1.93
1988 Major League Equivalency	22	128			74	72	121	9	107	71	5.06
1989 Edmonton (Pacific Coast League-Class AAA)	26	168	12	8	80	71	160	11	144	72	3.80
1989 California (American League)	1	3⅓	0	0	4	3	5	1	4	1	8.10
1989 Major League Equivalency	26	168			88	78	171	12	137	79	4.18

Interpretation
The two Major League Equivalencies suggest that Fetters is a good strikeout pitcher who probably is only one season away from being an effective starter at the big-league level.

JOHNNY ARD

Minnesota Twins
Pitcher
Twins' First-Round Pick, June 1988 Draft

Personal
Height: 6-5   Weight: 220
Throws right, bats right
Born: June 1, 1967

School: Manatee Junior College in Bradenton, Fla.

Ratings

	Present	Future
Fastball	4	5
Curve	4	5
Changeup	4	5
Control	3	5
Stamina	4	5
Poise	4	5
Fielding	4	5

Rating Key
7 Outstanding
6 Major League Caliber, High
5 Major League Caliber
4 Minor League Caliber, High
3 Minor League Caliber
2 Below Average
1 Poor

General
The Twins appear committed to bring Ard along slowly and let him accumulate experience at each level. He's tasted only success in each of his first two seasons, most recently in the Class A California League. Ard tied for the league high with 13 victories at Visalia and ranked fifth in the circuit with 153 strikeouts. At 6-foot-5, 220 pounds, he has the size and demeanor to be an intimidating pitcher, yet his pitches don't have the velocity usually associated with players his size. He is a good competitor who was focused and dedicated in his first full minor league season. Drafted out of the junior college ranks, he was the 20th pick overall in 1988.

Pitching Tendencies
Ard has a good one-two combination, featuring a sinking fastball and a slider that keeps getting better. His fastball isn't overpowering, but he has good movement on the pitch and changes speeds effectively. Even at this stage, Ard had pretty good command of his deliveries and isn't afraid to challenge hitters. He's surrendered only 6.9 hits per nine innings in two seasons. Scouts like the way his arm held up last year, when Ard tied for the California League lead with 28 starts and ranked second with 186 innings pitched.

Fielding/Holding Runners
Despite his size, Ard is a good athlete who fields his position well. He gets off the mound quickly and covers the bag on plays to the first baseman. He has a decent move to the bases.

Projection
Ard and fellow Twins prospect Willie Banks are on the same timetable. Both are scheduled to pitch at Class AA Orlando in 1990 and likely will arrive in the major leagues in 1992.

Career Statistics

	G	IP	W	L	R	ER	H	HR	SO	BB	ERA
1988 Elizabethton (Appalachian League-Rookie)	9	59⅓	4	1	17	13	40	2	71	26	1.97
1988 Kenosha (Midwest League-Class A)	4	25⅔	3	0	3	3	14	0	16	4	1.05
1989 Visalia (California League-Class A)	28	186	13	7	87	68	155	13	153	84	3.29

(Projections unavailable because player has not competed at Class AA or Class AAA levels)

GLENN CARTER

California Angels
Pitcher
Angels' Third-Round Pick, June 1988 Draft

Personal
Height: 6-0   Weight: 175
Throws right, bats right
Born: November 29, 1967

School: Triton Junior College in River Grove, Ill.

Ratings

	Present	Future
Fastball	4	5
Curve	4	5
Changeup	3	5
Control	4	5
Stamina	4	5
Poise	4	5
Fielding	4	5

Rating Key
7 Outstanding
6 Major League Caliber, High
5 Major League Caliber
4 Minor League Caliber, High
3 Minor League Caliber
2 Below Average
1 Poor

General
Based on Carter's first full season in the minors, scouts are high on his big-league potential. He is an aggressive pitcher who isn't afraid to challenge hitters or throw inside. Consequently, he gets results. Named the righthanded pitcher on the Midwest League's 1989 All-Star squad, Carter struck out a league-leading 190 batters and led the Class A Quad City staff with 15 victories. His 2.05 earned-run average was among the best in the minors and he led the Angels' minor league system in all three pitching categories. Drafted in 1988 after one season in the junior college ranks, he was the second player picked by California after Jim Abbott.

Pitching Tendencies
Carter relies mostly on two pitches, an average-speed fastball that has some movement and a good curveball. He can move the ball around the plate without risking many walks (he averaged only three per nine innings in 1989) and has a strong arm. Carter does need to develop an effective changeup and learn more about pitching, both of which the Angels believe he'll do with experience. He outclassed most hitters at the Class A level, holding opponents to a .187 batting average on 109 hits in 166⅔ innings. Overall, he allowed only 9.07 baserunners per nine innings.

Fielding/Holding Runners
Carter fields his position well and showed a very good move to the bases in 1989. Midwest League opponents succeeded on only 53.6 percent of their stolen base attempts (15 steals in 28 tries).

Projection
The Angels figure to promote Carter to Class AA Midland in 1990. He is at least two years away from the major leagues.

Career Statistics

	G	IP	W	L	R	ER	H	HR	SO	BB	ERA
1988 Bend (Northwest League-Class A)	9	45	3	4	25	23	46	6	47	15	4.60
1989 Quad City (Midwest League-Class A)	25	166⅔	15	6	48	38	109	10	190	57	2.05

(Projections unavailable because player has not competed at Class AA or Class AAA levels)

BLAINE BEATTY

New York Mets
Pitcher
Baltimore Orioles' Ninth-Round Pick, June 1986 Draft

Personal
Height: 6-2 Weight: 185
Throws left, bats left
Born: April 25, 1964

School: Baylor

Ratings

	Present	Future
Fastball	5	5
Curve	5	5
Changeup	5	5
Control	5	6
Stamina	5	5
Poise	4	5
Fielding	4	5

Rating Key
7 Outstanding
6 Major League Caliber, High
5 Major League Caliber
4 Minor League Caliber, High
3 Minor League Caliber
2 Below Average
1 Poor

General
Beatty won't overpower hitters with his arsenal. Better yet, he'll overmatch them. He is a placid-looking John Tudor-type who relies on excellent control and good movement of his pitches. Thus far, he's put up some impressive numbers at each stop of his minor league career. Traded to the Mets for Doug Sisk after the 1987 season, Beatty emerged as the Texas League's 1988 Pitcher of the Year. In 1989, his pinpoint pitching foiled hitters all through the Class AAA International League. At season's end, he ranked among the league leaders in wins, starts, shutouts, complete games and innings pitched. For that kind of pitching, Beatty earned a promotion to New York for the Mets' September stretch drive.

Pitching Tendencies
Beatty is a control pitcher with an excellent knowledge of pitching. He has good command of his pitches, the best being the fastball he spots with precision and a sharp curveball that serves as more than a diversionary pitch. The lefthander has proved his durability as a starter in each of his last three seasons, averaging nearly 202 innings pitched and 28 starts per year. Although he's not a strikeout pitcher in the traditional sense, his career strikeouts-to-walks ratio is an excellent 3-1. Beatty does fit the mold of the pitcher who won't beat himself, allowing only 97 walks in 499⅓ innings at the Class AA and AAA levels.

Fielding/Holding Runners
Beatty is an efficient fielder and has an excellent pickoff move to first base.

Projection
Beatty likely will be competing for a spot on the Mets' major league roster in 1990.

Career Statistics and Major League Equivalencies

	G	IP	W	L	R	ER	H	HR	SO	BB	ERA
1986 Newark (New York-Penn League-Class A)	15	119⅓	11	3	37	28	98	6	93	30	2.11
1987 Hagerstown (Carolina League-Class A)	13	100	11	1	32	28	81	7	65	11	2.52
1987 Charlotte (Southern League-Class AA)	15	105⅔	6	5	38	36	110	2	57	20	3.07
1987 Major League Equivalency	15	105⅔			35	33	108	2	56	19	2.81
1988 Jackson (Texas League-Class AA)	30	208⅔	16	8	64	57	191	13	103	34	2.46
1988 Major League Equivalency	30	208⅔			74	65	208	16	101	40	2.80
1989 Tidewater (International League-Class AAA)	27	185	12	10	86	68	173	14	90	43	3.31
1989 New York (National League)	2	6	0	0	1	1	5	1	3	2	1.50
1989 Major League Equivalency	29	191			99	78	193	17	91	52	3.68

Interpretation
Beatty has posted impressive Major League Equivalencies for three successive seasons. By that token, he should be ready to pitch in the major leagues. His MLEs show excellent control and a hits-allowed total of about nine per game.

RHEAL CORMIER

St. Louis Cardinals
Pitcher
Cardinals' Sixth-Round Pick, June 1988 Draft

Personal
Height: 5-10   Weight: 185
Throws left, bats left
Born: April 23, 1967

School: Rhode Island
Junior College

Ratings

	Present	Future
Fastball	4	5
Curve	4	5
Changeup	4	5
Control	4	5
Stamina	4	5
Poise	4	5
Fielding	4	5

Rating Key
7 Outstanding
6 Major League Caliber, High
5 Major League Caliber
4 Minor League Caliber, High
3 Minor League Caliber
2 Below Average
1 Poor

General
Cormier may not have the physical build of a dominant pitcher, but he is a competitor with a good knowledge of pitching. The fact that he's a lefthander doesn't hurt his big-league chances, either. Cormier pitched for the Canadian Olympic team in the 1988 Summer Games and, consequently, did not pitch in the minors until last season. He spent the entire year at Class A St. Petersburg and was one of two lefthanders named to the Florida State League's All-Star team. A native and resident of New Brunswick, Canada, he works as a lumberjack during the off-season.

Pitching Tendencies
Cormier has four pitches—fastball, curve, forkball and changeup—and throws them all for strikes. He isn't overpowering, with his fastball in the 87-mph range, but still is able to strike out hitters because of the good movement and location of his pitches. An aggressive pitcher who gets the most out of his ability, Cormier also proved to be durable in his first professional season, pitching 169⅔ innings and four complete games in 26 starts at St. Petersburg. He ranked third among pitchers in the Florida State League with a 2.23 earned-run average and topped his staff with 12 victories.

Fielding/Holding Runners
Like many young hurlers, Cormier needs to master a better move to the bases. His seven balks last season are proof positive. He is, however, a good fielder.

Projection
Cormier likely will begin the 1990 season at Class AA Arkansas. From what he's shown in his single minor league season, he's probably two years away from the majors.

Career Statistics

	G	IP	W	L	R	ER	H	HR	SO	BB	ERA
1989 St. Petersburg (Florida State League-Class A)	26	169⅔	12	7	63	42	141	9	122	33	2.23

(Projections unavailable because player has not competed at Class AA or Class AAA levels)

MIKE STANTON

Atlanta Braves
Pitcher
Braves' 13th-Round Pick, June 1987 Draft

Personal
Height: 6-1 Weight: 190
Throws left, bats left
Born: June 2, 1967

School: Alvin Community College in Alvin, Tex.

Ratings

	Present	Future
Fastball	6	6
Curve	5	5
Changeup	..	..
Control	4	5
Stamina	5	5
Poise	5	5
Fielding	5	5

Rating Key
7 Outstanding
6 Major League Caliber, High
5 Major League Caliber
4 Minor League Caliber, High
3 Minor League Caliber
2 Below Average
1 Poor

General
At the very least, Stanton joined the upper echelon of the Braves' stable of pitching prospects with a stellar late-season stint at Atlanta in 1989. Many believe he nailed down the Braves' lefthanded closer's job. Relieving in 20 games, Stanton fashioned a 1.50 earned-run average and picked up seven saves, second on the club only to Joe Boever's 21 saves. A starter for most of his first two minor league seasons, Stanton made the transition to reliever in 1989 and jumped from the Class AA level to the majors within the year. In a stop at Class AAA Richmond, he didn't allow a run in 13 appearances and saved eight games. He was drafted out of the junior college ranks in Alvin, Tex., the town that gained a measure of notoriety for turning out another hard-throwing pitcher: Nolan Ryan.

Pitching Tendencies
Stanton's pitches have excellent velocity. His fastball has good sinking movement and his curve has a sharp break. He's had some control problems at times, averaging 4.4 walks per nine innings in his career. But he's also been a good strikeout pitcher, fanning 357 batters in 345 career innings. The Braves like his arm strength and are convinced his major league showing in 1989 was for real. Stanton has the perfect reliever's mentality—he wants the ball in critical situations and he's loaded with confidence.

Fielding/Holding Runners
Stanton is regarded as a solid fielder (he was errorless in the minors in 1989) and has a good move to the bases.

Projection
Stanton is the No. 1 candidate to fill the Braves' lefthanded closer's job in 1990.

Career Statistics and Major League Equivalencies

	G	IP	W	L	R	ER	H	HR	SO	BB	ERA
1987 Pulaski (Appalachian League-Rookie)	15	83⅓	4	8	37	30	64	7	82	42	3.24
1988 Burlington (Midwest League-Class A)	30	154	11	15	86	62	154	7	160	69	3.62
1988 Durham (Carolina League-Class A)	2	12⅓	1	0	3	2	14	0	14	5	1.46
1989 Greenville (Southern League-Class AA)	47	51⅓	4	1	10	9	32	1	58	31	1.58
1989 Richmond (International League-Class AAA)	13	20	2	0	0	0	6	0	20	13	0.00
1989 Atlanta (National League)	20	24	0	1	4	4	17	0	27	8	1.50
1989 Major League Equivalency	80	95⅓			16	15	60	1	100	62	1.42

Interpretation
Stanton has literally blown away hitters at his last three minor league stops. His Major League Equivalency is completely consistent with his 1989 record in 20 games with the Braves.

KEITH RICHARDSON

Pittsburgh Pirates
Pitcher
Pirates' Second-Round Pick, June 1988 Draft

Personal
Height: 6-4   Weight: 218
Throws right, bats right
Born: January 24, 1967

School: Georgia Southern

Ratings

	Present	Future
Fastball	4	5
Curve	4	5
Changeup	3	5
Control	4	5
Stamina	4	5
Poise	4	5
Fielding	4	5

Rating Key
7 Outstanding
6 Major League Caliber, High
5 Major League Caliber
4 Minor League Caliber, High
3 Minor League Caliber
2 Below Average
1 Poor

General
The Pirates took heart when Richardson bounced back from a dubious start at the Class AA level and finished with a strong second half for Harrisburg in 1989. Pitching his first full season in the minors, Richardson made the jump to Double-A after opening the year with a 4-0 record at Class A Salem in the Carolina League. He didn't get discouraged by a 1-5 start at Harrisburg and concluded his Eastern League tour with an 8-10 record and 96 strikeouts in 117⅔ innings. It was a valuable experience for the big righthander, who had tasted only success in 1988 with a combined 9-2 record and 1.03 earned-run average at three stops.

Pitching Tendencies
Armed with a live 90-plus mph fastball, Richardson can fill the role of a power pitcher. He has good command and control of his hard stuff but needs to find consistency with his two other pitches, a potentially good curveball and a changeup. At 6-4, 218 pounds, he can be an intimidating figure on the mound, and he isn't afraid to go after hitters and challenge them. He does need to pay close attention to his mechanics and stay with his proper delivery. When he gets his fastball up, he can get taken deep (15 home runs allowed in 21 games at Harrisburg). Overall, he's had good control, with a strikeouts-to-walks ratio of nearly 3-1 in two minor league campaigns.

Fielding/Holding Runners
Richardson is a good athlete who committed only one error last season and two in 1988. He's made progress improving his move to first base.

Projection
Richardson likely will return to Class AA Harrisburg in 1990 and could be pitching in the major leagues within two years.

Career Statistics and Major League Equivalencies

	G	IP	W	L	R	ER	H	HR	SO	BB	ERA
1988 Watertown (New York-Penn League-Class A)	8	44⅔	6	1	11	6	29	0	35	8	1.21
1988 Augusta (South Atlantic League-Class A)	4	29⅓	3	1	3	1	18	0	17	4	0.31
1988 Salem (Carolina League-Class A)	2	13	0	0	4	3	8	2	13	3	2.08
1989 Salem (Carolina League-Class A)	5	32	4	0	3	3	30	0	26	10	0.84
1989 Harrisburg (Eastern League-Class AA)	21	117⅔	8	10	63	60	131	15	96	39	4.59
1989 Major League Equivalency	21	117⅔			75	72	146	18	91	46	5.51

Interpretation
With just part of one season at the Class AA level—and not a very good stint at that—Richardson isn't ready to move up to the major leagues. His Major League Equivalency bears that out.

FRANK CASTILLO

Chicago Cubs
Pitcher
Cubs' Sixth-Round Pick, June 1987 Draft

Personal
Height: 6-1   Weight: 180
Throws right, bats right
Born: April 1, 1969

School: Eastwood High
in El Paso, Tex.

Ratings

	Present	Future
Fastball	4	5
Curve	4	5
Changeup	4	5
Control	5	5
Stamina	4	5
Poise	4	5
Fielding	4	5

Rating Key
7 Outstanding
6 Major League Caliber, High
5 Major League Caliber
4 Minor League Caliber, High
3 Minor League Caliber
2 Below Average
1 Poor

General
Castillo is not the type of pitcher who will impress you with the radar gun clocking, yet all he does is win. He bounced back from a fractured right shin suffered in spring training in 1988 and made the climb from from Class A ball to Class AA Charlotte last season. Starting the year at Winston-Salem, he worked eight complete games in 18 starts and pitched a two-hit game and three-hitter within a week. In 1988, he was nearly invincible when he returned from his injury, posting a 6-1 record and 0.71 earned-run average with Peoria. Castillo was named the Player of the Year in the rookie Appalachian League in 1987.

Pitching Tendencies
Castillo is not overpowering but gets hitters out with cunning and outstanding control. His knowledge of pitching is well advanced for a player his age. His average fastball looks harder than it is because of his aggressiveness. He's able to change speeds effectively and get his breaking pitches in the strike zone. The Cubs can't help but move him along because of his track record. In three minor league seasons, Castillo has a strikeouts-to-walks ratio of nearly 5-1. He has averaged nearly a strikeout every inning and has pitched 19 complete games in 49 minor league starts.

Fielding/Holding Runners
Castillo ranks among the very best fielding pitchers. Thus far, he has played with four minor league teams and committed an error with only one: at Winston-Salem (three errors) in 1989. Otherwise, he's been flawless. The righthander's move to first base gets good marks.

Projection
Castillo likely will resume his career at Class AA Charlotte in 1990. He is probably two years away from Chicago.

Career Statistics and Major League Equivalencies

	G	IP	W	L	R	ER	H	HR	SO	BB	ERA
1987 Wytheville (Appalachian League-Rookie)	12	90⅓	10	1	31	23	86	4	83	21	2.29
1987 Geneva (New York-Penn League-Class A)	1	6	1	0	1	0	3	0	6	1	0.00
1988 Peoria (Midwest League-Class A)	9	51	6	1	5	4	25	1	58	10	0.71
1989 Winston-Salem (Carolina League-Class A)	18	129⅓	9	6	42	36	118	5	114	24	2.51
1989 Charlotte (Southern League-Class AA)	10	68	3	4	35	29	73	7	43	12	3.84
1989 Major League Equivalency	10	68			34	28	73	7	41	12	3.71

Interpretation
Although it is based on a small sample of innings, the Major League Equivalency depicts Castillo as a prospect who is close to being ready. He has very good control but his MLE shows him with a hits-allowed total that needs to come down.

JOSIAS MANZANILLO

Personal
Height: 6-0 Weight: 190
Throws right, bats right
Born: October 16, 1967

Ratings

	Present	Future
Fastball	4	5
Curve	4	5
Changeup	4	5
Control	4	5
Stamina	3	5
Poise	4	5
Fielding	4	5

Rating Key
7 Outstanding
6 Major League Caliber, High
5 Major League Caliber
4 Minor League Caliber, High
3 Minor League Caliber
2 Below Average
1 Poor

Boston Red Sox
Pitcher
Signed by Red Sox as a Non-Drafted Free Agent, January 1983

General
Though he'll pitch in 1990 at just 22, Manzanillo has been in the Boston system for what seems like forever. Signed out of the Dominican Republic at age 16, he has been in the organization for seven seasons. Two of those years were particularly trying. Manzanillo missed all of 1988 and pitched just 10 innings in 1987 due to a shoulder injury that eventually required surgery. He made a successful comeback in the Class AA Eastern League in 1989, leading the New Britain staff with nine victories. He pitched a no-hitter against Reading in July and fired a one-hitter in his next start. Manzanillo had just begun to assert himself before the injury, ranking second in the Florida State League in 1986 with a 2.27 earned-run average.

Pitching Tendencies
Manzanillo delivers an above-average fastball in the 90-mph range, along with a good breaking ball and slider. He threw all of his pitches with slightly better command last season but still had his lapses. He topped the Eastern League with 16 wild pitches and so far has a career average of 5.9 walks per nine innings. His strikeout total was down in 1989, but the Red Sox can live with that if he starts finding his control. His shoulder held up well, allowing him to tie for the Eastern League lead with 26 starts.

Fielding/Holding Runners
Manzanillo is considered a complete pitcher with decent fielding ability and a good move to first. Despite his layoff, he helped catch 11 of 32 opponents who tried to steal against him in 1989.

Projection
The Red Sox will give Manzanillo a look in their 1990 spring camp, but he'll likely start the season at Class AAA Pawtucket.

Career Statistics and Major League Equivalencies

	G	IP	W	L	R	ER	H	HR	SO	BB	ERA
1983 Elmira (New York-Penn League-Class A)	12	38⅓	1	5	44	34	52	7	19	20	7.98
1984 Elmira (New York-Penn League-Class A)	14	25⅔	2	3	24	15	27	1	15	26	5.26
1985 Greensboro (South Atlantic League-Class A)	7	12	1	1	13	13	12	1	10	13	9.75
1985 Elmira (New York-Penn League-Class A)	19	39⅔	2	4	19	17	36	1	43	36	3.86
1986 Winter Haven (Florida State League-Class A)	23	142⅔	13	5	51	36	110	3	102	81	2.27
1987 New Britain (Eastern League-Class AA)	2	10	2	0	5	5	8	1	12	8	4.50
1987 Major League Equivalency	2	10			6	6	9	1	11	9	5.40
1988	Injured—Did Not Play										
1989 New Britain (Eastern League-Class AA)	26	147⅔	9	10	78	60	129	11	93	85	3.66
1989 Major League Equivalency	26	147⅔			110	84	156	15	89	120	5.12

Interpretation
Manzanillo's Major League Equivalencies take into account the good hitting background in Fenway Park. Since batters see the ball so well, they'll work a wild thrower like Jose for a load of walks.

PAT MAHOMES

Minnesota Twins
Pitcher
Twins' Sixth-Round Pick, June 1988 Draft

Personal
Height: 6-1   Weight: 175
Throws right, bats right
Born: August 9, 1970

School: Lindale High
in Lindale, Tex.

Ratings

	Present	Future
Fastball	4	5
Curve	4	5
Changeup	3	5
Control	3	5
Stamina	4	5
Poise	4	5
Fielding	4	5

Rating Key
7 Outstanding
6 Major League Caliber, High
5 Major League Caliber
4 Minor League Caliber, High
3 Minor League Caliber
2 Below Average
1 Poor

General
Mahomes, playing most of the 1989 season at age 18, blew away his share of hitters in the Class A Midwest League. He displayed admirable poise for a pitcher his age, and some scouts claimed he had the best velocity in the league. A note of warning to hitters: Mahomes has the potential to throw even harder once he physically matures. He has averaged more than one strikeout per inning in two professional seasons. As a minor league rookie in 1988, he fanned at least 10 batters four times in 13 starts. He had a 15-strikeout game with Kenosha in 1989, surrendering only one hit along the way.

Pitching Tendencies
Mahomes relies mostly on his lively fastball, but he's steadily gaining command of his curveball and changeup. Formerly just a thrower, he is learning the importance of varying his pitches and hitting spots. He still has a way to go, however. Last season, he walked a Midwest League-high 100 batters, or 5.75 walks per nine innings. His average of 9.6 strikeouts ranked fourth among the league's starters. Mahomes has been a durable pitcher who doesn't run out of gas in the late innings. Considering the success he's had at this stage of his development, his big-league prospects appear promising.

Fielding/Holding Runners
Mahomes was a multitalented athlete in high school whose agility serves him well on defense. He is able to hold runners close with a good move to the bases.

Projection
Because of his youth, Mahomes figures to remain at the Class A level in 1990, perhaps moving to Visalia in the faster California League. He appears to be three years away from the major leagues.

Career Statistics

	G	IP	W	L	R	ER	H	HR	SO	BB	ERA
1988 Elizabethton (Appalachian League-Rookie)	13	78	6	3	45	32	66	4	93	51	3.69
1989 Kenosha (Midwest League-Class A)	25	156⅓	13	7	66	57	120	4	167	100	3.28

(Projections unavailable because player has not competed at Class AA or Class AAA levels)

WAYNE EDWARDS

Chicago White Sox
Pitcher
White Sox's 10th-Round Pick, June 1985 Draft

Personal
Height: 6-5   Weight: 185
Throws left, bats left
Born: March 7, 1964

School: Azusa Pacific
University in Azusa, Calif.

Ratings

	Present	Future
Fastball	4	5
Curve	4	5
Changeup	4	5
Control	5	5
Stamina	4	5
Poise	5	5
Fielding	5	5

Rating Key
7 Outstanding
6 Major League Caliber, High
5 Major League Caliber
4 Minor League Caliber, High
3 Minor League Caliber
2 Below Average
1 Poor

General
Save for 11 scattered relief jobs, Edwards toiled as a strong-armed starter through five seasons in the White Sox's minor league ranks. He was brought up to Chicago last September only when injuries thinned out the Sox's bullpen corps. One month later, Edwards' major league future was looking up—as a relief pitcher. In seven relief appearances with Chicago, the minor league veteran struck out nine batters and allowed only two of seven inherited runners to score. He was one of two lefthanders named to the Class AA Southern League's 1989 All-Star team after going 10-4 at Birmingham, primarily as a starter. In 1987, he pitched 15 complete games in 28 starts in the Class A Florida State League.

Pitching Tendencies
The White Sox like Edwards' potential as a reliever because of his ability to throw strikes, especially with his curveball late in the count. He has good command of his fastball, which he consistently throws in the high 80s, and he spots his changeup effectively. He appears to have the makeup you want in a reliever, with good poise and a bulldog attitude. Scouts say he is learning now that he can get people out without relying on the strikeout. Last season, for the first time since his rookie year, he surrendered less than a hit per inning. And he still picked up his 120-plus strikeouts.

Fielding/Holding Runners
Edwards is adequate in the field (he committed five errors in 24 games at Birmingham in 1989) but has a good move to the bases.

Projection
Edwards will report to spring training with the White Sox in 1990 and contend for a spot on their big-league roster.

Career Statistics and Major League Equivalencies

	G	IP	W	L	R	ER	H	HR	SO	BB	ERA
1985 Sarasota White Sox (Gulf Coast League-Rookie)	11	68⅔	7	3	26	19	52	0	61	18	2.49
1986 Peninsula (Carolina League-Class A)	24	128⅓	8	8	80	60	149	10	86	68	4.21
1987 Daytona Beach (Florida State League-Class A)	29	199⅔	16	8	91	80	211	4	121	68	3.61
1988 Birmingham (Southern League-Class AA)	27	167	9	12	108	91	176	9	136	92	4.90
1988 Vancouver (Pacific Coast League-Class AAA)	2	3	0	0	0	0	0	0	2	0	0.00
1988 Major League Equivalency	29	170			125	105	193	10	131	106	5.56
1989 Birmingham (Southern League-Class AA)	24	158	10	4	69	56	131	6	122	65	3.19
1989 Chicago (American League)	7	7⅓	0	0	3	3	7	1	9	3	3.68
1989 Major League Equivalency	31	165⅓			73	62	144	7	125	72	3.38

Interpretation
Edwards' Major League Equivalency for 1989 indicates a breakthrough season. His walks and hits allowed totals were both under control, a sign he's ready to move from the Class AA level to the major leagues. His trial with Chicago agrees.

MARK CLARK

St. Louis Cardinals
Pitcher
Cardinals' Ninth-Round Pick, June 1988 Draft

Personal
Height: 6-5 Weight: 225
Throws right, bats right
Born: May 12, 1968

School: Balyki High
in Bath, Ill.

Ratings

	Present	Future
Fastball	4	5
Curve	4	5
Changeup	4	5
Control	4	5
Stamina	4	5
Poise	4	5
Fielding	4	5

Rating Key
7 Outstanding
6 Major League Caliber, High
5 Major League Caliber
4 Minor League Caliber, High
3 Minor League Caliber
2 Below Average
1 Poor

General
Despite pitching in the shadow of John Ericks at Class A Savannah in 1989, Clark saw his own stock rise tremendously. He's now regarded as one of the Cardinals' top pitching prospects, having come out of nowhere to lead the Savannah staff (and the South Atlantic League) in victories while turning in one good start after another. Among pitchers in the St. Louis farm system, Clark ranked third in victories and second in strikeouts (behind Ericks) and innings pitched (trailing only veteran Bob Tewksbury).

Pitching Tendencies
Clark has four pitches—fastball, slider, forkball and changeup—and throws them all for strikes. With a strikeouts-to-walks ratio last season of nearly 3-1, he demonstrated he can effectively work the strike zone. The tall, strapping righthander has the size and stamina to be a dominant and durable pitcher. At Savannah, he hurled four complete games and ranked second in the South Atlantic in innings pitched. Including stints in the winter instructional league, Clark has posted an earned-run average above 3.00 only once: a 3.05 mark in 1988 in the New York-Penn League. The Cardinals believe Clark will continue to rise through the organization.

Fielding/Holding Runners
Clark is a solid fielder and has been fairly successful at holding baserunners close to the bag. Pitching with a runner on first, he is able to shorten his delivery and get the ball to the plate quickly—a big plus for a big man.

Projection
Clark likely will begin the 1990 season at Class AA Arkansas and probably is two years away from the majors.

Career Statistics

	G	IP	W	L	R	ER	H	HR	SO	BB	ERA
1988 Hamilton (New York-Penn League-Class A)	15	94⅓	6	7	39	32	88	10	60	32	3.05
1989 Savannah (South Atlantic League-Class A)	27	173⅔	14	9	61	47	143	8	132	52	2.44

(Projections unavailable because player has not competed at Class AA or Class AAA levels)

JOE AUSANIO

Pittsburgh Pirates
Pitcher
Pirates' 11th-Round Pick, June 1988 Draft

Personal
Height: 6-1 Weight: 202
Throws right, bats right
Born: December 9, 1965

School: Jacksonville University
in Jacksonville, Fla.

Ratings

	Present	Future
Fastball	4	5
Curve	..	..
Changeup	4	5
Control	4	5
Stamina	4	5
Poise	5	6
Fielding	4	5

Rating Key
7 Outstanding
6 Major League Caliber, High
5 Major League Caliber
4 Minor League Caliber, High
3 Minor League Caliber
2 Below Average
1 Poor

General
Ausanio has the perfect psyche for a short reliever, exuding an even-keeled presence. Deep down, he is an outstanding competitor who likes the challenge of pitching with a game on the line. He was the Pirates' minor league Pitcher of the Year in 1989, his first full professional season. Pitching at Class A Salem in the Carolina League, he saved 20 games and finished 51 contests, both league-leading totals. Voted to a league All-Star berth, he also strung together 21 consecutive scoreless innings over 10 games. He had similar success as a stopper in the New York-Penn League in 1988, saving a league-best 13 games.

Pitching Tendencies
Ausanio is a power pitcher who combines a fastball and a nasty split-fingered pitch. His fastball has plenty of pop and good movement, but he gets most of his strikeouts with the split-finger. In two seasons in the minors, he has fanned 153 batters in 136⅔ innings. Ausanio has a bulldog attitude, coming right at hitters with his best stuff. He is sometimes guilty of trying to overthrow his pitches, and that's when his consistency suffers. If he unloads his pitches naturally, he has good command and can throw strikes at any point in the count. The Pirates expect he'll get the measure of discipline he needs with experience.

Fielding/Holding Runners
A good all-around athlete, Ausanio has committed only one error in his two minor league stints. His move to first base is rated average. Although he seldom gets a chance to bat when he's in relief, he is a good-hitting pitcher.

Projection
Ausanio is on schedule to move to the Class AA level in 1990 and could be pitching in the majors sometime during the 1991 season.

Career Statistics

	G	IP	W	L	R	ER	H	HR	SO	BB	ERA
1988 Watertown (New York-Penn League-Class A)	28	47⅔	2	4	10	7	29	1	56	27	1.32
1989 Salem (Carolina League-Class A)	54	89	5	4	29	21	51	9	97	44	2.12

(Projections unavailable because player has not competed at Class AA or Class AAA levels)

ROGER SMITHBERG

Personal
Height: 6-3 Weight: 195
Throws right, bats right
Born: March 21, 1966

School: Bradley

Ratings

	Present	Future
Fastball	4	5
Curve	4	5
Changeup	4	5
Control	3	5
Stamina	4	5
Poise	4	5
Fielding	4	5

Rating Key
7 Outstanding
6 Major League Caliber, High
5 Major League Caliber
4 Minor League Caliber, High
3 Minor League Caliber
2 Below Average
1 Poor

San Diego Padres
Pitcher
Padres' Second-Round Pick, June 1987 Draft

General
Smithberg spent his first full season in the professional ranks at the Class AAA level. A 1987 draftee who didn't report to the Padres until spring training was completed in 1988, Smithberg was assigned to Class AAA Las Vegas last season to make up for lost time. He held up reasonably well, fashioning a 7-7 record with four complete games in 22 starts. Smithberg went the distance in five of 15 starts in 1988, when he was 9-2 in the Class A California League. Instructors say he is filling out physically, which should make him stronger and a more dominating type of pitcher.

Pitching Tendencies
Smithberg has three quality pitches in his repertoire: a fastball, good breaking ball and excellent split-fingered fastball. He has pretty good command of all three (he's averaged only 2.5 walks per nine innings in the minors), but just needs to pitch more to polish them for the major league level. He was hit hard at times in the Pacific Coast League, allowing 10.4 hits per nine innings after limiting California League opponents to 7.8 hits in 1988. He wasn't a big strikeout pitcher at either level but doesn't necessarily have to be. Instead, he has a sharp knowledge and a very good temperament.

Fielding/Holding Runners
With Sandy Alomar Jr. catching at Las Vegas, Smithberg didn't have many opponents running against him. Instructors say he has a good move to first and is steady in the field.

Projection
Smithberg likely will return in 1990 to Class AAA Las Vegas to polish his game and appears destined to make a bid for the major leagues in 1991.

Career Statistics and Major League Equivalencies

	G	IP	W	L	R	ER	H	HR	SO	BB	ERA
1988 Riverside (California League-Class A)	15	103⅓	9	2	52	38	90	2	72	32	3.31
1989 Las Vegas (Pacific Coast League-Class AAA)	22	137	7	7	79	68	159	9	58	35	4.47
1989 Major League Equivalency	22	137			72	62	155	8	55	32	4.07

Interpretation
Unlike many young pitchers, Smithberg has exhibited very good control. He did, however, surrender far too many hits at Class AAA Las Vegas. His Major League Equivalency reflects that, although his earned-run average adjusts down when he's away from the hitter-friendly Pacific Coast League.

SHAWN BOSKIE

Chicago Cubs
Pitcher
Cubs' First-Round Pick, January 1986 Draft

General
Boskie is a strapping righthander who had played mostly third base until the Cubs turned him into a pitcher in rookie ball. He has the raw ability to dominate hitters with hard stuff, and he's shown steady progress making the adjustments necessary to pitch at the big-league level. While he's learned, Boskie has been able to taste some success. He led the Southern League in strikeouts in 1989, his first season at the Class AA level, and topped Charlotte's starting rotation with 11 victories. In 1988, he wound up fifth in the Class A Carolina League with 12 victories and was second in strikeouts, earning league All-Star honors for his showing.

Pitching Tendencies
Boskie has good velocity on all of his pitches but needs to throw them consistently for strikes. He has struggled some with his control, walking an average of 4.2 batters per nine innings over the last two seasons. He's also given up a lot of hits, including a league-high 196 in 181 innings at Charlotte in 1989. While he's absorbed his share of ups and downs, Boskie has never quit. He ranked second in the Carolina League with 186 innings pitched in 1988 and fourth in the Southern last season. Then there are the tell-tale strikeout totals of a power pitcher: 164 in each of the last two seasons. The Cubs are looking for Boskie to develop some consistency, which they believe will come with experience.

Fielding/Holding Runners
Being a converted third baseman, Boskie has a fielder's instincts. He has improved his move but, overall, still needs to hold runners closer.

Projection
If he continues to develop, Boskie is destined to reach the major leagues within two seasons.

Personal
Height: 6-3 Weight: 205
Throws right, bats right
Born: March 28, 1967

School: Modesto Junior College in Modesto, Calif.

Ratings

	Present	Future
Fastball	4	5
Curve	3	5
Changeup	3	5
Control	3	5
Stamina	4	5
Poise	4	5
Fielding	4	5

Rating Key
7 Outstanding
6 Major League Caliber, High
5 Major League Caliber
4 Minor League Caliber, High
3 Minor League Caliber
2 Below Average
1 Poor

Career Statistics and Major League Equivalencies

	G	IP	W	L	R	ER	H	HR	SO	BB	ERA
1986 Wytheville (Appalachian League-Rookie)	14	54	4	4	41	32	42	4	40	57	5.33
1987 Peoria (Midwest League-Class A)	26	149	9	11	91	72	149	12	100	56	4.35
1988 Winston-Salem (Carolina League-Class A)	27	186	12	7	83	70	176	9	164	89	3.39
1989 Charlotte (Southern League-Class AA)	28	181	11	8	105	88	196	10	164	84	4.38
1989 Major League Equivalency	28	181			102	86	197	10	156	85	4.28

Interpretation
Boskie's progress is normal for a pitcher. His Major League Equivalency indicates he needs to allow fewer hits and walks, but also indicates he pitched in a tough park in Charlotte since his projected earned-run average for Wrigley Field goes *down*. At least he'll be prepared.

RICHIE LEWIS

Montreal Expos
Pitcher
Expos' Second-Round Pick, June 1987 Draft

Personal
Height: 5-10 Weight: 175
Throws right, bats right
Born: January 25, 1966

School: Florida State

Ratings

	Present	Future
Fastball	4	5
Curve	4	5
Changeup	3	5
Control	4	5
Stamina	3	5
Poise	3	5
Fielding	4	5

Rating Key
7 Outstanding
6 Major League Caliber, High
5 Major League Caliber
4 Minor League Caliber, High
3 Minor League Caliber
2 Below Average
1 Poor

General
Each of Lewis' three seasons in the Montreal system have been cut short due to elbow problems. After a promising start in 1989 at Class AA Jacksonville, he missed the season's final two months with a sore elbow and underwent surgery in November. Aside from the major concern about Lewis' arm, the Expos are high on his big-league chances. He was a dominating pitcher in college, helping Florida State to the College World Series in 1987. Lewis led Division I pitchers that year with 196 strikeouts and tied for the lead with 15 victories. Rewarded out of college with an assignment to Class AAA Indianapolis, he made only two appearances due to his ailing arm.

Pitching Tendencies
When he's healthy, Lewis ranks among the best strikeout pitchers. He fanned 105 in 94⅓ innings at Jacksonville in 1989 and surrendered just 80 hits. He has improved his tempo and reduced his pitch count, helping him stay in games longer and learn about situational pitching. Previously, he tended to take too long between pitches, which sometimes took the edge off the defense behind him. He also improved his control last season, reducing his walk total to 55 after putting on 56 batters in 61⅓ innings in 1988. The fact that he hasn't quit in the face of his arm troubles shows well for his competitive nature.

Fielding/Holding Runners
Scouts say Lewis is an adequate fielder although he has committed six errors in 31 chances in the minors. He has a good move to first base.

Projection
If he's ready to pitch this spring, Lewis could open the season at Class AAA Indianapolis. He probably needs two seasons to get to the major leagues.

Career Statistics and Major League Equivalencies

	G	IP	W	L	R	ER	H	HR	SO	BB	ERA
1987 Indianapolis (American Association-Class AAA)	2	3⅔	0	0	4	4	6	2	3	2	9.82
1987 Major League Equivalency	2	3⅔			4	4	6	2	3	2	9.82
1988 Jacksonville (Southern League-Class AA)	12	61⅓	5	3	32	23	37	2	60	56	3.38
1988 Major League Equivalency	12	61⅓			35	25	40	2	57	61	3.67
1989 Jacksonville (Southern League-Class AA)	17	94⅓	5	4	37	27	80	2	105	55	2.58
1989 Major League Equivalency	17	94⅓			46	33	91	2	100	68	3.15

Interpretation
Lewis' injuries aside, his recent Major League Equivalencies indicate he has progressed beyond Class AA ball and may be ready for Montreal. He does, however, have high projected walk totals.

NARCISO ELVIRA

Milwaukee Brewers
Pitcher
Purchased by Brewers from Mexican League's Leon club, 1987

Personal
Height: 5-10 Weight: 160
Throws left, bats left
Born: October 29, 1967

School: Pasteje, Mexico

Ratings

	Present	Future
Fastball	4	6
Curve	4	5
Changeup	2	4
Control	4	5
Stamina	4	5
Poise	4	5
Fielding	4	5

Rating Key
7 Outstanding
6 Major League Caliber, High
5 Major League Caliber
4 Minor League Caliber, High
3 Minor League Caliber
2 Below Average
1 Poor

General
For obvious reasons, Elvira has been compared with Brewers lefthander Teddy Higuera. They have similar pitching styles, nearly the same build and both were purchased by Milwaukee from Mexican League clubs. What's more, Elvira admits he has patterned himself somewhat after Higuera. Coincidentally, both pitchers struggled early in the 1989 season, Higuera as he recovered from back surgery, Elvira because of painful tonsils. With his concentration suffering due to that ailment, Elvira managed only a 2-2 record and 7.64 earned-run average to begin the year at Class AA El Paso. After his tonsils were removed, he saw his health and pitching both improve. Elvira finished 8-5 for Class A Stockton, pitching a two-hitter and two three-hit games.

Pitching Tendencies
Elvira can be a terror on the mound with his hard fastball, slider, sharp curve and competitive drive. He led the Brewers' minor league system in strikeouts in each of the last two seasons and allowed fewer hits than innings pitched each year. In 1988, despite a tender shoulder, he surrendered just 5.8 hits per nine innings. He was more consistently in the strike zone last season, but scouts say he still needs to come up with a good off-speed pitch.

Fielding/Holding Runners
Elvira is fundamentally sound in the field and has developed a good move to the bases. Opponents trying to steal against him last season were thrown out 15 times in 23 attempts.

Projection
Depending on his spring showing, Elvira will start the 1990 season either at El Paso or Class AAA Denver. He figures to be pitching in the major leagues in 1991.

Career Statistics and Major League Equivalencies

	G	IP	W	L	R	ER	H	HR	SO	BB	ERA
1987 Beloit (Midwest League-Class A)	4	27	3	0	5	4	15	1	29	12	1.33
1988 Stockton (California League-Class A)	25	135⅓	7	6	49	44	87	7	161	79	2.93
1989 Stockton (California League-Class A)	17	115⅓	8	5	45	39	92	5	135	43	3.04
1989 El Paso (Texas League-Class AA)	7	33	2	2	34	28	48	4	18	23	7.64
1989 Major League Equivalency	7	33			32	26	47	4	17	22	7.09

Interpretation
Elvira's Major League Equivalency is on par with his Texas League line, since both Milwaukee and El Paso play in hitters' ball parks. His projected walk total is an unacceptable six batters per game.

PAT GOMEZ

Atlanta Braves
Pitcher
Chicago Cubs' Fourth-Round Pick, June 1986 Draft

Personal
Height: 5-11   Weight: 185
Throws left, bats left
Born: March 17, 1968

School: San Juan High
in Citrus Heights, Calif.

Ratings

	Present	Future
Fastball	5	5
Curve	3	4
Changeup	4	5
Control	3	5
Stamina	4	5
Poise	4	5
Fielding	4	5

Rating Key
7 Outstanding
6 Major League Caliber, High
5 Major League Caliber
4 Minor League Caliber, High
3 Minor League Caliber
2 Below Average
1 Poor

General
Acquired by Atlanta last September in the Paul Assenmacher trade, Gomez is a four-season veteran of the Chicago Cubs' farm. He didn't exactly clear a path to the majors his first three years, posting a combined 8-19 record with a 4.89 earned-run average. In 1989, however, he caught the Braves' eye at the Cubs' Class A Winston-Salem club. Gomez started throwing strikes with confidence and earned a late-season promotion to the Class AA level. The lefthander has as much physical ability as any pitcher in the minors. For now, he needs only to establish his consistency to make the jump to the major leagues.

Pitching Tendencies
Gomez has pitched as a starter and reliever in the minor leagues but entrenched himself as the ace of the Winston-Salem rotation in 1989. His pitches have good velocity, with his fastball nudging the radar gun near 90 mph. For a young pitcher, he has an above-average changeup that he's mastering with experience. The off-speed pitch makes his fastball look even better, and he's making progress with a slider. Gomez has been able to strike out hitters in a pinch and ranked fifth in the Carolina League in 1989 with 127 strikeouts. In 1988, he fanned 97 batters in 78⅔ innings, appearing mostly as a reliever. Instructors will keep a close watch on his mechanics to help him develop some consistency with his control.

Fielding/Holding Runners
Gomez has a good move to first base and is improving his overall fielding skills.

Projection
Gomez is ticketed to start the season at Class AA Greenville and is probably two years away from the majors.

Career Statistics

	G	IP	W	L	R	ER	H	HR	SO	BB	ERA
1986 Wytheville (Appalachian League-Rookie)	11	54	3	6	51	31	57	4	55	46	5.17
1987 Peoria (Midwest League-Class A)	20	94	3	6	55	45	88	4	95	71	4.31
1988 Charleston (South Atlantic League-Class A)	36	78⅔	2	7	53	47	75	1	97	52	5.38
1989 Winston-Salem (Carolina League-Class A)	23	137⅔	11	6	59	42	115	6	127	60	2.75
1989 Charlotte (Southern League-Class AA)	2	14⅓	1	0	5	4	14	0	11	3	2.51

(Projections unavailable due to player's limited experience at Class AA level)

SCOTT RADINSKY

Chicago White Sox
Pitcher
White Sox's Third-Round Pick, June 1986 Draft

Personal
Height: 6-3 Weight: 190
Throws left, bats left
Born: March 3, 1968

School: Simi Valley High in Simi Valley, Calif.

Ratings

	Present	Future
Fastball	4	5
Curve	4	5
Changeup	3	5
Control	4	5
Stamina	4	5
Poise	4	5
Fielding	4	5

Rating Key
7 Outstanding
6 Major League Caliber, High
5 Major League Caliber
4 Minor League Caliber, High
3 Minor League Caliber
2 Below Average
1 Poor

General
Radinsky came back from shoulder surgery with an iron will in 1989. After pitching just 3⅓ innings in 1988, he saved 31 games last season for Class A South Bend and was an All-Star pick in the Midwest League. Radinsky ranked third among the league's relievers with a strikeout ratio of 12.1 batters per nine innings and finished second in saves. At one point, he made 18 consecutive appearances without allowing a run. What impressed the White Sox perhaps even more than those results was the way he worked to recover from the surgery. Radinsky convinced the organization he is healthy and holds promise for the immediate future. He steadily grew as a relief closer, a role he filled for the first time in his four-year career.

Pitching Tendencies
Radinsky's fastball is consistently in the high 80s and occasionally tops 90 mph. He's still working to improve his curveball and changeup, both of which he needs to throw with more confidence. Otherwise, he has good control and usually throws a strike when he needs to, especially late in the count. In 61⅔ innings in 1989, he allowed just 39 hits, walked 19 and posted a 1.75 earned-run average, by far the best season of his career. He is a very disciplined worker and an intelligent pitcher.

Fielding/Holding Runners
Radinsky is regarded as a good fielder and holds runners on base well. Last season, opponents were cut down five times in 10 stolen base attempts.

Projection
Radinsky received an invitation to the White Sox's major league spring camp in 1990 but likely is better suited for a job at the Class AA or AAA level. He could advance to the majors in 1991.

Career Statistics

	G	IP	W	L	R	ER	H	HR	SO	BB	ERA
1986 Sarasota White Sox (Gulf Coast League-Rookie)	7	26⅔	1	0	20	10	24	0	18	17	3.38
1987 Peninsula (Carolina League-Class A)	12	39	1	7	30	25	43	2	37	32	5.77
1987 Sarasota White Sox (Gulf Coast League-Rookie)	11	58⅓	3	3	23	15	43	1	41	39	2.31
1988 Sarasota White Sox (Gulf Coast League-Rookie)	5	3⅓	0	0	2	2	2	0	7	4	5.40
1989 South Bend (Midwest League-Class A)	53	61⅔	7	5	21	12	39	1	83	19	1.75

(Projections unavailable because player has not competed at Class AA or Class AAA levels)

ERIC GUNDERSON

San Francisco Giants
Pitcher
Giants' Second-Round Pick, June 1987 Draft

Personal
Height: 6-0 Weight: 175
Throws left, bats right
Born: March 29, 1966

School: Portland State

Ratings

	Present	Future
Fastball	5	6
Curve	4	5
Changeup	4	5
Control	4	5
Stamina	4	5
Poise	3	4
Fielding	4	5

Rating Key
7 Outstanding
6 Major League Caliber, High
5 Major League Caliber
4 Minor League Caliber, High
3 Minor League Caliber
2 Below Average
1 Poor

General
Gunderson has been a starter (save for one game) through his first three seasons in the minors, but some scouts envision him as a reliever at the major league level. He doesn't have the tricky second pitch that would make him doubly effective in a closer's role, but Gunderson does have the weapon of choice to subdue a lineup in relief: a live, hard fastball. Scouts, however, say he needs to improve his temperament to take full advantage of his talent. Gunderson started the 1989 season at Class AA Shreveport, where he posted an 8-2 record in 11 starts to earn a promotion to Class AAA Phoenix. He was an All-Star pick in the Class A California League in 1988, when he was 12-5 at San Jose with a league-leading four shutouts.

Pitching Tendencies
Gunderson's best pitch is a hard fastball that has excellent movement. He is particularly tough on lefthanded hitters and is consistently in the strike zone. He has a career strikeouts-to-walks ratio of 2.5-1 and has fanned eight batters per nine innings pitched. If the Giants use him as a starter, they'll have a durable one. Gunderson worked 186 innings in 1988 and pitched five complete games in 20 starts for San Jose. As a minor league rookie, he went the distance five times in 15 starts.

Fielding/Holding Runners
Gunderson committed just one error last season, and his ability to hold runners at bay was stunning. Working with good catchers at Shreveport and Phoenix, he helped erase 15 runners in 17 stolen base attempts.

Projection
Gunderson figures to begin the 1990 season at Class AAA Phoenix but could be in the major leagues by season's end.

Career Statistics and Major League Equivalencies

	G	IP	W	L	R	ER	H	HR	SO	BB	ERA
1987 Everett (Northwest League-Class A)	15	98⅔	8	4	34	27	80	4	99	34	2.46
1988 San Jose (California League-Class A)	20	149⅓	12	5	56	44	131	2	151	52	2.65
1988 Shreveport (Texas League-Class AA)	7	36⅔	1	2	25	21	45	1	28	13	5.15
1988 Major League Equivalency	7	36⅔			29	25	50	1	27	15	6.14
1989 Shreveport (Texas League-Class AA)	11	72⅔	8	2	24	22	68	1	61	23	2.72
1989 Phoenix (Pacific Coast League-Class AAA)	14	85⅔	2	4	51	48	93	7	56	36	5.04
1989 Major League Equivalency	25	158⅓			82	76	172	9	111	64	4.32

Interpretation
Gunderson's Major League Equivalencies don't add much to the overall statistical picture. He gets promoted during each season to a level he doesn't appear to be ready for, although he gets his game in order by the same point the following year. His tough stint at Class AAA Phoenix in 1989 hurt his MLE.

WILLIE SMITH

New York Yankees
Pitcher
Signed by Pittsburgh Pirates as a Non-Drafted Free Agent, July 1986

Personal
Height: 6-5 Weight: 225
Throws right, bats right
Born: January 27, 1965

School: Savannah High
in Savannah, Ga.

Ratings

	Present	Future
Fastball	5	6
Curve	4	5
Changeup	..	..
Control	4	5
Stamina	5	6
Poise	4	5
Fielding	4	5

Rating Key
7 Outstanding
6 Major League Caliber, High
5 Major League Caliber
4 Minor League Caliber, High
3 Minor League Caliber
2 Below Average
1 Poor

General
Smith has been described as a clone of major league stopper Lee Smith. His physique is certainly similar and he throws almost as hard—blue darts that have been clocked at 96 mph. Scouts believe he can be just as dominating in a short-relief role. Smith's trials as a starter were marked by control problems and he was moved back to the bullpen each time. He overcame one such test in the Pirates' chain last season. After a 1-4 start at Class A Salem, Smith regrouped as a closer and earned a promotion to the Class AA level. The Yankees picked him up with pitcher Jeff Robinson in a trade for catcher Don Slaught in December.

Pitching Tendencies
Smith can be overpowering when he's properly used. He can enter a game in relief, blow smoke by hitters for a few innings and pick up saves. His calling card is pure power: an intimidating fastball and a slider that registers close to 90 mph. With his velocity, two pitches are all he needs as a short reliever. He has struck out 191 batters in 192⅓ innings covering four minor league seasons. At this stage, instructors believe Smith just needs to pitch and develop some consistency. He is sometimes guilty of overthrowing the ball, which he doesn't have to do with his stuff. When he does overthrow, he falls victim to stretches of wildness.

Fielding/Holding Runners
Smith is a good athlete who fields his position well. He keeps runners close to first with a good pickoff move.

Projection
If the Yankees prescribe seasoning for Smith, he'll open 1990 at the Class AA level. A good spring could get him a ride to Class AAA Columbus. Either way, he could reach the majors before year's end.

Career Statistics and Major League Equivalencies

	G	IP	W	L	R	ER	H	HR	SO	BB	ERA
1986 Bradenton Pirates (Gulf Coast League-Rookie)	7	21⅔	1	0	8	6	16	0	13	6	2.49
1987 Bradenton Pirates (Gulf Coast League-Rookie)	10	19⅓	2	1	4	3	12	0	27	11	1.40
1987 Watertown (New York-Penn League-Class A)	5	20⅓	2	0	13	10	15	1	24	10	4.43
1988 Augusta (South Atlantic League-Class A)	30	48⅓	1	4	20	16	35	0	48	29	2.98
1989 Salem (Carolina League-Class A)	23	64⅓	4	5	26	21	46	4	58	40	2.94
1989 Harrisburg (Eastern League-Class AA)	12	18⅓	3	0	5	5	11	1	21	10	2.45
1989 Major League Equivalency	12	18⅓			5	5	11	1	18	12	2.45

Interpretation
Smith's 1989 Major League Equivalency shows the same kind of success he enjoyed at the Class AA level. The adjustments cancel out each other from Harrisburg to Pittsburgh due to the clubs' similar ball parks.

TERRY BROSS

New York Mets
Pitcher
Mets' 13th-Round Pick, June 1987 Draft

Personal
Height: 6-9 Weight: 235
Throws right, bats right
Born: March 30, 1966

School: St. John's

Ratings

	Present	Future
Fastball	4	5
Curve	3	5
Changeup	3	5
Control	2	5
Stamina	4	5
Poise	4	5
Fielding	2	4

Rating Key
7 Outstanding
6 Major League Caliber, High
5 Major League Caliber
4 Minor League Caliber, High
3 Minor League Caliber
2 Below Average
1 Poor

General
The Mets are trying to develop Bross as a short reliever. And for good reason: intimidation. At 6-foot-9, he looks as if he can hand the ball to the catcher. Bross turned to baseball even though he had pitched just 24 innings in two collegiate seasons at St. John's, where he was known more for his exploits as a starting forward/center on the basketball team. After swinging between the bullpen and starting rotation in two tours through the short-season New York-Penn League, he emerged as a top-flight closer in 1989 at Class A St. Lucie.

Pitching Tendencies
First, there's the intimidating presence he casts simply by standing on the mound. Then there's the fastball that smokes in at 90-plus mph, the hard slider and split-fingered pitch. It all spells s-t-o-p-p-e-r when you talk potential, yet there is room for improvement. Though his mechanics are sound given his size, Bross needs to have better command of his pitches and reduce his walk total, which is high for a short reliever (84 walks in 141⅓ minor league innings). Nevertheless, he's managed to stay out of big trouble thus far, keeping both his earned-run average and hits-allowed total low. He seems destined to refine and develop his skills with experience.

Fielding/Holding Runners
Because of his height, Bross sometimes has trouble reacting quickly to balls hit back up the middle and fielding taps in front of the mound. He'll need to sharpen that area of his game. His move to first is said to be adequate.

Projection
Bross likely will pitch at Class AA Jackson in 1990 and is probably two years away from reaching the major leagues.

Career Statistics

	G	IP	W	L	R	ER	H	HR	SO	BB	ERA
1987 Little Falls (New York-Penn League-Class A)	10	28	2	0	23	12	22	3	21	20	3.86
1988 Little Falls (New York-Penn League-Class A)	20	55⅓	2	1	25	19	43	2	59	38	3.09
1989 St. Lucie (Florida State League-Class A)	35	58	8	2	21	18	39	1	47	26	2.79

(Projections unavailable because player has not competed at Class AA or Class AAA levels).

Statistical Explanation

The statistical formulas used in this book are loosely based on the work done by Bill James for his 1985 Baseball Abstract. I have tinkered with the formulas and used them in ways that Bill had not evisioned, so if you don't like the work, I deserve the blame. If, however, you find them interesting, a lot of the credit should go to James, who did all of the ground work.

In the statistical boxes for each player, a "Major League Equivalency" line appears at the end of each season in which the player appeared at the Class AA, Class AAA and/or major league levels. The MLE line attempts to translate how the player's minor league performance would have looked for that season with his respective team in the major leagues. The basic formula for computing MLEs, unchanged from James' 1985 method, is a complicated series of adjustments and calculations designed to project a player's success at the major league level.

The biggest adjustment is to individual ballparks and that's why the player MLEs can't be compared directly to each other. Some parks inflate statistics, others deflate them. But they do give a more accurate picture of what the player might be able to achieve when he is called up by his parent club.

For pitchers, the MLE process converts their statistical lines to "batting" stats and then applies the batting MLE process. But when the time comes to apply the difference in quality of play between the major leagues and the minors, it is used to inflate the batting stats rather than deflate them. Thus, the batter against whom the pitcher is presumed to be pitching gets better, not worse.

The MLE process for pitchers has not been fully tested, but one test the pitching MLEs do pass is that of plausibility. None of the results seem obviously wrong. There are no ERAs of 0.03 or 75.00, nobody adjusts from 20 homers to two or 200, and no minor league pitcher projects to win the Cy Young Award. Further testing will no doubt refine the process, but it does seem reasonable now.

There are Peak Projection lines for hitters in addition to the various MLEs. The peak lines are generated by a process that bears some resemblance to James' 1985 Brock2 career projection system. This system took whatever seasons a major league player had already compiled and produced a projection of what the remaining seasons of his career might reasonably look like, including such features as reductions in playing time, player ages and career-end falloff.

I have fiddled considerably with this method. First, I identified the age at which the Brock2 process gave a player his best year—the "peak" year of his career. According to Brock2, that year should occur when the player is 27.

To get reasonable peak lines, however, a series of adjustments need to be made on a player's MLEs. I won't get into these complicated computations here, but I think it's important to point out one key adjustment that was made for purposes of this book. Because some of the players had so little MLE data to work with (some had less than a full season at either the Class AA or AAA levels), it was difficult to translate their numbers into a reasonable peak projection. So, working on the assumption that the players appearing on these pages are all top-quality athletes with excellent chances of making an impact at the big-league level, I forced their "Games" column when necessary to 154, thus forcing the rest of their numbers to match up accordingly.

It is imperative that the reader keep in mind that the intention of these peak projections is to give a general grasp of what the top-end potential of a given player might be if his career develops without such distortions as injuries and sudden power surges.

A key factor is a player's age. The growth potential of a 20-year-old is much different from a player who is 26. The latter already is near his peak while the other still is in an early developmental stage. If two such players compile similar seasons in the minor leagues, it is likely they will become much different players at the major league level. Getting a handle on that—deciding whether a player is likely to be a star or journeyman—is the purpose of the peak line. It is not meant to be an accurate projection of what he "will" do.

There are no Peak Projections for pitchers. The Brock2 method could not be stretched to project young hurlers who still are fighting their control. Pitchers change the shape of their statistics much more than batters and their major league careers will not strongly resemble their minor league years.

It's important to reemphasize the experimental nature of all this. Of the methods used here, only the batter MLE system has been thoroughly tested. Even that method works much better with full seasons of data than the skimpy samples some of the young players here have turned in. The pitcher MLEs come from a reasonable extension of the batter MLE process, but the method has not been seriously tested. The Peak Projections are the result of an experimental version of a method that is designed to be applied to much larger samples of live data than we have here.

While there certainly is information to be gained from all this, rigid attempts to treat the results as guarantees are unjustified. The MLEs and projections are here for you to read, enjoy and keep for future evaluation.

—Brock Hanke